A WORLD
OF
STRANGERS

A WORLD OF STRANGERS

Order and Action in Urban Public Space

LYN H. LOFLAND

Basic Books, Inc., Publishers / NEW YORK

73 74 75 76 77 10 9 8 7 6 5 4 3 2 1

For
E. K. WILSON and J. LOFLAND

The ocean is something every inland Indian has heard of and has some sort of picture of in his mind. . . . Ishi was looking forward to seeing it, but when the car stopped on the bluff above the Cliff House, giving onto a wide view of ocean, surf, and beach, Ishi's breath drew in, not because of the great rolling Pacific but because of the thousands of people who covered the beach below and spilled over into the surf. . . . He said over and over softly, half-whisperingly, Hansi saltu, hansi saltu! Many white people, many white people! He had not known so many people could inhabit the earth at one time; the shock of sheer numbers obliterated every other impression.

Kroeber, 1967:138–139

PREFACE

This is a book about cities—or, more precisely, about one aspect of what it is like to live in cities. Writing about cities and about the ways people live in them is a controversial occupation these days. Perhaps it always was. In any case, whenever one is nervy enough to write with presumed sociological detachment on a controversial topic, one owes to one's readers some honesty about hidden axes that might be grinding away. Thus:

I am an unashamed cityphile. I would prefer to live in a city, despite the dirt, than in a rural paradise or honeysuckled small town. I share the concern of many of my contemporaries over the deteriorating physical environment, over the insane population increase, over the destruction of the earth's life support system. I share with them some of their critiques of industrial society, of technology run wild, of sprawling suburbanization. But I do not share the antiurban sentiment which is increasingly a part of these concerns and critiques. I was reared in a small town in a wilderness area and have no illusions about the inevitably idyllic and utopian character of such settlements. The small town and the rural countryside may be sites of leisure, of contentment, of peace. They can also be sites of parochialism, of bigotry, of spiritual narrowness. The city may be harsh, but it is exciting. It may be cruel, but it is tolerant. It may be indifferent, but it is a blessed indifference. In sum, I share the Aristotelian judgment of the urban world: "Men come together in cities in order to live. They remain together in order to live the good life."

It is perhaps also appropriate to give the reader, as either encouragement or discouragement, some conception of what is to be found in the pages that lie ahead. I have said that this is a book about one aspect of what it is like to live in cities. The character of that aspect of focus is contained in the title, *A World of Strangers*. To live in a city is, among many other things, to live surrounded by large numbers of persons whom one does not know. To experience the city is, among many other things, to experience anonymity. To cope with the city is, among many other things, to cope with strangers. This is a book, then, about that very peculiar social situation.

The fact that the social situation of city living is "peculiar" may not, in an age of worldwide urbanization, be evident. Chapter One attempts to make it so. It sets the stage for all that is to follow. If one can conceive of a book as a kind of journey, with the author as guide, then to understand what is happening en route, the reader must see what the author sees, must make problematic what the author makes problematic. It is the goal of Chapter One to do this.

I shall argue that, given certain social psychological assumptions about human beings and given certain anthropological and historical evidence about nonurban peoples, there is very good reason to ask: how is city life possible? I shall argue that a situation of "pure" anonymity would be intolerable. I shall argue that humans can live in cities only because they, in fact, know a great deal about the strangers who surround them. And I shall argue that this knowledge—this *sine qua non* of urban living—is itself made possible by an "ordering" of the city's populace such that appearances and locations provide relatively dependable clues to "identities."

The locus of the city as a world of strangers resides in the city's public space. It is here, primarily, that the drama of strangers in the midst of strangers is played out. And it is here that we must look if we are to understand how the drama is played at all. In Part 1, we shall explore just what is going on in this public space. We shall discover that "what is going on" has undergone a historical change, and that this change is intimately linked to the matter of what clues are most reliable in the crucial task of identifying strangers. Chapter Two focuses on the preindustrial city. It argues that in this city, public spaces contained such a conglomeration of persons and activities that locational clues were of little value. Appearances, however, were fairly reliably hooked to identity. Chapter Four focuses on the modern city. It argues that in the modern city, the opposite is true. Here, public spaces "specialize" in certain persons and activities, while appearances can be highly deceiving. Each type of city, that is, has its characteristic type of order, which allows its citizens to make relatively accurate identifications of one another. The preindustrial city is characterized by the dominance of appearential ordering; the modern city, by the dominance of spatial ordering. And the early industrial city, which is the focus of Chapter Three, is the locale wherein the historical transformation from one sort of order to another occurred and is the locale to which we must look if we are to begin to understand the dynamics of this transformation.

The theme of Part 1, then, might be said to be an answer to the question: given the stranger-filled character of cities, how is it possible for people to live in them? The theme of Part 2, in contrast, is a partial answer to the question: within the context of the order that makes city living possible, how do people live? Here, that is, the concern shifts from ordering to "acting." Chapter Five explores urban learning. In it we shall be looking at the process by which both the knowledge of city meanings (which allows the individual to identify surrounding strangers) and the skills (which allow him to utilize his knowledge as he moves among these strangers) are acquired.

City dwellers, of course, like all humans, vary in their scholarly attainments. And they vary also in their need for urban scholarship. The remaining chapters of Part 2 (Six, Seven and Eight) attempt, then, to specify some of the parameters of this variation. Chapters Six and Seven focus on some of the devices that urbanites use to avoid the world of strangers and thereby reduce the necessity to use or even to acquire complex urban know-how. As we shall see, these devices are a heterogeneous lot. Their analytic unity resides in their consequence: each transforms public space—the locus of the world of strangers—into private or semiprivate space. Each allows its user, for long or short periods of time, to a greater or lesser degree, to avoid the difficulty and the challenge that are the essence of the city as a world of strangers.

Chapter Eight, in contrast, is concerned not with avoiding, but with adventuring; not with escape, but with excitement. Here we shall be watching the Phi Beta Kappas of urban learning as they use their knowledge and skills to confront the world of strangers head-on and to engage, in the midst of this world, in some conventional and some not-so-conventional fun and games.

That, in brief, is what the pages ahead are about. We begin in Chapter One with the tribal human confronting, with fear and suspicion, the infrequent stranger. We end in Chapter Eight with the cosmopolitan human confronting, with ease and ability, the constant stranger. And in Chapter Nine, I shall try to draw out some of the implications of that fact.

While there is, I trust, unity and coherence among the eight chapters that make up the crucial core of this volume, there is also, I am certain, considerable diversity. This diversity is most clearly reflected in the multiplicity of types and sources of materials utilized in developing the analysis. Chapters One through Three rely heavily on the work of anthropologists, historical sociologists, and historians. Chapter Four draws upon a motley collection of newspaper articles, published works of sociology and history, and my own interviews and observations. The materials for Part 2 are predominantly the interviews and observations of my own first-hand research,* but even here I attempt to extend the range of my vision and hearing by calling upon the sights and sounds preserved in the written record. I admit, that is, to a certain promiscuity in my data collection. I admit also to a certain analytic ruthlessness. The focus herein is on "the city," not specific cities. The focus is on "urbanites," not particular urbanites. Those who prefer their sociology set within the finite dimensions of a concrete place existing within a particular span of real time and peopled by a specific cast of characters may find what follows somewhat disconcerting. I trust they will not find it unconvincing.

Finally, a few words seem in order regarding footnotes and sex. First, as to footnotes. I use the modern method of referencing throughout, so that footnotes are reserved exclusively for asides, additional references, clarifications, qualifications, and just interesting little items that I couldn't figure out where else to put. The book can be read quite well without them, especially Chapter One, where they are liberally sprinkled to say the least, and where they refer largely to matters of how this or that does or does not relate to esoteric sociological disputes.

Last, as to sex. I have attempted to avoid as much as possible the use of the term "man" to stand for all human beings. I have also attempted to avoid excessive use of the pronouns "he," "his," and "him" when referring to both men and women. Neither attempt has been particularly successful. Stylistic convention makes "man," "he," "him," and "his" difficult words to avoid. At one point, I considered substituting "woman," "she," "her," and "hers" in all the appropriate places, but finally decided that female chauvinism is no improvement over the male variety. In addition, in reading over a sentence or paragraph

---

* Beginning in 1965, many hundreds of hours were spent observing in public places in a variety of American cities, especially Ann Arbor, Michigan; Detroit, Michigan; and San Francisco, California. During 1969 and 1970 some 50 persons living in San Francisco and surrounding communities were interviewed—some individually, some in groups—relative to various aspects of their experiences in cities. A detailed account of this research may be found in L. Lofland, 1971, pp. 298–310.

where I had made such a substitution, I found that, because of the strangeness of the phrasing, the words drew attention to themselves and even I lost track of what was being said. If language is truly a living entity, perhaps in the not-too-distant future we can expect more neutral terms to emerge, and we shall then be spared the idiotic practice of using the masculine gender to designate all human beings. But since that future time has not arrived, I must apologize to those of my readers who find this practice irritating and degrading. I do so myself.

1973   L.H.L.

CONTENTS

1

Urban Public Order:
The Historical Transformation

2

Urban Public Behavior:
City Dwellers in Action

A WORLD
OF
STRANGERS

CHAPTER ONE

THE PROBLEMATIC
WORLD OF STRANGERS

A city is many things. It is a geographical and social location—a collection of relatively large numbers of people in a relatively small space. It is a political entity—an administrative unit with various relationships to other administrative units. It is a magnet—a place of ambition and hope. It is a repellent—a place of inconvenience and fear. It is a place where people live and work and expend their leisure, a place where other people visit and leave their money. In all of this, except for size, a city does not differ much from other kinds of places where people are born, live out their lives, and die. Small towns and villages are also geographical and social locations, political entities, magnets to some and repellents to others; residential, work, and play sites; and places to visit.

But in one respect, at least, the city is not like other kinds of places. The city, because of its size, is the locus of a peculiar social situation: the people to be found within its boundaries at any given moment know nothing personally about the vast *majority* of others with whom they share this space. Each knows of the aggregate existence of all these others, of course, but he does not know of their individual existence: he does not know their names or their personal histories or their hopes or preferences or fears.

The city then, among all the other things that it may be, is also a world of strangers, a world populated by persons who are personally unknown to one another. It is this peculiar characteristic of the city which is of concern here. It is this which is the starting point of all that is to follow. Beginning with this observation that the city is a world of strangers, we shall pursue, through time and across space, the question which this observation raises: how can it be?

Strangers as Exceptional: The Historical Situation

To large numbers of contemporary humans, there is nothing peculiar in the situation of living out one's life amid persons one does not know. In an urban, urbanizing, and increasingly crowded world, this state of affairs is expected and tolerated, if not always appreciated. But to large numbers of other humans—some now living, most long deceased—this state of affairs would appear very peculiar indeed. For throughout a major part of human history (and prehistory), in most times and most places, men and women have lived out their lives not in great cities or urban sprawls, but in small and isolated worlds—in bands or tribes or villages or towns. However varied the human condition in these little worlds—and it varied enormously—they shared one crucial characteristic: the absence of anonymity. Their peoples were born and reared, they reached adulthood and married, propagated, grew old and died, surrounded always and almost exclusively by persons who knew them and who were known to them.[1]

The arrival of a stranger or group of strangers in these little enclaves of personal knowing was (and in some parts of the world still is) a truly remarkable and momentous event. Just how remarkable and how momentous depended on numerous related factors: the degree of the group's isolation, past experience with such events, the extent to which the stranger's appearance differed from that of the receiving group,[2] the group's social organization and belief system, and so forth. But never were such appearances merely routine. They always occasioned the interruption, to some degree, of everyday activities.

If the group were sufficiently isolated, it might conceive itself to be the only group of humans in the world. As such, any stranger who might appear could only be, quite logically, a nonhuman. And in no human society is the appearance of a humanlike nonhuman a routine event. Special measures are always called for. Among some groups, like the Tiwi, who inhabited two islands off the coast of Northern Australia, killing the intruder appeared the most satisfactory solution:

Tiwi tradition is firm and certain that before the white man's arrival there was no contact between the islands and the mainland. To them, the dimly seen coastline of Australia was *Tibambinumi*, the home of the dead, to which all Tiwi souls went after death. It follows from this that they regarded the inhabited world as composed of their own two islands and on those islands they lived a self-contained and exclusive existence. Occasionally outsiders appeared, either castaways from surrounding areas, including presumably the Australian mainland, and in recent centuries, fishing boats and pirates from Indonesia, loosely called "Malays" in the literature. To such visitors from outside, the Tiwi were consistently and implacably hostile. Their own traditions and what little written history there is of "Malay" penetration into the Arafura Sea both tell the same story. Outsiders who landed on the island were massacred or vigorously resisted. Whether they were classified as *Malai-ui* ("Malays") or *Wona-rui* (Australian aborigines from the mainland) they were not Tiwi and hence not real people, or at least not human enough to share the islands with the chosen people who owned them. (Hart and Pilling, 1966:9–10)

Among other groups, the intruding nonhumans might be viewed as ancestral ghosts and treated with whatever ceremonial propitiation was deemed necessary. Thus:

In the Andaman Isles . . . "the natives had not the faintest knowledge of even the neighbouring coast of Burmah, much less the world at large. . . . The few voyagers who from time to time ventured near their shores were regarded as deceased ancestors who, by some dispensation, had been permitted to revisit the earth. . . . In confirmation of this may be cited the name by which the natives of India are to this day called, viz. *chawgala* (literally, departed spirits)." (quoted in Levy-Bruhl, 1923:359)

To less isolated peoples who had established relations with their neighbors and who no longer conceived themselves as the only inhabitants in the world, a newcomer of strange appearance might still be viewed as anything but human. The accounts of early European voyagers to out-of-the-way parts of the globe tell again and again of their being received by the native populations with fear, astonishment, apprehension, ceremonies of propitiation, protective rituals, fainting, and so forth—the exact emotion and behavior of the hosts depending on just what they conceived these strange white objects to be. Sometimes the voyagers were thought of as ghosts or ancestors from the normally unseen world, sometimes as beings from the world of occult powers, sometimes as spirits of the dead or persons raised from the dead, sometimes as malevolent gods (Levy-Bruhl, 1923:355–64; Wood, 1934:77–84), and in one possibly apocryphal case of one lone white man, as a sacred white monkey:

The late Doctor Stutterheim, Government Archeologist in Java, used to tell the following story: Somewhat before the advent of the white man, there was a storm on the Javanese coast in the neighborhood of one of the capitals. After the storm the people went down to the beach and found, washed up by the waves and almost dead, a large white monkey of unknown species. The religious experts explained that this monkey had been a member of the court of Beroena, the God of the Sea, and that for some offense the monkey had been cast out by the god whose anger was expressed in the storm. The Rajah gave orders that the white monkey from the sea should be kept alive, chained to a certain stone. This was done. Doctor Stutterheim told me that he had seen the stone and that, roughly scratched on it in Latin, Dutch, and English were the name of a man and a statement of his shipwreck. Apparently this trilingual sailor never established verbal communication with his captors. He was surely unaware of the premises in their minds which labeled him as a white monkey and therefore not a potential recipient of verbal messages: it probably never occurred to him that they could doubt his humanity. He may have doubted theirs. (Ruesch and Bateson, 1951:204–5, n. 1)

Even among peoples with greater knowledge of the world and all its diversities, the lurking suspicion that the stranger might be other than human died hard. " 'Beggars and strangers,' says Homer, 'come from Zeus' " (Haarhoff, 1948:1). Or, in the New Testament version: "Be not forgetful to entertain strangers, for thereby some have entertained angels unawares" (Hebrews 13:2).

The humanity of the stranger was not always doubted. Yet even when it was not, his arrival still managed to break the routine of everyday activities. Among the Australian aborigines, such an arrival necessitated the collection of some rather detailed information:

> At every moment of the life of a member of an Australian tribe his dealings with other individuals are regulated by the relationship in which he stands to them. . . . Thus in any part of the continent when a stranger comes to camp the first thing to be done, before he can be admitted within the camp, is to determine his relationship to every man and woman in it, i.e., to determine what is the proper term of relationship for him to apply to each of them. . . .

Social relations of any type [could not be] established with strangers unless these could demonstrate that they were connected by kinship ties with someone within the horde. A stranger from an unknown tribe, unless he came accredited as a sacred messenger, would most probably be promptly speared. (Wood, 1934:65–66 [Wood is quoting from Radcliffe-Brown, 1931.])

And unlike as they may have been in other respects, American Southern Mountaineers shared with these Australian aborigines a similar lack of "civil disattention" to strangers:

As you approach a cross-roads store, every idler pricks up to instant attention. Your presence is detected from every neighboring cabin and cornfield. Long John quits his plowing, Red John drops his axe, Sick John . . . pops out of bed and Lyin' John . . . grabs his hat with "I jes' got ter know who that feller is!" Then all Johns descend their several paths, to congregate at the store and estimate the stranger as though he were so many board-feet of lumber in the tree or so many pounds of beef on the hoof. (Kephart, 1913:202)

Having completed their visual inspection, the verbal interrogation could proceed:

Whar are you gwin? What did you say your name was? What mought you-uns foller for a living? What you aimin' to do up hyur? How much money do you make? Whar's your old woman? (Kephart, 1913:201, 204)

Among many peoples, a stranger—however human—was believed to be possessed of special powers. Sometimes these powers were thought to be malevolent, sometimes benevolent, sometimes both; whatever the case, extraordinary ceremonies, often involving long periods of time, were called for (Van Gennep, 1960:26–35; Frazer, 1922:226–230). And even when the stranger was not thought to have magical powers, he was often viewed with a fear or joy or some mixture of both emotions. He might, for example, be an enemy in disguise and require close observation, as in the twelfth century injunction to "Beware of strangers while thou have an enmye, and see welle to his wayes" (Saint Bernard, *Le Regisme de Mesnaige*, c. 1130). Or, he might be a welcome novelty in an otherwise restricted life and thus deserving of the utmost in hospitality:

From the great landed proprietors to the small tobacco grower [in Colonial America], Southern planters were renowned for the hospitality they showed travelers: "They are not easy," remarked a newcomer to Maryland, "till you have given them an opportunity to show you a kindness." In fact, they took such delight in entertaining visitors that innkeepers frequently complained that the competition from private houses was putting them out of business. . . .

In South Carolina, the planters often posted Negro slaves along the road with instructions to invite travelers to stop for refreshment and lodging. (Miller, 1966:104–5)

Frequently, as in the American Frontier, the stranger was greeted with a mixed emotional and behavioral response:

The frontiersmen joined hospitality to strangers with a suspicion of them. They were suspicious that the stranger might in some way infringe upon their rights, or that his or her presence might in some way prove to be a disturbing factor in the new community. . . . But there also existed a certain obligation to treat the stranger hospitably since it was recognized that in the wilderness he was altogether dependent upon such good will. Moreover, if the stranger proved an agreeable person, his visit was a welcome break in the monotony of the social life of the frontier and was more than welcome. (Wood, 1934:183–84; see also Kephart, 1913:chap. IX)[3]

And even in settlements where strangers were somewhat more routinely expected, their appearance might still be the occasion for excited expressions of curiosity, gossiping, and gaping. Thus, an American woman, now in her thirties, recalling her childhood in a small Utah village, can report:

You knew when a strange car came into town. You have friends sitting down on main street—there's a new car in town, you know. It would go all over town.[4]

If the appearance of a stranger today, in our urban and mobile and tourist-haunted world, is less frequently evocative of wonder, curiosity, astonishment, hostility, hospitality, suspicion, and delight than was the case in times past, such responses have not disappeared altogether. There are still places, isolated from the comings and goings of modern life, where a stranger might be killed or feasted or gaped at or gossiped about. Sometimes these little pockets of preserved history are to be found, in modified form, in the middle of great cities. More frequently they linger on amidst inaccessible mountains, vast jungles, frozen wastes, or broiling deserts. How much longer they will continue to exist one cannot say. That will depend on the course of history, and I leave predicting the future to others. Anyone wishing to visit such places, however, is probably well advised not to delay the trip too long.

The Emergence of Cities: Multiplication of Strangers

In the discussion above, it has been my intent to point up the fact that for most human beings throughout most of the species' time on this earth, the stranger has been the exception, not the rule. The ways in which he has been defined, the emotions and behavior which his arrival has evoked, have varied enormously.[5] But in all this variation there appears a common thread: his arrival is always sufficiently infrequent to be disruptive to routine and to call forth extraordinary behavior.[6] Now this state of affairs is perfectly acceptable and workable as long as the number of strangers to be encountered remains minimal. And the number of encountered strangers remains minimal as long as persons live in small bands or towns or villages of relatively stable population and as long as they are relatively isolated from other persons in other small bands or towns or villages. But this state of affairs becomes unacceptable and unworkable with the appearance of cities.

Exactly when and where and how the first cities arose remains a matter of conjecture. Received scholarly wisdom has it that the emergence of cities—of relatively large human settlements in which residents did not provide their own food—was dependent upon certain developments in technology, especially the invention of writing and the plow.[7] The first cities are usually said to have appeared between 4,000 and 3,000 B.C., or perhaps somewhat later—the estimates vary according to how the archeological evidence is read, how the investigator defines a city, and so on—and they are usually placed in Mesopotamia.[8] A few scholars have lately challenged this conventional truth, arguing that recent archeological work in Turkey—at the mound known as Catal Hüyük—indicates that cities may have existed as long ago as 7,000 B.C. or earlier (Mellaart, 1964). And, basing her thesis on the Catal Hüyük findings, Jane Jacobs (1969) has argued that rather than the agricultural revolution's making possible the emergence of cities, cities made possible the agricultural revolution.

It is not my intention to embroil myself in such controversies. The only important point here is that sometime, somewhere, somehow, a new form of human settlement—the city—came into being. And when it did, for the first time, human beings were faced with a social situation unlike anything they had known before. For the first time, human beings were faced with a situation in which the stranger was not the exception, but the rule.[9]

Before proceeding, it would seem advisable to consider in some detail the relation between population size and the possibilities for personal knowing, and to confront the difficult question of the point at which, in the growth of a settlement, one can say that a city, a world of strangers, has emerged.

As long as a human settlement remains small, it is a very simple matter for everyone living in it to know personally everyone else living in it. But as it begins to increase in size, this becomes more and more dif-

ficult until, at some point, knowing everyone in the settlement is totally impossible. And as the population continues to increase, the proportion of the total that any given individual can know personally
becomes smaller and smaller until he is literally surrounded by strangers. This is hardly an earth-shaking observation. Everyone knows that
cities are "anonymous" sorts of places. But in asking why this should
be so, one is forced into some considerations that are more complex
than might at first seem the case. Let me suggest three reasons why
population increase should lead to anonymity.

(1) First, and probably most obvious, there would appear to be a
sheer *biophysical limitation* on the capacity of human beings to recognize, either by name or by face (i.e., to have personal knowledge of),
an infinite number of their fellowmen. I know of no research which
tells us the maximum numbers that can be known; human beings probably vary in their individual capacities in this regard.[10] My own guess
—and it is only a guess—is that the maximum number might be
three or four thousand, perhaps slightly more.

(2) As the population of a settlement increases, occupational differentiation becomes more complex, and with this differentiation, *structural limitations* to knowing begin to appear. Some part of the population becomes involved in relatively restrictive life rounds such that
their opportunities for encountering other residents of the settlement
are reduced. The warehouse clerk, for example, has less chance to meet
his fellow citizens than does the street merchant. The housewife knows
fewer people than does her shop-owning husband. In addition, these
spatial restrictions on the intersection of life rounds are reinforced and
compounded by status distinctions which make portions of the population "off limits" to other portions.

(3) Because of the peculiar character of larger settlements, *time limitations* to knowing also come into play. Large settlements have always
been those kinds of places which attract to themselves immigrants and
visitors.[11] Thus, at any given moment there are present fair numbers of
persons who have just arrived and/or who are just passing through. As
such, they have not had the opportunity to know or be known by any
significant numbers of the settlement's populace.

As the population of a settlement increases, these limitations to personal knowing grow in the intensity of their effect until at some point,
as I have said, the residents are literally surrounded by strangers. But
what is this point? How large does the settlement have to be before we

can say unequivocally that the small personal world has disappeared and the city, the world of strangers, has emerged? Again I must plead ignorance. In modern times, the question is almost meaningless. Ease of travel, suburbanization, and metropolitanization have blurred the distinctions between small settlements and large cities. And the enormity of the world's great cities has distorted our capacity to make these distinctions, even where they are not blurred. "I was raised in a small town," says the contemporary urbanite. "It had a population of only 50,000." But even considered from a historical perspective, from the perspective of a period when human settlements were more clearly separated by time and space, the question is difficult to answer. We are dealing here with a continuum, and while the extremes of a continuum are always clear cut, its middle points are notoriously hazy. I shall, therefore, have to be arbitrary. I shall say that once the population of the settlement reaches 8,000 to 10,000 persons, the transition to city has occurred.[12]

While this is an arbitrary figure, its choice is not entirely unreasoned. Eight to ten thousand persons is clearly too many, I think, for any individual to know personally. A settlement of this size must also involve a fair amount of occupational differentiation and thus structural limitations to knowing are operating. In addition, the reader should bear in mind that prior to industrialization, there were severe economic and population limits on the multiplication of cities. A settlement which reached a population of 8,000 or more was likely to dominate a large hinterland, precluding the growth of similar-size settlements nearby. It thus had no competition in attracting immigrants and visitors, and temporal limitations to knowing could play their part. London, in the twelfth century, for example, had an estimated population of between 20,000 and 35,000 (Comhaire and Cahnman, 1962), by today's jaundiced standards a mere village—hardly worth going out of one's way to see. But to a visitor of the period, it appeared quite a metropolis indeed and well worth the time and trouble it took to get there (Holmes, 1966).

A population of 8,000 to 10,000 persons is a *lower limit*. In discussing the emergence of cities and the consequent creation of a new social situation, I am generally talking about settlements of a much greater size. The Mesopotamian city of Ur is estimated to have had a population of 34,000 in the second millennium B.C., and Greater Ur (which would include the area immediately outside the city walls) is estimated at 360,000 (Wooley, 1954). The population of Babylon under Chaldean rule is thought to have been at least 200,000, perhaps as high as a million (Moholy-Nagy, 1968). Carcopino (1940, 1952) sets the population of Rome at the end of the first century A.D. at a million or more. Other scholars consider 200,000 a more reasonable figure (Russell, 1958; Sjoberg, 1960). There are, of course, no certainties in the business of providing population estimates for historical cities. Archeologists and urban historians battle mightily among themselves over the reasonableness of this or that figure for this or that city at this or that time. But even if only the most conservative estimates are taken seriously, most of the cities of history stand out quite clearly as large settlements, exceeding by some thousands my arbitrary figure of 10,000.

Let us now return to considering that new social situation which the rise of cities engendered: for the first time, strangers became not the exception, but the rule. Meeting strangers was no longer rare, it was a constant occurrence; and under these circumstances, the old ways of handling them were untenable.[13] It's one thing to kill such persons when they appear infrequently; it's another when they're continually about. It's quite possible to provide every stranger one meets with bed and board and good fellowship, but only as long as one doesn't meet too many. It's plausible to believe that the first stranger one sees is a god; it strains one's credibility to think that 100,000 gods have congregated in one place. One can take the time to interrogate the occasional stranger, but interrogating every person one meets in the street becomes a bit cumbersome. The old ways had served the people living in small personal worlds quite well; for the city dweller, however, they would not do. They required too much—psychically, temporally, and economically. The old ways worked well when the small personal group confronted the infrequent stranger. They would not work at all for the *stranger in the midst of strangers*.[14]

How then was city life to be possible? How has it continued to be possible for thousands of years and for increasingly larger numbers of people? How could human beings live out their lives in a world of strangers? To answer these questions, even to understand fully just what these questions mean, we must first turn to some matters of assumption, definition, and specification.

Analytic Groundwork

ASSUMPTIONS: THE NATURE OF HUMAN NATURE

Human beings are very peculiar animals indeed. Their peculiarity stems largely, I think, from their linguistic capacity—a capacity which gives them a freedom unknown to other animal species but which at the same time causes them no end of difficulty. Language frees them from the slavery of simple reactivity, from the bondage of stimulus–response. It enables them to control and direct their action vis-à-vis an object (or situation) because it enables them to name it, to confer meaning upon it rather than merely to receive stimulus from it. Language is freedom also because it makes possible a consciousness of self among individual members of the species: a consciousness, that is, of one's separation from the physical and biological environment. Different languages do this through varying devices (for example, pronouns, verb forms), and some languages allow a much greater sense of individual self than others (E. Becker, 1962:178). But in all human tongues this power to separate and thus liberate is present.

On the other hand, human linguistic ability also causes no end of trouble. Freedom, as everyone is always pointing out, is never easy. Thus, while it may be very nice to be freed from the clutches of simple reactivity, it also makes life more complicated. Since, in order to decide how he is going to act toward some object or event that confronts him, the human has first to name that object or event, to define it, getting through the day proves to be no simple task. If he is going to avoid standing around all the time with his finger in his ear wondering what to do next, he has to become terribly skilled at naming things, and this necessity sets up all kinds of possibilities for misunderstandings, confusions, and errors.

The linguistic creation of the self—of the consciousness of separate individual identity—also is as complicating as it is liberating. Like other complex animals, human beings experience fear and anxiety in the face of potential physical injury or death. Unlike other animals, human beings can also get upset in the face of potential nonphysical injury or "death." That is, they can be concerned not only with what is happening to their bodies, but also with what is happening to their selves. (In fact the linguistically created self can come to take such precedence over the biologically created body that the perceived destruction of the former, or the need to maintain its integrity may lead to the voluntary destruction of the latter.) The maintenance of biological life is a struggle for all living things. But only human beings compound the difficulties of life itself with existential crises, hurt feelings, insult, embarrassment, dishonor, shame.

These complications which language brings to the human life process are interrelated. How one acts relative to a given situation or object can be very important to the continued protection of the self, to the maintenance of self-esteem. And how one defines a given situation or object is crucial to how one acts. Errors in definition and thus in action can lead to all sorts of injuries to the self—one's own or another's. To avoid such errors, the individual needs (1) the rules for "coding" or defining, (2) accompanying behavioral repertoires which are appropriate to the coded object or situation, and (3) *enough information about the object or situation to be able to activate the coding rules.*[15] While the rules and repertoires are usually provided by the culture of his group, obtaining sufficient information is up to the individual himself. He has to utilize all his sensory apparatus, and, particularly when the object is a fellow human, often his linguistic powers as well.

It is not my intent here to delve into the full complexities of human defining and acting. These are multitudinous. Especially under heterogenous and rapidly changing life conditions, new objects and situations are continually appearing, new definitions continually emerging. Even in small, isolated groups there are undoubtedly interpersonal and interclique conflicts over coding rules and over appropriate behavior even when the rules are agreed upon. In the modern world, such conflicts are a routine feature of everyday life. Nor is it my intent to explore the intricacies of human acting and defining relative to physical objects or other animals. It is my intent, rather, to point up the crucial character of information—perceptual and verbal—in the coding and acting that human beings engage in vis-à-vis one another. As can be seen from what has been said above, if that information is insufficient or if it is unreliable, the individual will code the other (or the situation in which the other is involved) "erroneously," will behave "inappropriately," and will open himself and/or the other to the possibility of embarrassment, shame, dishonor, insult—or any of the other multitudinous ills to which the self is subject.

In the last few pages we have moved a long distance from the topic of city dwellers and their stranger-filled lives to consider briefly some basic assumptions about the nature of human beings.[16] The reader is undoubtedly wondering at this point just what the importance of information in human coding and acting and "self-protecting" has to do with the question of how people are able to live in the anonymous world of the city. But bear with me a while longer. Before the connection can be made, we need to make some further inquiries into this matter of information. That is, we need to consider some different types of knowing; we need to define some terms.

DEFINITIONS: CATEGORIC KNOWING, PERSONAL KNOWING, AND STRANGERS

In the foregoing pages, I have used terms like "personally-known others" and "strangers" without being very exact about just what they imply. Assuming that the common sense understandings of the reader would be sufficient for him to follow the narrative, I have not wanted to clutter it with matters of definition. The time has come, however, when such matters can no longer safely be ignored. If we are to come to grips with the situation of the city dweller, we must spend some time considering the various ways human beings can know one another, the various kinds of information they can possess about one another. First, however, a word of warning is appropriate. Analytic distinctions and definitions are intended to create clarity out of the confusion of reality. To the extent that they are successful, to that extent "reality" has been distorted. Nonetheless, they are indispensable intellectual tools, the *sine qua non* of human thought. But the reader must not confuse them with the raw reality they are designed to elucidate.

Categoric Knowing. By categoric knowing, I refer to knowledge of another based on information about his roles or statuses, to use the standard sociological jargon. That is, one knows who the other is only in the sense that one knows he can be placed into some category or categories.[17] One knows that the other is a policeman or a whore or a female or an American Indian or a student or a Frenchman or a king, or some combination thereof. The particular conceptions of what categories are possible, of what things there are in the world for a human being to be, will, of course, vary with various groups. So will the extensiveness of the available categories and so will the indicators of who goes where. All this variation should not be allowed to obscure the basic fact, however, that for all human groups, categoric knowing is a primary mode of apprehension. To know another at all is to know him always and at least as an instance of a category.

Categoric knowing may be said to be *simple*, when it is based exclusively on information that can be obtained visually. Thus, in the United States, information about the age and sex of another usually requires no more than visual apprehension. Categoric knowing may be said to be *complex* when it is based on information that is obtained both visually and verbally. Thus, merely seeing a young man on the street will not be sufficient for determining that he is a father. To know that, one would have to be told, either by the person himself or by another.

Personal Knowing. By personal knowing, I refer to knowledge of another based on information not only about his roles and statuses, his categories, but on information, however slight, about his biography as well. To know another personally is always to apprehend him as a unique historical event. It is always to recognize him either by face or by name or by some other means and to be able to connect with this face, or name, or whatever, bits and pieces of accumulated material.

Personal knowing may or may not involve actual acquaintance. Celebrities, for example, are those sorts of persons who are personally known to large numbers of people about whom they know nothing at all. And all of us carry in our heads, in addition to numerous national and local celebrities, individuals who are made personally known to us by our friends and intimates. Thus I have personal knowledge of Joe, my cousin Mary's friend, because she tells me about him. I even know, from the picture on her piano, what he looks like. But I have never met him myself.[18]

The dead, as well as the living, populate our personally-known world. Again, these may be celebrities, whose memory is perpetuated through books and songs and stories. Or they may be more "common folk," made available to me in the same way that my cousin Mary makes the living Joe available.

This population of concrete individuals that we carry in our heads is a shifting one. New additions are constantly being made; old inhabitants are constantly being discarded. Those most easily forgotten are probably those about whom we have the least information. But this is not always the case. There may be persons, for example, whom we see only once, whom we never meet, but who, for some reason, become indelibly etched in our brains, never to be discarded.

Humans vary, of course, not only in what it takes to make a concrete individual unforgettable, but in what it takes to make another personally known in the first place. Many of us have had the rather discrediting experience of being introduced to another two or three times and being aware that on the second or third occasion, the other has no memory of us at all, that as far as he or she is concerned, we are being introduced for the first time. And humans vary also, as was discussed above, in their capacities for personal knowing. Some persons can just barely manage to keep track of a few hundred concrete individuals; others manage to keep up with, perhaps, several thousand.

For most of us, the most important personally-known others are those with whom we are at least acquainted, that is, those whom we have met, with whom we have shared time and space and information. These are the persons of whom we commonly say, "I know him," as distinct from those of whom we say, "I know of him." [19] These are the persons whom we know casually, those with whom we are familiar, and those with whom we are intimate. These are the persons who are our acquaintances, our associates, our friends, and our families. These are the individuals who share our personal worlds.

To know another personally is not to eliminate knowing him categorically. Personal knowing supplements categoric knowing; it adds temporal events, nuances of meaning, relational depth to the stark outline of the other's roles and statuses. It adds adjectives and adverbs and qualifying phrases, as it were, to the simple sentence that is categoric knowing. In some instances, to carry the analogy further, the noun and the verb themselves lack meaning without their modifiers and qualifiers. That is—and the importance of this point will become clear soon—complex categoric knowing is frequently dependent upon personal knowing, categorical placement being dependent upon biographical information.

Strangers. The term stranger, in its popular as well as its scholarly uses, has a variety of meanings. It is often used to mean anyone with whom we are not acquainted, whom we have never met, even though we may possess a great deal of biographic information about the person. Sometimes it is used in a more philosophic sense to suggest human loneliness or separateness as in the Thomas Wolfe phrase "which of us not forever a stranger and alone." Less frequently, the term refers to persons who are "different" in some way from an established group, the latter being used as the point of reference. (See, for example, Williams, Dean, and Suchman, 1964.) Thus, one might speak of the Jews in a "Christian" community as strangers. Or, conversely, in the Old Testament, the word is often used to designate anyone not a Jew, anyone not sharing religious beliefs and rituals.

My use of the term is different from any of these. By stranger I refer to any person who is personally unknown to the actor of reference. Thus, as we have seen, while a celebrity is personally known to many persons, the majority of these are not personally known to him. In this sense, to all of us most of the world's three billion people are strangers.

Out of this vast reservoir of personally-unknown others, the average human being in his lifetime encounters—actually shares immediate time and space with—only a minuscule proportion. These are the persons of whom we can possess simple categoric knowledge. And these are the persons who are meant when I speak of strangers.

In this more restricted sense, then, *a stranger is anyone personally unknown to the actor of reference, but visually available to him.*[20]

The line between stranger and personally-known other is a fluid one, and social life teems with transformations from one to another. In fact, if looked at too closely, the distinction breaks down altogether. Let us imagine, for example, two persons walking along a deserted city street, each approaching the other. Let us assume that neither has ever seen or at least has no recollection of having seen the other before. They catch sight of one another as each is at either end of the block. And, since there is nothing else especially to attend to, they attend to one another (if this is contemporary America, they do so surreptitiously, of course). Each notes, at minimum, the other's age and sex, and each places the other accordingly. They come closer, they each glance, for a brief second, at the other's face. They pass, each going his separate way, each out of the other's thoughts, never again to be remembered. Now, in terms of the definitions given above, this is a clear instance of visual access and simple categoric knowing. Here are two persons, clearly strangers to one another. And yet, look more closely. For a very brief period of time, each possessed a small piece of biographical information which could be added to the information picked up visually. That is, one knew, for as long as the other remained in consciousness, that this other, whom one saw, did, at this particular time, on this particular day, in this particular street, walk along the block and pass oneself in the middle. For a brief second, each perceived the other as a concrete individual, a historical event. For a brief second, each was personally known to the other.

Despite such analytic nit-picking, the distinction between strangers and personally-known others remains, for all practical purposes, a meaningful one. The fact that the distinction is unstable, that strangers can be transformed instantly into personally-known others is one of the fascinating dynamics of social life—a dynamic that we shall have occasion to consider in more detail in Part 2. For now, however, the more static view, which clearly demarcates the one from the other, will be most serviceable.

SPECIFICATIONS: URBAN PUBLIC SPACE
AS THE LOCUS OF STRANGER ENCOUNTERS

Up to this point, I have referred repeatedly to cities as "worlds of strangers." I have spoken of the city as a place where persons find themselves to be "strangers in the midst of strangers." This is poetic license. It is time now to be more specific.

The city is not, everywhere and always, a world of strangers. The city dweller is not, everywhere and always, in the midst of strangers. He lives, as do all human beings, in the most emotionally significant parts of his life, in a world of personally-known others. He does not, because he happens to reside in a city, suddenly become devoid of spouse and children, relatives and friends, neighbors and work associates, drinking buddies and casual acquaintances. In fact, his personal world may be much more heavily populated than ever was that of the isolated islander, mountaineer, or villager. The personal worlds of these latter persons, however, were coextensive with their spatial worlds. When the villager left his home or the homes of his relatives, friends, or enemies and moved into the street, he was still surrounded by enemies, friends, and relatives. When the city dweller leaves his home or the homes of people he knows personally, he is surrounded by strangers. More precisely put, *the world of strangers which is the city is located in the city's public space.*

By public space, I refer to those areas of a city to which, in the main, all persons have *legal access*.[21] I refer to the city's streets, its parks, its places of public accommodation. I refer to its public buildings or to the "public sectors" of its private buildings. Public space may be distinguished from private space in that access to the latter may be *legally restricted*. A private club may deny access to all but its members and invited guests. A home owner or tenant may legally lock his door to the unwanted visitor. But a city may not restrict entrance to a public street.

This definition is admittedly crude. The line between public and private space, like the line between strangers and personally-known others, is a fluid one. Is a bar public if access is restricted to certain categories of age or sex or race? Is a park public if police systematically clear it of sleeping men? Is the sidewalk in front of a home public if the elderly resident of the house continually chases away the neighborhood children who try to play there?

Despite the crudity of this definition, it will serve for the time being. Just as we shall be concerned later with the dynamics of transforming strangers into personally-known others, so we shall also be concerned with the dynamics of the shifting definitions of public and private space, with the dynamics of claims to access and counterclaims to restriction, with the dynamics of power and powerlessness in struggles over territory. For now, however, the reader's common sense understanding is sufficient.[22]

I have said that the city's public space is the locus of the world of strangers. This remains true whether a given portion of public space is at a given time either actually or potentially populated by persons who are personally unknown to one another. If I walk outside the door of my house and stand on the sidewalk, I may see no one except two or three friends and neighbors. Nonetheless, I have still entered the world of strangers. At any moment someone I do not know may appear. If I live on a heavily trafficked street, the likelihood of that occurring is much greater than if I reside in an isolated *cul de sac*. But in either case, having crossed the common sense threshold from private to public space, I have entered the world of strangers, and in it I must somehow make my way.

Making Strangers Routine: Ordering the Urban Populace

Some pages back, it was suggested that with the emergence of cities, with the emergence of large settlements, the old ways of handling strangers which had been used by persons living in small personal worlds were no longer viable. Given this fact, it was asked, how was city life to be possible? Having completed the analytic groundwork, we are in a position not only to understand just what was meant by that question, but to begin seeking an answer as well.

Let the reader cast his mind back to the beginning of this chapter and to the descriptions of various ways in which various groups of isolated and semi-isolated persons dealt with the occasional strangers who appeared in their midst. Sometimes the strangers were killed, sometimes interrogated, sometimes feasted, sometimes gossiped about, sometimes involved in long and tedious ceremonies. Always the everyday routine of activity in which the group engaged was disrupted. But why? Why all this attention to the stranger? The reason is this: For these peoples *continued co-presence without personal knowing was impossible. In order to relate to strangers beyond the initial seconds of the encounter, the people living in small personal worlds had to transform them into the only kind of human objects they were familiar with—personally-known others.* In order for coding to occur and the appropriate behavioral repertoires to be activated, biographical information had to be obtained, and to obtain it, attention had to be diverted from routine activities. Consider, for example, the Australian Aborigines. Behavioral repertoires were hinged to placement of the other in available kin categories. To know who the other was in any sense at all meant to know how the two of you were related. That is, complex categoric knowing, on which interaction depended, was itself dependent on personal knowing. One could not place the other without biographical information, without personal knowing. Sometimes, of course, as we have seen, the obtained biographical information only proved that no placement could be made at all, in which case the intruder was simply killed.[23]

Fortunately, at least from the point of view of the incoming stranger, few groups have been as restrictive as the Aborigines in their available coding schemes. Most have been quite capable of dealing with persons other than kin. But they have still required that the stranger somehow be transformed. Direct interrogation, utilized by the mountaineers as well as the Aborigines, is one way. One transforms the stranger by simply asking him straight out for biographical information. More subtle means include long ceremonies, "rites of passage" as Van Gennep called them, through which the strange other can be observed, conversed with in ritual terms, and gradually incorporated into the group as a familiar, known object. More immediate hospitality will also do the trick. Offer a stranger the comforts of one's home and one acquires the right and the opportunity to "find out" about him, to discover "who he is" in the personal sense.

Now, as we have seen, with the emergence of cities, this transformation of strangers into personally-known others ceased to be a viable course of action. One could still do it with some limited numbers, of course; but not everyone in the settlement with whom one was likely to come into contact could be handled in this way. There were just too many. Yet—and this is what was meant by the question of how city life was possible—without biographical information, how were city dwellers to know "who" their fellow residents were? Without access to biographical information, how were these strange others, encountered every time one entered the city's public space, to be coded? How were behavioral repertoires to be activated? Human beings, if they are to act at all, must define. And if they are to avoid hurts to their fragile selves, they must define with a relatively high degree of accuracy. *Yet all the city dweller had to go on, to know anything at all about these other people, was the information he could glean by looking at them.*[24]

That he needed to know who these others were in order to survive in a large settlement should be obvious. Buying one's food, making one's way through the streets, getting rid of one's wastes, securing water—all of these things and many more required that most people, at least on occasion, had to move outside their private little worlds. One's inability to transform all these strangers encountered there into personally-known others did not enable one simply to ignore them altogether.[25]

What the city dweller required then, was some kind of arrangement whereby the amount and reliability of his knowledge of his fellow residents could be maximized with a minimum of information. He required an arrangement whereby simple categoric knowing of others would be enough to enable him to make his way among them.

The answer to the question of how city life was to be possible, then, is this. *City life was made possible by an "ordering" of the urban populace in terms of appearance and spatial location such that those within the city could know a great deal about one another by simply looking.* A potentially chaotic and meaningless world of strangers was transformed into a knowable and predictable world of strangers by the same mechanism human beings always use to make their worlds livable: it was ordered.[26]

It is, of course, true that the capacity to know another on the basis of visual information alone did not originate in the city. What city living necessitated was the capacity to know another *human being* on the basis of visual information alone. The Tiwi didn't find it necessary to engage intruders in conversation before deciding what to do about them. Any such newcomers were clearly not human and had to be killed. Other groups who defined newcomers as gods or ghosts or whatever also needed no more than visual evidence to determine who these strangers were. But this capacity for "immediate recognition," as it were, depended on the belief that one's group or other known groups like one's own were the only inhabitants of the earth. Wherever that belief did not exist, or wherever it collapsed (and it was likely to collapse the moment people began arriving with any frequency), strangers had to be dealt with as fellow human beings. For most people, in most places, throughout major portions of time, dealing with human beings has meant dealing with personally-known others.

But in the city, the ways in which humans could know and thus deal with one another were extended. In the city, by ordering themselves, humans made it possible to live with and relate to larger and larger numbers of other humans. In the city, the parochial tribalist died. In the city, the sophisticated cosmopolitan was born.

What, then, was the character of this ordering? What did it entail? How did it operate? How was it maintained? To these and other related questions we now turn.

1

Urban
Public Order:
The
Historical
Transformation

In the three chapters that comprise Part 1, we shall be concerned with analyzing the character of urban public order, which, as I have argued in the preceding pages, is crucial to city living. As we shall see, this ordering of the urban populace has its basis in two quite different principles, producing two types of order: the principle of appearance, which produces what I shall call *appearential ordering*, and the principle of location, which produces what I shall call *spatial ordering*. Put simply, appearential ordering allows you to know a great deal about the stranger you are looking at because you can "place" him with some degree of accuracy on the basis of his body presentation: clothing, hair style, special markings, and so on. In contrast, spatial ordering allows you to know a great deal about the stranger you are looking at because you know a great deal about "who" is to be found in the particular location in which you find him. In either instance, you know how to act toward this stranger (acting toward, of course, may involve either interaction or avoidance) because having defined the object, your common sense world provides you with a behavioral repertoire. In Part 2, we shall be interested, among other things, in such matters as how individuals come to learn the "meanings" attached to various body presentations or locales, and in such matters as the difficulties that can be encountered when such learning is inadequate or when rapid change interferes with its reliability. For now, however, our primary concern is with the ordering itself.

In making his way through a world of strangers, *the city dweller, in all times and places, appears to utilize simultaneously, both principles of ordering. Cues to the identity of the strange other are simultaneously provided by his appearance and his location,* each piece of information reinforcing, correcting, or adding to, the other.* Nevertheless, it seems to be the case that there has been historical variation in the ease with which one or the other principle could be reliably uti-

---

* And, to a limited degree, by his behavior—a fact which until Chapter Five, we shall conveniently ignore.

lized. The trend of urban history, I am suggesting, is away from appearential ordering and toward spatial ordering. The preindustrial city, characterized by *mixed public space use* and *overt heterogeneity of populace*, is the site of the dominance of appearential ordering. The modern city, with its *specialized space use* and *masked heterogeneity of populace*, is the site of the dominance of spatial ordering. In Chapter Two, the preindustrial city is our focal point. Chapter Four is concerned with the modern city, and in Chapter Three, we shall consider the dynamics of the transformation from the dominance of one type of order to another.

Before proceeding, a few words of qualification. There is nothing uniquely urban in the utilization of body presentation and location as indicators of identity. Even in small personal worlds, persons commonly alter their appearance in accord with certain categories of identity to which they lay claim. Among the Toda, for example, only the women may tattoo themselves (Queen and Habenstein, 1967:35). So, too, in the small personal world certain locations may be defined as "appropriate" only for certain persons. Again among the Toda, only males have access to the "sacred dairies" (Queen and Habenstein, 1967:34). In the city, however, this common human linking of appearance and space to identity is emphasized, refined, and extended. It takes on complexities and importance unknown in the small personal world. As William Form and Gregory Stone have so nicely phrased it with regard to appearance and status:

The urbanite may frequently rely upon appearance rather than reputation: status may be temporarily appropriated by the "correct" display and manipulation of symbols, while in the small town it is more permanently manifested by the direct enactment of rights and duties. The bestowal of status in the city is often an inference from symbolism to social position; in the small town the bestowal of status proceeds from the evaluation of rights and duties appropriate to social position, and the relevant symbolism is basically symptomatic. (1964:335; see also, Goffman, 1951)

Enough said. Let us turn now to the preindustrial city itself to try to understand one historical solution to the problems engendered by the world of strangers.

CHAPTER TWO

THE PREINDUSTRIAL CITY
Appearential Ordering

City living is possible only because a city is not, in fact, a totally anonymous sort of place. While personal knowledge of the vast majority of others with whom the urbanite shares time and space is impossible, categoric knowledge is well within his grasp. The multitudes of strangers forming the urbanite's public milieu may not be personally knowable, but they are most certainly categorically *identifiable*, and as such, capable of being acted toward. That is, one can live as a stranger in the midst of strangers only because important elements of "strangeness" have been removed.

There is a crucial difference, of course, between simply identifying a strange other and identifying him with some degree of accuracy. It is the function of what I have called "urban public order" [1] to make that crucial difference. In the preindustrial city, the most accurate identifications were based on the strange other's appearance. It is the task of this chapter to suggest why and how that should have been the case. We shall begin by examining two of the preindustrial city's many characteristics: its mixed public space use and its overtly heterogeneous population.

Characteristics of the Preindustrial City

In utilizing one term to cover all cities prior to the onset of industrialization (and many cities or sections of cities untouched by industrialization even today), I am following Gideon Sjoberg. In *The Preindustrial City* (1960), Sjoberg argues that despite their many differences, these historical and contemporary urban settlements were and are sufficiently similar in important respects to justify considering them as representative of a single constructed type. Type formulations, since they seek unity in diversity, always obscure variation. And it is certainly true that preindustrial cities, as historical entities, varied enormously. They varied, among other ways, in size, function, societal type in which they were embedded (Lenski, 1970), and relationship to their surrounding societies (see, for example, Pirenne, 1925). In the face of all this diversity, it is perhaps not surprising that Sjoberg's unitary concept has been subject to criticism (see, for example, Cox, 1969; Pahl, 1970).

Although in adopting Sjoberg's usage, I am open to the same sort of criticism, I feel justified in doing so. Granted that for some purposes a more complex typology of cities would be more appropriate, with regard to the two characteristics in which I am interested—mixed public space use and overt heterogeneity of populace—all the cities of which I have any knowledge show a remarkable similarity. This is not to say that they are identical. But when contrasted with the modern city (see Chapter Four), preindustrial cities do appear all of a piece.[2]

COMPOSITE PORTRAIT OF THE PREINDUSTRIAL CITY

Before we begin our more analytic investigation of the preindustrial city's relevant characteristics and before we pursue the relationship of these characteristics to the dominance of appearential ordering, let us take a brief journey backward in time and visit a preindustrial city, not an actual one, but a kind of composite city—a mythical sort of place that brings together many of the sights and sounds we might have seen and heard had we been able to visit a wide range of settlements across a broad spectrum of time. This will be, by no means, a complete tour. We shall not enter the homes or other private sectors of the city but shall concentrate our attention on what is happening in its public parts, especially in its streets. And even after so limiting ourselves, we shall not have time to see and hear everything that might be seen or heard. We must be content with merely "getting a sense" of the flavor of a kind of city living very unlike anything we are apt to have known.

Picture yourself then, a modern urban human, dropped by means of a time machine, in the midst of some mythical composite preindustrial city. You are struck, first of all, by the sheer amount of activity there. Merchants, operating out of little cubbyholes, have spread their wares in the street. Next to them, a school of some type appears to be in session and you wonder how the students can concentrate. A wandering vendor is coming toward you, shouting out the wonders of his wares, and out of the hubbub of the street noises, you can just make out the shouts of other wandering vendors moving through the other streets. A man stops the vendor and they begin haggling over the price of an item. Then you notice that the more immobile merchants are also engaged in such haggling, some of it of long duration. Here and there, such an encounter has drawn a crowd and bystanders have involved themselves in the interaction. Everyone is shouting, with many insults passing back and forth.

Down the street, a beggar, his eyes obviously sightless, his face scarred by burns, keeps up a steady stream of requests for aid. As you pass through the streets you note that they are teeming with beggars. Some appear to be members of religious orders, others are lame or maimed, but many seem to have no bodily afflictions. Of the beggars, many are children; some are with adults, but large numbers "work" alone.

You turn a corner and are struck with a sight repulsive to your modern eyes: a man has been nailed by his ear to a door. Upon inquiry, you discover that this is his punishment for cheating his customers. He is a merchant and he has been nailed to the door of his own establishment. Now a huge cry attracts your attention and you turn another corner to discover three people, stripped naked, being driven through the streets with whips and brushes. Later, at the outskirts of the city, you see the remains of bodies hanging in chains in some sort of elevated cage. One or two of the chains support whole bodies; from the rest, hang only "quarters."

Back in the city itself, a wandering actor or street singer or story teller has attracted a crowd and is in the midst of a performance. In one plaza, you note a public reader who is droning on and on about absolutely nothing and you marvel at the patience of his listeners.

Suddenly a town crier appears, shouting to all he passes that a fire is underway at such and such a place. You follow the crowd and, arriving at the scene, watch the citizenry attempt to cope with the flames. No one special seems to be in charge, and efforts to either contain or put out the fire appear hopeless. People are bringing things from their houses to help—bowls or buckets—running to the well with them and running back to toss the water on the flames. All is chaos. Eventually, after destroying many of the buildings in the area where it started, the fire burns itself out.

Watching the people running for water, you follow them and stop awhile at a nearby well or fountain, where you see men and women bathing, washing clothes, exchanging gossip. You see men with large buckets come by to fill their containers and then hurry off to deliver the water to nearby houses. And you see women coming with jars to get their own water.

The initial shock of this strange place having begun to wear off, you begin to note things that at first did not attract your attention. The sheer filth of the streets appalls you. Everywhere there seems to be refuse, garbage, human and animal excrement. And then you note for the first time the large numbers of animals in the streets—pigs eating the garbage, insects attracted to the excrement, dogs tearing at bones. There are larger animals too, horses and oxen drawing carts through the crowded, narrow streets, and other animals being driven to the marketplace. And everywhere children: playing in the streets, running up and down the narrow alleyways; taunting the lame and maimed beggars, poking sticks at an obviously feeble-minded man who is helpless to protect himself. Here and there they are joined in their "games" by an adult, and your modern "sensitivities" are stung by the discovery that human beings can find the suffering of others so amusing.

Suddenly, pushing its way through the crowd comes an enclosed litter. It is being carried by four huge men and is richly appointed. Surrounding it are four other men carrying weapons. Much of the crowd makes way for the litter as it passes. Those who do not do so voluntarily are pushed aside roughly by the guards. You cannot see inside but you are told by one of the passersby that this litter is carrying one of the city's elite.

Night begins to fall and more and more people disappear from the streets. No lamps light the impending darkness. The sounds diminish with the light and you are suddenly afraid. For a while, nothing stirs. You can hear the occasional step of the night-watch, patrolling the deserted streets, the occasional cry of the watchman that all is well. You move along. Suddenly you note that a huge gate within the city that had been open earlier in the day is closed and that a whole section of the city has been sealed off. You cannot enter that section for it is walled. Now, should this city you are visiting be like Rome, new sounds begin, and the carts and wagons banned from the streets during the day make their appearance, bringing into the city the supplies it needs to stay alive. The lanterns of these trains of wagons provide a welcome glow in the oppressing darkness, and the sounds of the "teamsters'" voices are comforting. But if this city is not like Rome, it is probable that very little beyond an occasional scream breaks the darkness and stillness of the night. Somehow you avoid the lurking men, waiting in the darkness to rob you if possible, to kill you if necessary. You move from place to place, stumbling here and there across the outstretched legs of sleeping men. These are the homeless ones, huddled against walls and doorways, seeking warmth and shelter from the night.

At last, morning comes. Life begins with daybreak. And now it seems that there are even more people on the streets than there were the day before. You learn that today is a holiday, one of the many throughout the year, a day of public ceremony and festivity. The actors, street singers, storytellers, readers, and beggars are out in even greater numbers and are attracting even greater crowds. Again, if this city is a "Roman" sort of place, you might go to the Coliseum or to the Circus Maximus to enjoy the amusements provided you by the rich and mighty of the city. But if it is not a "Roman" sort of city, the streets and plazas and squares themselves are likely to be turned into places of amusement. Perhaps there is some religious ritual; perhaps the elites will show themselves by parading through the streets. Perhaps there will be dancing or human sacrifice or animal sacrifice or battles between men or between men and animals or between animals. Or perhaps the spectacle will be as simple as watching someone beat a dog with a stick. But whatever there is to be seen, it will be enjoyed with great gusto. And it will be free.

Suddenly you feel tired. The multiplicity of sights and sounds, the pushing and shoving and shouting of the crowd, the smells—particularly the smells—all of this begins to seem "too much." Too many people are crowded into too small a space; too many odors, most of them offensive; too many sights, most of them vile. You can't get away from the beggars and vendors. They accost you wherever you go. You can't escape the crippled limbs, the scarred faces, the running sores. Your person seems never safe from the constant assaults of the pickpockets. Everything seems jumbled together. Rich and poor, health and disease, young and old, house and business, public and private. All seems disorder. All seems chaos. Dizzy, frightened, confused, you step back into the time machine and are returned again to what now seems the orderliness and cleanliness of your own crowded, car-congested, smog-ridden, crime-obsessed modern city.[3]

MIXED PUBLIC SPACE USE

The above portrait particularly emphasized one characteristic of the preindustrial city: the multiplicity of uses to which public space was put. It is this characteristic which imparts to the modern eye, confronting the city through the works of historians and archeologists, an overwhelming impression of disorder. Some critics, disenchanted with what they consider the sterility of the modern city, have even suggested that our contemporary metropolises could well benefit from the importation of a little of this historical "disorder" (see, for example, Sennett, 1970). I do not share in this judgment of the preindustrial city as disordered. It may appear so to us, but only because the principle of its ordering, only because the dominant type of order, differs from that to which we are accustomed. Nevertheless, there is no question but that in contrast to the modern city, the public spaces of historic urban settlements were sites of an incredible mixture of activities and persons. Let us now explore this characteristic in some detail.

The Spatial Integration of Activities. In the preindustrial city, many human activities that we moderns think of as more appropriately housed in private or semiprivate space often occurred in public. *Educating the young* was one such activity. In ancient Rome, for example, primary school was typically conducted on the street, "under the awning outside some shop and invaded by all the noises of the street from which only a screen or tent cloth separated it" (Carcopino, 1940:105).[4] Or, in twelfth century Paris, where older students from all over Europe came to study with individual scholars, much of the instruction was of a highly public character. In warm weather, teacher and students, seeking relief from the breathless heat of the scholar's small house, held their lectures and discussions out of doors, clustering, perhaps, around one of the benches that were placed here and there along the city's streets. In winter, instruction moved inside but the door to the teacher's house remained open, encouraging all passersby who cared to, to stand about the entranceway and listen (Holmes, 1966:67–69).

Education, however, was hardly a major human activity in times past, and of the little that did occur, much undoubtedly took place in more private surroundings. A more ubiquitous public activity was the *elimination of body wastes.* This is not to say that private facilities were never available. The Roman elites had a version of indoor plumbing, well-to-do homes in many places and times were equipped with detached but semiprivate outbuildings, and even the common folk had recourse to the chamber pot for nighttime use. Nevertheless, going to the bathroom in the preindustrial city was not the almost exclusively private affair that it is today. A good deal of this activity probably took place on the street in full view of anyone who happened to be about. If, as Chastenet tells us, the seventeeth and eighteenth century Parisian gentleman considered it perfectly acceptable to conduct an "audience" while seated on his *chaise percee* (1952:231), there is no reason to suppose that our urban ancestors were inhibited by any "false modesty." Given the fact, as we shall see, that city streets were frequently the dumping grounds for human wastes, a little direct contribution to such "piles" would not appear unreasonable. Some cities, with perhaps more fastidious elites, were equipped with public latrines. While these at least moved some of the elimination activity indoors, they were hardly citadels of privacy. In Rome, for example, the seats of the latrine were not separated from one another with any sort of partitions. Carcopino suggests that in the Roman *forica*, "people met . . . , conversed, and exchanged invitations to dinner without embarrassment" (1940:41).

To a modern human, the most distasteful of the preindustrial city's public activities would perhaps be the *punishments* and *executions*. The stocks, the pillory, and the whipping post were all standard urban features. Most often located in the city's busiest sector, their associated activities were expected to attract an appreciative audience. Colonial Boston had three well-patronized whipping posts, and whipping was one of the more popular spectator sports in America at the time (Miller, 1966:256). Public punishment was not, however, limited to the pain of the lash or the indignity of the stocks and pillory. Sjoberg reports that in "the medieval city of Prato, thieves and prostitutes were birched naked through the streets" (1960:248). And we have already noted above that a merchant found guilty of cheating his customers might be nailed by his ear to the door of his shop (Sjoberg, 1960:248).

The ultimate punishment—death—was also often carried out in public. A foreign visitor to London in the early 1700s reported that "[public] executions are frequent in London, they take place every six weeks, and five, ten or fifteen criminals are hanged on these occasions" (quoted in Chancellor, 1907:62). In medieval France, the "gibbet" was a permanent fixture in every city and town, and after the hanging, the corpse was allowed to remain till it crumbled:

One can easily imagine the strange and melancholy aspect of this monumental gibbet [called Montfaucon and located at the outskirts of Paris] if one thinks of the number of corpses continually attached to it, and which were feasted upon by thousands of crows. On one occasion only it was necessary to replace *fifty-two* chains, which were useless; and the accounts of the city of Paris prove that the expense of executions was more heavy than that of the maintenance of the gibbet, a fact easy to be understood if one recalls to mind the frequency of capital sentences during the Middle Ages. Montfaucon was used not only for executions, but also for exposing corpses which were brought there from various places of execution in every part of the country. The mutilated remains of criminals who had been boiled, quartered or beheaded, were also hung there, enclosed in sacks of leather or wicker-work. (Lacroix, 1963:424)

Executions were frequently preceded by "parades" in which the condemned were pushed, dragged, prodded, or carried through the streets en route to the death site, as in Roman Jerusalem prior to crucifixion or in medieval Prato, where "forgers and heretics were dragged behind carts to be burned alive in the open square" (Sjoberg, 1960:248). Sometimes the spectators were allowed to participate as when, for example, the condemned was stoned to death. More frequently, their role was limited to that of a rather demanding audience.

New Yorkers had a way of dealing with Negro slaves who rebelled against their masters. In 1712, a number of Blacks set fire to a house in New York and killed the Whites as they hurried to extinguish the flames. For this crime, 21 slaves were executed: "some were burnt, others hanged, one broke on the wheel, and one hung alive in chains in the town." Those who were burned were roasted over a slow fire in order to prolong their torment for eight or ten hours. . . .

   One batch of condemned slaves [arrested in connection with an alleged anti-White plot], although they were given an opportunity to save themselves by confessing, steadfastly maintained their innocence until they were brought to the stake. At this point their resolution gave way and they admitted their guilt. But the crowd that had turned out to watch the execution was too large and its demands for vengeance too strong to permit the Negroes to escape by a last-minute confession: the sentence of the court was duly carried out and the Negroes were chained and burned at the stake. (Miller, 1966:159, 160) [5]

   Adding to the hubbub of the preindustrial city's public space were a number of activities which modern technology has since rendered unnecessary. *Water collection* is an example. The wells and the fountains of the city were the scene of much coming, going, and staying. Household water had to be collected there, either by the individual householder or by commercial water sellers. Laundry was frequently washed at the site of the water supply, providing the occasion for visiting and gossiping. And the ubiquitous fires led to much dashing back and forth between flame and water (Carcopino, 1952:37; Rowling, 1968:68–90).

Garbage and waste disposal also involved a good deal of public coming and going. Not all of this was human. The situation which Frances Trollope described for early nineteenth century Cincinnati was equally true of many preindustrial cities:

No pump, no cistern, no drain of any kind, no dustman's cart, or any other visible means of getting rid of the rubbish which vanishes with such celerity in London that one has no time to think of its existence; but which accumulated so rapidly at Cincinnati that I sent for my landlord to know in what manner refuse of all kinds was to be disposed of.

"Your help will just have to fix them all into the middle of the street, but you must mind, old woman, that it is the middle. I expect you don't know as we have got a law that forbids throwing such things at the sides of the streets; they must just all be cast right into the middle, and the pigs soon takes them off."

In truth, the pigs are constantly seen doing Herculean service in this way through every quarter of the city; and though it is not very agreeable to live surrounded by herds of these unsavoury animals, it is well they are so numerous, and so active in their capacity of scavengers, for without them the streets would soon be choked up with all sorts of substances in every stage of decomposition. (Trollope, 1960:38–39)

Pigs must have been as common a sight in the cities of times past as the automobile is today. Davies, writing of sixteenth and seventeenth century Madrid speaks of "the privileged pigs of St. Anthony [who] roved about everywhere grubbing for garbage" (1952:192–93). In the medieval European city, "pigs were left to roam the streets . . ." (Rowling, 1968:68), and the "hogreeve" was an important official in Colonial Philadelphia (Miller, 1966:125). Dogs, birds, and other animals also performed scavenger duty, but where these and the pigs were insufficient to their task, the result was an odd one: "Excavations at Ur [in Mesopotamia] reveal a continual rising of the street level due to the accumulation of refuse, so much so that many houses whose doorways were left below the street level had to be equipped with higher entrances" (Sjoberg, 1960:35).

All this nonhuman street activity was called for because the preindustrial city was never able to solve its short-run disposal problem. (The modern city has, of course, been successful in this, but has thereby created a long-run problem of rather incredible proportions.) Garbage and waste disposal was largely an individual problem, and most individuals appear to have considered street dumping the most convenient solution. In some cities, some residents, at least, made an attempt to presage the modern solution by throwing their garbage and wastes over the city's wall or outside the gate, but many of their neighbors undoubtedly considered this unnecessarily time-consuming (Sjoberg, 1960:93). Here and there commercial enterprise made a minor dent in the accumulation, as with the Roman fuller who collected the urine which city dwellers brought to him and which he needed in his trade (Carcopino, 1940:42), or with other businessmen in other cities who distributed human excrement to the outlying farms (Sjoberg, 1960:94).

Given the lack or minimal use of the printed word and given the generally low levels of literacy among the populace, the public space of the preindustrial city understandably enough was further enlivened by the *distribution and collection of news*. Town criers relayed elite pronouncements to the citizenry, warned of fires or other dangers, and spread news of interesting, if mundane, events:

The town crier [in medieval Prato] . . . hurried from one street corner to the next, to spread the day's news: births and weddings, and deaths, bankruptcies and emancipations, lists of lost property and lost cattle, even applications for wet nurses—while more important official news was imparted by three trumpeters on horseback, dressed in the colours of the commune, who blew a treble blast on their trumpets before announcing the sentences of the courts of law—banishments and fines, and sometimes executions. (Origo, 1957:59, quoted in Sjoberg, 1960:287)

And while no foreign correspondents provided news of the doings in other lands, while no *Wall Street Journal* informed the businessmen of price fluctuations, the travelling merchants, who could be found in the marketplaces of the city, might do so in their stead (Sjoberg, 1960:289).

Where the level of literacy was somewhat higher but where paper was hard to come by or expensive, the walls of buildings served as a medium for personal announcements, public notices, local news, and, of course, that most eternal form of human communication, advertising (Tanzer, 1939:5). Advertising was also the source of much of the din of the public space, for without access to radio, television, or mass-circulation newspapers, merchants took it upon themselves or hired others to run about the streets shouting out the wonders of their wares.[6]

Activities which, in the modern city, tend to be relegated to specialized public locations, were, in the preindustrial city, piled upon one another, as it were. *Buying and selling*, for example, often took place in the street itself, for the wandering vendors were everywhere.[7] Even where the businessmen had stalls or cubbyholes, both their goods and/or their activities tended to overflow, thus throwing up one obstacle after another to the innocent pedestrian. In Rome, edict after edict attempted to control this spill-over, but to little or no avail (Carcopino, 1940:47).

Ancient Rome, of course, had its Coliseum, its Circus Maximus, and its theaters, but in most preindustrial cities, no such specialized locations were provided for *entertainment and public pageantry and ceremonials*. Instead, these activities took place in the squares and plazas and streets. Even in Rome, those "public readers" who could not afford to hire a hall or room made themselves right at home in less costly settings:

As soon as they spied a group of people anywhere whose curiosity at least they might pique, they would mingle with them and unblushingly unroll their manuscript—in the forum, under a portico, or among the crowd at the baths. The *recitatio* had invaded even the crossroads. Examining the contemporary literature, we soon get the impression that everyone was reading something, no matter what, aloud in public all the time, morning and evening, winter and summer. (Carcopino, 1940:197)

In cities as diverse in time and place as eighth century Damascus and sixteenth century London, actors, storytellers, musicians, and street singers were ever-present, giving their performances whenever and wherever they could collect a crowd.[8] Public pageantry and ceremonials were frequent, far more frequent than in the modern city and far less likely to be spatially restricted or confined. One has the impression, reading historical descriptions of these cities, that events like the New Orleans Mardi Gras were scheduled with some regularity, albeit with more religious excuse.[9]

Wherever the rule of the elites was less than absolute, the city's streets and plazas and marketplaces were also the scenes of *political meetings and discussions*. Athens in the fifth century B.C. is perhaps the most well-known exemplar of this tendency, but it is by no means the only one (Bowra, 1952:12–13; G. and C. Charles-Picard, 1961:44).

Nor was *individual religious expression* confined to the city's temples, churches, or other sacred areas. In twelfth century Venice, for example, "small tabernacles were placed at many corners, wherein a lamp was lighted to honor a saint [and, incidentally] to illuminate passersby at the same time" (Comhaire and Cahnman, 1962:62).

Finally, note must be made of those activities which, while still occurring in the public space of the modern city, do so with much less frequency than was the case in the city of preindustrial times— *"hanging about,"* for one. As we shall see in the next section, preindustrial cities contained large numbers of organizationally unattached persons, floating populations as they are called. In twelfth century London, they were referred to as the *ribauz* and they spent their time

always on the edge of a crowd. They begged and plundered at the slightest provocation. They hung around outside the door of the banquet hall when a large feast was held. The king of England had three hundred bailiffs whose duty it was—though not all at one time—to keep these people back as food was moved from the kitchens to the hall, and to see that guests were not disturbed. Frequently in twelfth-century romances a beautiful damsel is threatened with the awful fate of being turned over to the *ribauz*. Nothing more horrible can be imagined. (Holmes, 1966:37; see also Chastenet, 1952:232)

Given the economic plight of persons such as the *ribauz*, it is not surprising that *begging* should also be a constant feature of public space activity. As we shall see later, beggars were an interesting (and not always pitiable) addition to the hodgepodge of persons crowding the streets of historic cities.

Residences in the preindustrial city were likely to be rather cramped, unpleasant places by modern standards. The elites, of course, were rather differently housed and they often had access to private courtyards. But for the vast majority of the urban populace—adult and child—"going out" was probably preferable to "staying in." As a consequence, a great deal of *socializing and playing* appears to have occurred in public space. Helen Tanzer's description of the small towns of southern Italy in the late 1930s seems equally applicable to the historic city:

The people spend a great part of their time in the streets, or so it seems to the traveler. All day long and far into the night, and especially in the early evening, the streets are full of people, sitting and standing about, and, for the most part, talking, eating or preparing to eat. In the evenings the workers swell the crowds so that it is hard to believe that so many people really belong in so small a town. (Tanzer, 1939:41)

In Imperial Rome, the public baths, as well as the *taverna* were great sites for socializing (Carcopino, 1952:46–47), as were the taverns of Colonial Boston (Miller, 1966:127–28). And everywhere, the children played. Writing of Elizabethan London, Byrne speaks of the "swarms of small boys [who] dashed in and out between the throngs and bumped into everyone and generally made a thorough nuisance of themselves" (1961:98).

Walking was undoubtedly the most constant of activities. Only the rich could afford litters or horses and although many working people had access to carts, in the narrow streets and alleys they were probably more of an impediment than a convenience. No telephones, telegraphs, or regular postal services sped messages across space. If one had anything to say to anyone, one went to see him. Securing water and food (no refrigeration), getting rid of garbage and wastes, inviting a friend to dinner, all such myriad activities in which humans engage, all required walking. It is true, of course, that distances were probably not great. Preindustrial cities, lacking efficient transportation means, were compact (and thus densely populated) places. Still, we moderns can wonder at the stamina of these urbanites. Consider Bill Sikes, for example. His city—nineteenth century London—has already begun its industrially induced outward march, the compact area of its earlier years left far behind. Yet there he is, setting out before dawn, young Oliver Twist dragging behind him, trudging along hour after hour, his toil broken only by occasional short rides on passing wagons, arriving long after nightfall at his destination. Does he then rest? Only briefly. He must be off and away again, walking several more miles to the goal of all this toil: the scene of the crime. And after all this not only is he not successful but he must then spend several hours more running to escape his pursuers (Dickens, 1961:chaps. XXI–XXII).

The Spatial Integration of Persons. If, as we have seen, so many activities in the preindustrial city occurred in relatively nonspecialized public space, it is hardly surprising that this same space should contain within it a great mix of persons. Enough has been said already about the various types of *entertainers*, about *beggars* (some belonging to mendicant religious orders), and about the *children*, all of whom were likely to be encountered almost anywhere within the city's public areas. Mention has been made, too, of the omnipresent *wandering ven-*

dors, although perhaps I have insufficiently emphasized their number and variety. Sjoberg's partial listing of the itinerant peddlers in Peking some decades ago should rectify this: "Glutinous rice cake peddlers, pomegranate blossom peddlers, turnip and radish peddlers, sesame oil peddlers, gate god peddlers, reed horn peddlers, 'moon cake' peddlers, jew's harp peddlers and charcoal peddlers" (1960:202). We have also met the *ribauz*, twelfth century London's version of the economically destitute and organizationally unattached *floating populations* that were to be found throughout all preindustrial cities.[10] Just how these persons survived at all is not clear. Sometimes, as Holmes reported above, they begged, sometimes they stole, but much of their time appeared to have been spent hanging about waiting to involve themselves in whatever was happening. Surely their numbers provided much of the manpower for the preindustrial city's many riots. In Rome, under Tiberius, for example, "the mob came to blows over the comparative merits of rival actors and the riot became so serious that several soldiers, a centurion and a tribune were left dead on the streets." [11] Or in Boston, in 1721 when the city fathers were attempting to inoculate the citizenry against smallpox, "the last six people to be inoculated were in such danger of meeting with violence at the hands of the mob that they had to be removed to an island in the Bay for safety" (Miller, 1966:248–49).

Yet even if the reader imagines all these sorts of persons jumbled together, he will still have an incomplete sense of the extent of the mix of persons in the preindustrial city's public space. The *maimed*, the *lame*, the *feeble-minded*, the *blind*, the *scarred*, and the *diseased* were also present to a degree incomprehensible to a modern Westerner.[12] The Charles-Picards write of the bone defects still visible in the skeletal remains of the citizens of Carthage (1961:155–56). Runciman tells us of the great number of "mutilated men to be seen in the streets" of tenth and eleventh century Constantinople (1952:77–78). In twelfth century London and Paris "the diseased and handicapped people were in evidence everywhere" (Holmes, 1966:227). Given the state of medical knowledge, given the generally unsanitary conditions of urban settlements, given the prevalence of mutilation as a punishment for even minor infractions, given the lack of hospitals and other welfare institutions, and given the rough character of much everyday sport, we should perhaps not be surprised at such widespread suffering, so visibly displayed.

But the mix of the preindustrial city was more extensive still. For its characteristic jumbling of stores and residences, of slums and palaces, of monasteries and warehouses, constantly brought together in all its streets and other public areas peoples of *all classes, occupations*, and *age grades*. Carcopino describes the situation for Rome:

Warehouses, workshops and the workmen's dwellings alternated oddly with private mansions and blocks of flats. (Carcopino, 1940:180)

The fourteen districts of the urbs did not offer that sharp contrast between working-class and wealthy districts which may be seen in modern capitals, and there was the same kind of accidental egalitarianism in the Rome of the Caesars as there was later in the Rome of the Popes, with wretched apartment houses and magnificent palaces built next door to each other, and millionaires and men of modest means living on different floors under the same roof. (Carcopino, 1952:33–34)

In tenth and eleventh century Constantinople, "in every quarter, palaces and monasteries, shops and slums had grown up side by side" (Runciman, 1952:67), and in Paris of the seventeenth and eighteenth centuries:

There was little distinction between the richer and the poorer quarters. Obviously the houses of the rich were more numerous in some parts of town than in others, but even in the noblest mansions, although the principal floor would be occupied by the wealthy, it was usual for the upper floors to be divided up and let out to the families of artisans. (Chastenet, 1952:230)

And a Chinese working woman, telling of her life in the city of P'englai in the late 1890s informs us matter-of-factly that "the house in which my master [a rich civil official] lived was in the north of the city near the North Gate. On that street there lived a poor scholar who had passed his first examination but had no money to study further" (Pruitt, 1967:120).[13]

Adding to all this was the practice of combining work and residence in a single dwelling. The scholars of twelfth century Paris lived and taught in the same small building (Holmes, 1966:67–69). Many merchants and artisans followed a similar pattern, and Sjoberg considers this work–home mix one of the main features of "preindustrial-urban life from the earliest cities in Mesopotamia down to the present day" (1960:103). As late as 1906, until the earthquake and fire destroyed the city and a way of life, San Francisco shared this characteristic with earlier urban centers.[14]

Thus, as a consequence of all this "jumbling," the historic city dweller had only to step outside the door of his house or apartment or shack to encounter persons representing a broad range of classes, occupations, and ages.

OVERT HETEROGENEITY OF POPULACE

In the preceding section, we have considered one characteristic of the preindustrial city: the mixed usage of its public space. We turn now to a second. To suggest that the preindustrial city was characterized by the overt heterogeneity of its populace is first of all to suggest that its populace was heterogeneous—overtly so or not. On that score, the sophisticated modern urbanite, viewing the past from the standpoint of his own cosmopolitan milieu, might be inclined to harbor some doubts. Yet we have already seen evidence of this diversity in the foregoing pages: great wealth and incredible poverty existing side by side, occupational differentiation of considerable complexity, health and disease rubbing shoulders in the street.[15] Despite the historic fusing of church and state, then as now, cities were the breeding grounds for religious sectarianism, for revolts and talk of revolts. In the cities were the slaves and the freemen, women of "respectability" and their more adventurous sisters. In the cities (as we shall later see), the con man and the specialized thief came to maturity.

Yet the heterogeneity of the city was not limited to internal diversity within a genetically similar native population. Despite the difficulties and dangers of travel, cities drew to themselves adventurous souls from distant lands. Runciman describes the scene in tenth and eleventh century Constantinople:

As you passed through the bazaars you might meet a company of Russian traders, come to sell furs and wax and slaves, wandering with a police escort—for one could not trust such barbarians' behavior—or you might see Arab merchants treated with the deference that members of a sister-civilization deserved; or slick Italians, from Venice or Amalfi, fraternizing with the citizens but viewed always with a certain suspicion. Occasionally you might come across a group of Persians or slant-eyed men from Central Asia, or might watch members of the small Jewish colony welcome co-religionists from the Caspian or from Spain. In the main streets you might at any moment be pushed aside to allow the passage of some foreign ambassador and his train, come from Egypt or from Germany to present his credentials to the emperor; or it might be a vassal-prince from the Caucasus riding by in state. And in his hostelry or at the sacred shrines the pilgrim [Christian Europeans] would almost always find some of his own compatriots. (Runciman, 1952:70)

So, too, in Imperial Rome, one could see "the farmer of Rhodope . . . the Sarmatian fed on draughts of horse's blood, the Egyptian who quaffs at its spring the stream of first-found Nile . . . the Arab, the Sabaean, the Cilician, drenched in his own saffron dew . . . the Sygambrian with knotted hair, the Ethiopian with locks twined otherwise . . ." (quoted in Carcopino, 1940:248). To Rome also came the doctors, men of letters, scientists and philosophers from all over the Hellenic world (Haarhoff, 1948:257–58). Constantinople and Rome, of course, were centers of great political and commercial empires. Not every preindustrial city could match their exotic cosmopolitanism. Yet, in the twelfth century, it was said of the Mediterranean cities of Beziers, Agde, Narbonne, and Montpellier, that in them "every language in the world might be heard" (Lacroix, 1963:255–56). To thirteenth century Paris came students from all over Europe (Douglas, 1952:96). And even such inhospitable and xenophobic cities as Athens and Carthage contained large foreign colonies.[16]

Heterogeneity, per se, would appear to characterize city dwellers in all times and places. What is particularly interesting and peculiar about the heterogeneity of the preindustrial city's populace is its *overtness*. Socially defined differences among persons were emphasized in costuming, in body markings, and in language.[17]

Costuming. Elizabethan theater depended heavily on costuming to indicate the status or rank, occupation, and nationality of the characters being portrayed (Byrne, 1961:264–66). In this, it merely reflected "real-life" practices. To a degree unknown to moderns, the resident of the preindustrial city literally "donned" his identity. The Roman citizen, for example, expressed the fact of his citizenship by wearing, as decreed by law, the white toga (Tanzer, 1939:9). A "gentleman" in the Colonial cities of America was known by his "perriwig" (Miller, 1966:111). In Lhasa, Bokhara, and urban Korea he was known by his long sleeves, extending below the fingers (Sjoberg, 1960:185). City women of Afghanistan to this day lay claim to respectability by wearing

a shroud-like garment that envelops them from head to toe. A strip of gauze across the eyes enables the wearer to see where she is going but permits no one to view her features. Only marginal women like prostitutes, or occasionally lower-class working women on the order of shopkeepers have gone about unveiled. A recent study of Rowanduz, a town of northern Iraq, suggests that the ordinary unveiled peasant woman who neglected to put on a face veil when entering the community was placed by the local citizenry in the same category as the prostitute. (Sjoberg, 1960:167)

Urban elites everywhere struggled to differentiate themselves from their "inferiors" not only by the design of their dress, but by the materials as well. The cap of the medieval Frenchman was made of velvet for the elites, rough cloth for the poor (Lacroix, 1963:523). In Elizabethan England, "commoners were prohibited by law from wearing clothing fashioned from gold or silver cloth, velvet, furs and other 'luxury' materials" (Sjoberg, 1960:127). Hair length also indicated status. Among the Franks, only the elites had long hair. Males of lesser rank "wore theirs more or less short, according to the degree of freedom which they possessed, and the serfs had their heads completely shaved." [18]

The clothing of outcaste groups (including ethnic and religious minorities, members of certain occupations and persons with certain diseases) was often regulated by law. Sjoberg tells us that the Parsi minority in the Persian city of Yezd were forced, until the 1880s, "to twist their turbans instead of folding them, [were] denied various colors, and [were]prohibited rings, umbrellas and other items" (1960:134). Their situation was typical.

Occupation, too, was signaled by dress. The lawyers of medieval France, for example, were distinguished by their round caps or *mortiers* and the executioners of the period were forced to wear a special coat of red or gold so that they would be readily recognizable in a crowd (Lacroix, 1963:523, 413). Sailors in twelfth century London wore *braies* (wide underdrawers) and a snood cap in summer, donning a *gonne* or frock in colder weather (Holmes, 1966:35–36). Each of the various types of itinerant peddlers of Peking, whom we met above, wore a distinctive costume (Sjoberg, 1960:202), as did the clergy of twelfth century Europe and the members of religious sects in numerous preindustrial cities (Holmes, 1966:37; Sjoberg, 1960:263–64). Intraoccupational differences were also expressed in clothing, as among the bureaucrats of Tibet, traditional China, or Korea (Sjoberg, 1960:240). In late nineteenth century P'englai, China, even a relatively low-level military official had to have an elaborate wardrobe:

At least two times every month, the first and the fifteenth and sometimes oftener, my master put on his official robes and went to the temple with the other officials and worshiped. He looked very grand in his embroidered robes with the mandarin squares front and back and the waves of water around the hem. There were red tassels on his hat and a peacock tail. He was of such a rank that even my mistress had a peacock tail, a very small one, that she fastened to the knot of her hair when she went out on state occasions, and an official button to her hat. But my master looked most beautiful when he was dressed in full military robes to examine the candidates for military degrees or went three li outside the city to meet or escort a high official who was visiting or leaving the city. Then he wore his armour with the great wide shoulders and the embroidered front and his high helmet. (Pruitt, 1967:76–77)

Finally, visitors to the preindustrial city, as well as resident aliens, were identifiable not only by their skin color, features, or bone structure, but also by their "national" or regional garb. Thus a reporter, describing the scene in burgeoning San Francisco of gold rush days, could communicate the great mixture of adventurers to be found there by referring to the special dress of such groups as the native Californians, Chileans, Sonorians, Kanakes, Chinese, and Malays (O. Lewis, 1962).

Body Markings. As we have just seen, socially defined differences in status and rank, occupation and "nationality" were made clearly visible in the preindustrial city by means of costuming. Body markings and mutilations made visible another type of socially defined difference: moral difference. Punishment practices in many historic cities and in the broader societies of which they were a part, often made it difficult for a convicted criminal to escape his past.

In tenth and eleventh century Constantinople, "serious crimes were punished by the loss of sight or of the right arm, lesser offences by the loss of an ear or by branding" (Runciman, 1952:77–78). Mutilations, of course, could result from circumstances not involving criminality or punishment. An individual without an arm or hand or whatever might have merely had an accident. Moral differences were more reliably expressed by branding, especially where certain brands were reserved for certain offenses (see, for example, Lacroix, 1963:417). With the appropriate symbol burned onto his forehead, the "culprit" was forever proclaimed as such to all who saw him. The symbol system in use in Colonial America, given below in part, provides specific example of a widespread practice:

A = Adulterer or Adulteress
B = Blasphemer or Burglar

D=Drunkard
H=Hog Thief
 I=Incestuous Marriage
T=Thief
V=Venery
(Miller, 1966:185, 255, 257–58; see also Plotnicov, 1967:61 on
scars as identity marks in contemporary Jos, Nigeria—a city
both preindustrial *and* modern in its characteristics.)

Such body markings were not necessarily permanent. Especially
when elites were involved, the "sinner" might merely be forced to
wear the appropriate symbol sewn on his or her sleeve or bodice for a
designated period of time.[19] As Miller has noted, "had Hester Prynne
[*The Scarlet Letter*] been a serving wench she would not have gotten
off so lightly as she did" (1966:257).

Language. While our concern here is primarily with the visual expression of heterogeneity, a few words regarding its audial expression
in the preindustrial city should be added. Intrasocietal speech differences among classes, regions, or ethnic subgroups have hardly disappeared in the modern world. Yet it does appear to be the case that in
industrial and technological societies, there is some tendency toward
their minimization. But in the historic preindustrial city and its society
and in contemporary feudal orders:

Speech . . . is a highly sensitive status indicator. . . . Upper- and lower-
class persons employ quite divergent linguistic patterns, as do sub-groups
within classes: ruralites vs. urbanites, men vs. women, old people vs. young
people, and occupational groups, too. (Sjoberg, 1960:128)

The preindustrial city dweller had merely to open his or her mouth to
be placed immediately into the relevant socially defined categories.

Identifying Strangers in the Preindustrial City

THE DOMINANCE OF APPEARENTIAL ORDERING

For many pages now we have been giving detailed consideration to
two characteristics of the preindustrial city: its mixed public space use
and the overt heterogeneity of its populace. But our major concern is
not with the details of these characteristics, however interesting they
may be in themselves. Our major concern is with understanding how
the preindustrial city dweller made his way in a world of strangers,
how he knew "who" the strangers were who surrounded him. The an-

swer should already be clear: he knew who they were because their "identities," the expression of their socially defined categories, were literally "written all over them." Usually he could not tell who they were by *where* they were. But he could, with considerable reliability, tell who they were by how they looked. If the preindustrial city dweller did not know his or another's "place" in spatial terms, he certainly did in appearential terms. Gideon Sjoberg summarizes the situation at least with regard to status succinctly:

The distinctiveness of personal attributes in the non-industrial city makes it almost impossible to evade one's class (or other status ranking), whether in a strange locale or in a crowded city street. Individual or group anonymity is unachievable. In a city where the elite wear fashionable clothing and the poor mere rags and tatters, dress at a glance advertises one's class position. (Sjoberg, 1960:132)

The order which is found in human life may be created in a variety of ways. It may emerge through a series of mutual agreements and understandings. It may be imposed on the majority by a small group with a corner on power. It may simply develop without special intent on anyone's part. Or it may arise out of some combination of agreement, coercion, and "accident." However it is created, once in operation, order functions to make life relatively predictable and thus, in some senses, bearable. Just how the appearential order of the preindustrial city came to be, just how the socially defined identities of the urban populace came to be so overtly expressed, is lost in history. But once this order emerged, it served to make predictable, and thus bearable, the world of strangers that is the city.

THE LIMITED USE OF SPATIAL ORDERING

It was suggested at the beginning of this chapter that city dwellers in all times and places appear to utilize simultaneously both principles of ordering—appearance and location—in identifying the strangers who surround them. It has also been suggested throughout this chapter that in the preindustrial city the order was primarily appearential. The two statements are not contradictory. It is true that compared with the modern city dweller's, the historic urbanite's reliance on spatial clues was limited. The integration of persons and activities in his city's public space made the determination of "who" on the basis of "where" a rather risky business. Nonetheless, it is also true that some spatial segregation of persons and activities did occur in the preindustrial city. To the degree that this was the case, location could combine with appearance to provide information about the strange other.

The Limited Segregation of Persons. Some segregation of *ethnic, nationality, or religious groups* does appear to have been relatively common in the preindustrial city. The imposed segregation of Jews in Medieval Europe into "cities within cities," as described below, is only one example of a fairly widespread practice. Although the group being ghettoized might vary from city to city, the arrangement of the ghetto was relatively standard:

A Jewish community in an European town during the Middle Ages resembled a colony on an island or on a distant coast. Isolated from the rest of the population, it generally occupied a district or street which was separated from the town or borough. The Jews, like a troop of lepers, were thrust away and huddled together into the most uncomfortable and most unhealthy quarter of the city, as miserable as it was disgusting. There, in ill-constructed houses, this poor and numerous population was amassed; in some cases high walls enclosed the small and dark narrow streets of the quarter occupied by this branded race, which prevented its extension, though, at the same time it often protected the inhabitants from the fury of the populace.[20]

Voluntary ghettoes or ethnic colonies seem also to have existed. In late sixteenth and seventeenth century Seville, for example, the traders, brokers, and bankers who came to the city to live from all over Europe established residential enclaves based on nationality (Comhaire and Cahnman, 1962:78).

In some cities, *visiting foreigners* might be required to lodge in quarters specifically reserved for persons of their type. Thus, in tenth and eleventh century Constantinople, Christian pilgrims stayed at the Hospice of Samson, while Russian merchants were shuttled out to "specially reserved houses in the suburb of Saint Mamas" (Runciman, 1952:62). In Canton, China, in the seventeenth and eighteenth centuries, foreign merchants were barred from the city but were given permission to stay in "reservations" across the river and were allowed to conduct their business through specially designated mediators (Comhaire and Cahnman, 1962:115). This Cantonese arrangement seems extreme and untypical. More commonly in preindustrial cities, tourists, pilgrims, and businessmen were expected only to sleep in the visitors' quarters. During the day, they presumably were free to roam the city.

To some degree also, *occupational groups* might be segregated. Sjoberg tells us that various guilds were often localized into specific quarters or along certain streets, and the streets of preindustrial cities "commonly bear the names of their occupational groups—the street of goldsmiths, the street of glassworkers, and so on" (1960:101; see also, 189).

Status or class groups were likely, as we have seen, not to be residentially segregated in the preindustrial city. Here and there in the historical descriptions, however, are suggestions that if there was little exclusiveness in where one lived, there might be some in where one played. In the 1600s, London's Hyde Park, for example, became the setting for aristocratic get-togethers. In an area known as the Ring—a dusty circle of land in the middle of the park—the assembled "beautiful people" took rides in their coaches, some of the coaches going in one direction, some in the other, so that all had the opportunity to see and be seen (Larwood, 1881:47–48). So too in Paris, at about the same time, the Place Royale contained a "continuous procession of people of 'quality' on their way to pay calls, to shop or simply to show themselves off" (Chastenet, 1952:227).

Finally, although this appears to have been minor, there was some segregation on the basis of *moral categories*. Helen Tanzer, writing of Pompeii, tells us about the *popinae*, places where the meats left over from the sacrifices were served. "These had a very bad reputation, and no gentlemen could afford to be seen visiting them" (1939:41).

The Limited Segregation of Activities. In all cities, of course, some spatial segregation of activities takes place. A barber shop is a barber shop, whether in first century Rome or twentieth century Omaha. A restaurant is a restaurant whether the diners be Medieval Englishmen or nineteenth century industrialists. The Roman was no more likely to have his hair cut in a restaurant than the nineteenth century industrialist was to have a gourmet meal at his barber shop. What I have been suggesting in this chapter is not that activities in the preindustrial city were never spatially segregated from one another—but only that they were considerably less so than they are in the modern city.

Yet it is also the case that some preindustrial cities—especially if their elites were wealthy, "civic-minded," or desirous of propitiating as well as coercing the masses—did manage to set aside certain public spaces for certain public activities in what we would consider a very modern manner. Rome is the primary example, with its Coliseum, its Circus Maximus, its theaters, its baths. Rome also had "public gardens," the forerunners of Western city parks. Carcopino describes their effect:

The presence of these gardens at the centre as at the periphery of the *urbs* gave it a double aspect. There were two Romes in one; a Rome that was still involved in its ancient past, archaic and inchoate, stifled and twisted . . . ; and another Rome, which the emperors had tried to purge and modernize, which encroached upon and surrounded the first with its *horti* (gardens)—airy, peaceful and verdurous as the squares and parks of London. (Carcopino, 1952:35)

The Roman who desired a peaceful stroll, an outdoor game, or just some quiet sociability could escape the hurly-burly of the streets, at least for a time.

So, too, seventeenth century Madrid had wealth and space sufficient to devote one square exclusively to pageantry—including parades and executions (Comhaire and Cahnman, 1962:77). And by the early 1600s, London was blessed with its first park when Charles I ordered that his royal preserve be opened to the public (Larwood, 1881:17).

The designation of certain public spaces as being appropriate for certain activities was not, however, always so formal a matter. In London, during the seventeenth and eighteenth centuries, certain areas within the parks managed to get themselves defined as appropriate spots for the manly art of duelling, quite unassisted by royal proclamation (Larwood, 1881:81, 291). Imitation generally seemed sufficient for the creation of specialized public space, as in London, again, where during the 1700s, St. James Park became the setting for a whole series of highly improbable foot races. One of these—a typical example —took place in February of 1747 between

one Williams, a cook in Pall Mall remarkable for the bulk of his body, and a footman, who was to carry weight in order to make him as heavy as the cook. They had to run a hundred yards, the footman having a hundred and ten pounds fixed upon his body. Unfortunately he fell down, and some of the weights came off, whilst the fat cook in the meantime sped on to the goal and won without difficulty. (Larwood, 1881:404–6)

The Tenuous Nature of Appearential Order

One of the more fascinating aspects of any sort of order is that it seems always to be in the process of breaking down. Human beings, an intractable lot, are forever ignoring traditions, upsetting agreements, transcending rules, jumping boundaries, and just generally getting themselves into all sorts of mischief. It is to be expected, then, that the appearential order of the preindustrial city (like the spatial order of the modern city) should constantly be under assault. And so it was. A discussion of this matter more properly belongs in Part 2 where we shall be watching the city dweller in action, since one aspect of that action involves playing fast and loose with the ordering system. Nonetheless, a few words at this point should help to dispel any notion the reader might have that identifying strangers in the preindustrial city was a "sure bet."

The difficulty of so tightly connecting identity to appearance, as was the case in the preindustrial city, is that an individual can rather easily alter the one by altering the other. When identities can be donned, they can also be appropriated. And the appropriation of identities would appear to have been one of the favorite pastimes in the historic urban settlement.

In some cases the desire to "pass" may or may not have been present. The sixteenth century courtesans of Venice, for example, were said to be of such a "respectable" appearance that

when they went out accompanied by their maids, . . . it was said to be impossible to distinguish between them and their more honest sisters: a fact which aroused the indignation of the latter and led to attempts to prevent the courtesans wearing jewellery or silk dresses in the streets. (Cunard, 1952:180)

And in the second century A.D., the dress of Roman slaves and freemen became so similar that writers of the period insisted that unless the latter were wearing their togas they could not be told apart (Carcopino, 1940:59).

In other cases, identity appropriation was quite clearly not accidental. One of the standard identities in Medieval Europe was the pilgrim, who traveled to this or that sacred place and who was granted free board, room, and entertainment in the monasteries or urban hospices along the way:

Naturally, imposters and charlatans abounded to take advantage of the many earthly benefits accorded to genuine pilgrims. . . . Each had his script and burdon, that is, the wallet for food and the staff, with an iron point at one end and a knob at the other, carried by all pilgrims. But more important, his hooded gown would be covered with badges and brooches to prove he had visited the various shrines. . . . Aided by a vivid imagination and agile tongue, these rogues poured out lurid stories of the wonders seen on their travels, their well-filled scripts witnessing to the delight, gullibility or simple faith of their hearers. (Rowling, 1968:194–195)

As suggested above, the exact origin of the appearential order of the preindustrial city is lost in history. But while that is true, there is certainly no mystery regarding who struggled to maintain it, or at least that aspect of it relating to status. The elites waged a continual, and in the long run, losing battle to differentiate themselves from the "common herd." The fact that they could not even rely on tradition but had to have recourse to the repeated enactment of laws, suggests just how much of a battle it was. Wherever economic conditions allowed great wealth to concentrate in hands other than those of the nobility, the battle intensified. Witness the following French royal edict of 1294:

No bourgeois shall have a chariot nor wear gold, precious stones, or crowns of gold or silver. . . . The bourgeois possessing two thousand pounds or more may order for himself a dress of twelve sous six deniers, and for his wife one worth sixteen sous at the most. (Quoted in Lacroix, 1963:86)

The somewhat less than slavish obedience of the bourgeois may be gauged by the fact that each succeeding monarch found it necessary to issue similar edicts, and one century later Charles VII was "obliged to censure the excess of luxury in dress by an edict which was however, no better enforced than the rest" (Lacroix, 1963:86).

Colonial Americans apparently knew their "place" no better than the Medieval bourgeois, for in 1651 the Massachusetts General Court felt called upon to express its

utter detestation and dislike, that men or women of mean condition should take upon them the garb of gentlemen, by wearing gold or silver lace, or buttons, or points at their knees, or to walk in great boots; which, though allowable to persons of greater estates, or more liberal education, yet we can not but judge it intolerable in persons of such like condition.

It is therefore ordered by this court, and the authority thereof, that no person within this jurisdiction, nor any of their relations depending upon them, whose visible estates, real or personal, shall not exceed the true and indifferent value of two hundred pounds, shall wear gold or silver lace, or gold and silver buttons, or any bone lace above two shillings per yard, or silk hoods, or scarfs, upon the penalty of ten shillings for every such offense, and every such delinquent to be presented by the grand jury. (Quoted in Miller, 1966:114–15)

This battle to keep identities "properly" expressed was, as I have said, eventually lost. The appearential ordering of the preindustrial city did not survive the chaos and confusion of early industrialization. To watch the breakdown of one sort of order and the emergence of another, we turn now to the crucible of this change: the early industrial city.

CHAPTER THREE

THE EARLY INDUSTRIAL CITY
Confusion and the Dynamics of Change

The goal of this brief chapter is as follows: to touch here and there on just a part of "what was happening" in the early industrial city so as to suggest, tentatively, some of the factors that may help to account for the great urban transformation—the transformation from the *dominance* of appearential ordering to the *dominance* of spatial ordering, from a world in which stranger identities were signaled most reliably by appearance to a world in which they are signaled most reliably by location.

While no process of change can be precisely dated, let us, for simplicity, "bound" this transformation within the eighteenth, nineteenth, and early twentieth centuries. This is also the period we conventionally think of as the era of revolutions—industrial, technological, and urban (as well as political). And it seems hardly a coincidence that changes in the ordering of urban public space should coincide with other convulsive historical changes. Indeed, they seem each to be elements of a sweeping alteration in the human condition and, as such, interrelated and intertwined in a complex chain of mutual cause and effect.

Before we begin to unravel the small part of this complex chain that is of concern here, two comments are in order. First, in attempting to account for the change to the dominance of spatial ordering in the public space of the modern city, it is important to bear in mind that the key word is dominance. As we have seen, some elements of the spatial order already existed in the preindustrial city (just as, as we shall see, some elements of the appearential order remain in the modern city). The latent possibilities for its emergence, that is, were historically present long before the eighteenth century. Our concern, then, is not with understanding the creation of something new but with understanding the new dominance of that creation.

Second, as I am using the term, an industrial city—early or otherwise—is not necessarily a city in which heavy industry is located. It is a city, rather, that is itself located within an industrializing or industrialized social order. In this sense, San Francisco, for example, is as much an industrial city as Pittsburgh or Detroit; London—and we shall be paying a good deal of attention to London—is as much an industrial city as Birmingham or Manchester.

Let us turn now to a consideration of some of the things that were occurring in the early industrial city. Because of the availability of materials, we shall be looking, primarily, at the cities of England and the United States. But now and again in the text and footnotes, we shall transcend this rather narrow sample to see what is happening in contemporary early industrial cities in other parts of the world.

Confusion: Factors in the Decline of Appearential Order

ECONOMIC AND POLITICAL

As we saw in the last chapter, the maintenance of appearential ordering, or at least those aspects of it relating to the visibility of status, was largely in the interest of the aristocratic elites.[1] They were its watchdogs, its righteous guardians. We saw also that this guardianship had, for centuries, been no easy job. The assault had not come from the masses. They were much too poor to even consider aping the dress of their "betters." No, the assault had come from that minority in the old feudal orders who had been able to accumulate great wealth: the merchant bourgeois. This is not to suggest that this group was ideologically opposed to the visible display of status distinctions. Exactly the opposite. Where they were in control, as in Colonial America, they took great pains to institute costuming regulations quite similar to those extant in Europe. What this group wanted, rather, was merely to display an elite status which they felt, by right of wealth, they deserved.[2] However, as long as the major economic base of the larger society was agricultural, and as long as the aristocratic elites controlled this base, the princes of commerce could be held at bay.[3]

Whatever else the Industrial Revolution may have been, and it was certainly many things, it was primarily a shift in the economic base of the social order in which it occurred and a transfer of economic and political power to the new group which controlled that base: the bourgeois.[4] Thus, one of the "things that was happening" in the early industrial city was that the old elites were losing their grip. The old guardians of the appearential order, of the laws and traditions which sustained it, were in decline.

Had industrialization merely involved the transfer of power from one sort of elite group to another, the old appearential order might, with some modifications, have remained intact. As we have seen, the elites of the bourgeois were no less concerned with the visible display of status than were their aristocratic counterparts. But industrialization involved more than transfer; it also involved, to a degree, distribution. The preindustrial city had been largely divided between the very rich (aristocratic elites and bourgeois merchants) and the very poor. In the early industrial city, despite the continuation of grinding poverty among the majority of the population,[5] the petit bourgeois, the not-so-wealthy middle class, had begun seriously to emerge. These shopkeepers and tradesmen and clerks and their families shared in the riches that industrialization was making possible. As their numbers increased, they also began to collect a share of the power that industrialization had torn from the landed aristocracy. They too were concerned with status and, helped along by technological innovations (discussed below), they saw less and less reason for expressing their "proper place" through dress. With this group, we see the beginning on a massive scale of what is by now a common characteristic of modern life: the appropriation by one group of the dress style of another.[6]

DEMOGRAPHIC

Something else was happening in the early industrial city. It was growing by leaps and bounds. As we have seen, preindustrial cities were relatively large settlements; some of them, Rome for example, may have achieved a size that would be considered large even by today's jaundiced standards. But in the period under question, cities began to grow with a speed and to a size that was unique in the history of the world. This rapid and massive urbanization is often referred to as "the urban revolution," [7] a revolution that is most certainly still in progress. We moderns have become rather blasé about this phenomenon. It has, for many of us, become a part of our taken-for-granted worlds. But for those living during the initial period of great expansion, city growth, whether welcomed or viewed with dismay, must have seemed incredible. Take London, for example. In 1800, it had an estimated population of 800,000. Sixty years later, well within the lifetime of a single individual, it had grown to almost 3 million. And during the succeeding forty years, it grew to 4.5 million (Fulford, 1952). New York City in the 1840s (remember, industrialization came later to the United States than it did to England) contained 400,000 souls (Toll, 1969). By the turn of the century, again a leap of merely sixty years, it had 3.5 million (Fulford, 1952). In cities where the initial population base was smaller, growth may have, from a phenomenological perspective, had an even greater impact. In 1780, the population of Manchester was a mere 25,000. Within forty years it had doubled, and then doubled again; that is, by 1820 it had reached 100,000 (Comhaire and Cahnman, 1962). Boston's population in 1830 is estimated slightly in excess of 60,000. Thirty-five years later, and prior to the annexation of surrounding communities, it had reached almost 200,000 (Lane, 1967).

It is not my intent to bore the reader with a continuing recital of these statistics. I give these few examples only to suggest the enormity of the growth and the short period of time it took to occur (see further, A. Weber, 1899). Under the onslaught of these hordes, untutored in, or unsympathetic to, city meanings and ways, the appearential order was shaken. For the fact is that these cities were certainly not growing because of a tremendous upsurge in the fertility of urban women. (Cities have never grown to any appreciable degree through an excess of births over deaths. Their birth rates are always too low, and in preindustrial and early industrial cities their death rates were always too high. See Peterson, 1961:Part II; Freedman [ed.], 1964.) No, these cities were growing because they were receiving massive influxes of rural populations.

Cities had always received the excess population of the countryside. Persons who, for whatever reason (laws of inheritance, enclosure laws, and so forth), had been without a place in the traditional order of an agricultural world, had migrated to the cities. Many of them became a part of the organizationally unaffiliated mass, the "floating population" of the preindustrial city. But in the eighteenth, nineteenth, and early twentieth centuries, they came not only because they were pushed but because they were pulled. The disintegration of the feudal order, which, in England, had been proceeding for centuries, gave them the freedom to go. The "opportunities" of the developing industrial order gave them the desire to go.

Some of them undoubtedly found the city as full of opportunity as they had hoped, swelling the ranks of the not-so-rich middle class in their climb upwards. Others merely replaced their slavery to the land with their slavery to the machine. Still others, at least for a period, could not be absorbed by the industrial and industrially related organizations that had beckoned. Instead they became part of a "floating population," the likes of which even the preindustrial city had never seen.[8]

As we shall soon see, this floating population played what I consider to be a crucial part in the emergence of spatial ordering. For now, however, the main point to be made is simply that this massive influx of rural persons—whatever their urban destinies—challenged the already weakening appearential order simply by being ignorant or disdainful of it.

TECHNOLOGICAL

The third thing that was happening in the early industrial city involved technological advances in the manufacture of cloth, and eventually, the mass production of clothing (Smelser, 1959; Lenski, 1970:313–315). I suspect that these advances dealt the most crucial blow to the dominance of the appearential order for they eventually made available to a broad spectrum of persons quite inexpensive clothing that copied in design, if not in quality, the fashions of the elites. Without the availability of such clothing, the masked heterogeneity of the modern city (to be discussed in Chapter Four) might never have been achieved.

I am suggesting then that under the combined impact of the industrial, urban, and technological revolutions the appearential order of the public space of the preindustrial city was severely weakened. If cities can ever be said to be "disordered," surely the cities of the eighteenth, nineteenth, and early twentieth centuries were that. However, out of this confusion—in fact, as part of it—other things began to happen which pointed to the kind of order that would dominate the emerging modern city.

Dynamics: Factors in the Emergence of Spatial Order

AREAL

The early industrial city was growing not only in population; it was growing in area as well. London, for example, had begun its outward march, extending itself beyond the walls of the original city, long before the eighteenth century (George, 1965:1–3). But in the period under question, it did so with greater speed and more assurance. And London was typical. Between 1867 and 1873, Boston hungrily gobbled up Roxbury, Dorchester, Brighton, Charlestown, and West Roxbury —thereby, like some science fiction monster, growing larger in a very short time and with very little effort (Lane, 1967).

The crucial aspect of this areal expansion was that it made large-scale spatial segregation of activities and persons *possible* should it be deemed desirable. The preindustrial city might be likened to a family of ten living in a single room. All activities and persons, as long as they remained at home, were inevitably piled on top of one another. In the early industrial city, as it were, the family made the first of many moves to a larger house.

TECHNOLOGICAL

The outward march of the early industrial city was not alone in making spatial order possible. It was aided and abetted by a whole series of technological innovations. The trolley, the railroad, and eventually the automobile added fuel to the flame of urban expansion. Indoor plumbing not only moved a variety of activities indoors, it moved them from public to private space. Changes in building techniques, the use of electricity, and heating innovations made staying at home a good deal more pleasant for masses of people than it had ever been before. The same innovations probably also contributed greatly to the enclosing of much commercial activity. Inventions like the telegraph and the telephone made physical presence unnecessary for communication and thereby reduced the need to be out and about. Innovations in printing (combined with increasing literacy) strengthened reliance on newspapers as another medium of communication, and at least some huckstering activity moved out of the public space and into newspaper pages. Ironically, greater advances in technology, the radio, and television, would place the urban citizen far more at the mercy of the sellers than were his preindustrial counterparts. The latter, at least, could escape the "hard sell" by going home.[9]

SOCIAL

Granting the importance of factors such as those discussed above, it nevertheless seems to me that the most crucial dynamic in the emergence of spatial ordering involved the struggle between the growing nonelite middle class and those persons forever immortalized as "the dangerous classes." Just exactly who respectable England was referring to with this phrase is rarely clear. It seems generally to have covered everybody in dire economic straits, and in the early industrial city, that was quite a crew. Of this group, those who actually worked, when they worked, could hardly have been very dangerous. Descriptions of employment conditions at the time make very clear that anyone holding down a job would have neither the time nor the energy for "revolution." [10] But, as we have seen, not everybody was working. The potential work force of the early industrial city greatly exceeded the system's capacity to absorb it. In the cities of the period, the organizationally unaffiliated, the "floaters" were highly visible, and they must have seemed very dangerous indeed. Not only did these wretches have the effrontery to endanger that most holy of holies—private property, not only did they begin to show every indication of their willingness to radically alter the distribution of wealth,[11] but they had the gall to deny to the developing petit bourgeois the respect and status that the latter felt they deserved. Witness the following heart-rending scene:

On the King's birthday in 1800 there was another grand Volunteer review, and as usual it again rained heavily. Notwithstanding this, 12,000 volunteers made their appearance in the Park [London's Hyde Park]. The King, surrounded by his sons and a host of gallant generals and officers, reviewed the corps, and the whole ceremony of the year before was acted over again. It commenced at nine, and ended at eleven; all this time his Majesty, without even a great-coat for protection, remained exposed to the pouring rain, and continued in the Park until almost every corps had left. Thousands upon thousands of spectators also were willing "to bide the pelting of the pitiless storm." No umbrella could withstand four or five hours' unceasing rain and the light and airy summer toilets were in a pitiful state. . . . When the review was over the crush at the Park gates resembled that at the doors of a theatre when some Roscian phenomenon is to appear; and when, to the entire demolition of the careful labours of the toilet, the gate at last was passed, not a coach was to be found, not a porch, passage, or pent-house but was crowded to excess, and there was nothing for it. . . . It would have grieved a heart of stone to have witnessed so many highly respectable tradesmen, citizens and fathers of families, bespattered and bedraggled from head to foot, without a single dry thread on their bodies, the water running absolutely out of their breeches' knees. Then the dear wives of their bosom and their lovely daughters followed the fate of the husband and parent, their wet muslins adhering to the fair forms like the draperies of classic statues—now a few of them having lost their shoes in

this terrible rout. What with the volunteers hurrying home, women fainting, drums beating, bugles sounding, dogs barking, vehicles splashing, and
children half-drowned in the mud, the confusion was worse confounded
than that of the Christian army before Jerusalem during the merciless
storm of thunder and rain, which, according to Tasso, Beelzebub sent
against the Crusaders. *The female misery was aggravated by the heartless
jokes and course mirth of the mob through which the dripping fair had to
pass. One of the ammunition waggons of the Hon. Artillery Company left
the ground completely filled with fair disabled objects of this description.
But even this lamentable sight did not move the heartless crowd and jokes
and gibes were showered upon them, thicker and more unsparing than the
torrent itself.* (Larwood, 1881:205–6, italics added)

Lacking the means to insulate themselves from the "common people," the petit bourgeois were subject to continual harassment
whenever they ventured outside their homes. In 1814, for example,
they attended a festival in Hyde Park—only to have their delicate
sensibilities harshly offended:

The scenes of riot and debauchery to which this fair gave rise appear to
have been unparalleled. Drunkenness of course was the order of the day.
Cups and balls, E.O., and other low gambling tables, at first were innumerable, but these were soon stopped by the police. All the scum of London
. . . congregated in the Park: swindlers and pick-pockets abounded. . . .
Pugilistic encounters and desperate fights between milling amateurs were of
frequent occurrence. One young woman stripped herself naked, and was
going to bathe in the Serpentine in the presence of thousands upon thousands of men, but was for the honour of the sex carried off by main force
by a number of women. . . . In the House of Commons the fact was mentioned that these festivals in the Parks . . . had "given rise to incredible
scenes of vice and depravation, to the infinite annoyance of all the middle
classes of society." (Larwood, 1881:249)

More than just sensibilities were involved however. John Miller has
called eighteenth century England, "the most lawless country in the
civilized world" (1966:264), and it was undoubtedly the not-so-rich
middle class, who could afford no protective covey of servants and
guards, who bore the brunt of lawlessness. One writer, describing the
improved conditions of 1858, suggests something of what this unpro-
tected group had to endure during the eighteenth and early nineteenth
centuries.

No member of Parliament would now venture to say that it was dangerous
to walk in the streets of London by day or night. . . . Bad as the dens of
infamy in London still are, they are not to be compared with those older

places of hideous profligacy. . . . In the most disorderly part of the town, such as St. Giles, Covent Garden, and Holborn, the streets every Sunday morning exhibited the most outrageous scenes of fighting, drunkenness and depravity. . . . Crimes, too, are greatly diminished in atrocity. The large gangs of desperate robbers, thirteen or fourteen in number, now no longer exist. . . . (*Edinburgh Review*, July, 1858:12–13, quoted in Silver, 1967:5, n. 11) [12]

In addition to jeers and insults, embarrassments and shocks, and dangers to self and property, it seems likely that the petit bourgeois were also subject to another less threatening, but perhaps no less irritating, form of harassment: they were constantly accosted on the streets by the unemployed, begging, offering services, or asking for jobs. A recent visitor to Guatemala City (where—as in the historic early industrial city—massive numbers of rural immigrants are swelling the ranks of the unemployed) reports that it was impossible to walk down the streets without being subjected to a continual stream of offers to wash his car, polish his car, shine his shoes, bless his car, and so forth, and to a continual stream of requests for money. He adds that he soon found himself becoming irritated by all this "assault" on his self and wanted nothing so much as the right to be left alone (personal communication). The proud but defenseless middle class of an earlier period must have felt much the same way.[13]

Even in the preindustrial city, the bourgeois merchants and businessmen had never been very happy about having to rub shoulders with "the common herd." Because they did so, the elites relegated them to an outcaste status—a status from which great wealth alone could not free them. In fact:

The wealthy merchant who acquires prestige and entrée into the upper class seeks to insulate himself from the common man. One method is delegating all negotiation in the market place to brokers and middlemen. In this fashion the upper-class merchant is spared from direct contacts with the lower class and outcastes. (Sjoberg, 1960:184–85; also, 120, 136–37)

In so insulating himself, the socially ambitious merchant was merely imitating the elites. In fact, it might be argued that the spatial integration of persons and activities in the preindustrial city might never have been tolerated had the elites not had the power and the wealth to keep themselves "apart." Servants and slaves ran their errands; guards surrounded them or carried them in a litter when they ventured forth from their homes. In interaction with "the people" they were given a deference enforced not only by tradition and law but by their own private police.

The rising industrial elites of the early industrial city might very well have perpetuated this pattern. They were quite capable of commanding the necessary wealth and power to keep themselves apart. But the growing petit bourgeois could not. Not only could they not afford a phalanx of servants to protect them in their necessary travels about the city; they were doubly hampered by having no traditional or legal supports for the deference they undoubtedly felt they deserved. And even if they had, they were confronted by an enormous population of rural immigrant floaters who had little knowledge of, or respect for, city ways.

I am suggesting, then, that this not-so-rich middle class group, growing in numbers and power during the period under consideration, were crucial to the emergence of the spatial order.[14] I am suggesting that many of the instruments which created and which now maintain that order—the police, zoning, "humanitarian" organizations—were and continue to be the instruments of this group. I am suggesting that there is nothing coincidental about the fact that the first modern police force was created in England in 1829,[15] that in England and the United States, "humanitarian" concerns and zoning regulations were nineteenth and early twentieth century phenomena, and that this is the same period during which the middle class was struggling to differentiate and protect itself from the "dangerous classes." We shall be looking more closely at these instruments of spatial ordering in the next chapter. For now, it is enough to know that their births were a part of what was happening in the early industrial city.

In these brief pages, I have been discussing a period in human history that is perhaps unmatched in the enormity and complexity of its transformations. It is a period that has been studied, analyzed, and written about again and again.[16] Truly to understand the transformation from appearential to spatial ordering would require a detailed analysis of all the concurrent and related transformations. Such a study would fill at least one hefty volume, if not more. My aims for this chapter, then, have necessarily been modest. My intent has been merely to suggest some of the factors that may help to account for the emergence of that type of urban public order which dominates the modern city. To that city and its ordering we now turn.

CHAPTER FOUR

THE MODERN CITY
Spatial Ordering

We have been looking to the past. Now let us confront the present. For two chapters we have been concerned with our urban ancestors. In this chapter, we shall be concerned with ourselves.

In the preindustrial city the problem of identifying strangers was largely solved by an ordering of the populace such that appearances provided fairly accurate clues to identities. In the confusion and chaos of the early industrial city, however, that solution became increasingly untenable. Appearential clues might still be used, of course, but their reliability could not be counted upon. Fortunately (or unfortunately, depending on one's view of the desirability of urban living), concurrent with the decline of the old order, a new order began to emerge —an order incipient in the preindustrial city but capable of dominance only in the modern city. That order, as previously indicated, is spatial. In the great sprawling cities of the twentieth century, location, not appearance, becomes the major key to identification.

Characteristics of the Modern City

The "modern city" like the "preindustrial city" is an intellectual construct. Some contemporary urban settlements—Los Angeles and Detroit (together with their surrounding suburbs),[1] for example— probably are better exemplars of the type than others. And while throughout the world, modern cities are in the process of becoming,[2] it is in the most highly industrialized and technologically developed countries that they have attained their most advanced form. Not surprisingly, then, it is the cities of the United States which will be receiving the major share of our attention in the following pages.

Two of the modern city's many characteristics are of central interest: its tendency toward specialized public-space use and the tendency of its populace to mask their heterogeneity. Again, I ask the reader to bear in mind that any actual city may exhibit one or the other of these characteristics to a greater or lesser degree. My concern here, as throughout, is not with reproducing "reality," but with abstracting from it.

SPECIALIZED PUBLIC SPACE USE

In many respects, the ideal of the modern city is like the ideal of a well-ordered home: a place for everything and everything in its place.[3] And, as in the well-ordered home, the spatial distribution of activities and persons in the city is more complex than it might at first appear. Consider, for example, that in the home, the "place" for an item, person, or activity may be a wing, a floor, a room, a section of a room, a section of a section of a room, and so on. Additionally, certain areas may be designated as appropriate for a multiplicity of purposes and persons (for example, the recreation room). Others may be quite limited (children and dogs stay out of mother's bedroom; don't play in the living room). And, what may be appropriate at one time may not be at another (don't go into the study while brother is working; keep off the kitchen floor—it's just been waxed). In discussing the spatial segregation of the modern city, then, I am not merely making reference to such well-known phenomena as homogeneous neighborhoods or suburbs. I am referring more importantly to the designation of certain smaller locales (a bar, for example) as being appropriate for certain persons and activities; to the designation of different appropriate activities and persons at different times in the same locale (during the New Orleans' Mardi Gras, or New Year's Eve, or Halloween or in the morning rather than evening). I am referring also to the fact that within any given space—say a block-long street—a multiplicity of activities and persons designated as appropriate may exist side by side; that is, who and what are okay here may not be the same as who and what are appropriate next door. In sum, then, I ask the reader to bear in mind that spatial segregation may be in terms of large areas or neighborhoods, in terms of sections within larger areas, in terms of locales or places within sections, in terms of small spaces within locales, in terms of time within any area, section, locale, or small space, and so forth.

The Spatial Segregation of Activities. A good deal of what went on in the public space of the preindustrial city has simply disappeared from the public space of the modern city. It has moved into private or semiprivate quarters. Educating the young is now thought to be an activity requiring isolation and relative quiet and is largely relegated to buildings in which no other doings are permitted. And those few occasions when the young are brought "out in the world" are not always greeted with enthusiasm by the surrounding community. I recall being present at Greenfield Village in Dearborn, Michigan, during an invasion of grade-school age children on a "field trip." From the harried expressions on the faces of the accompanying teachers, the museum's personnel, and the adult visitors, I had the distinct impression that a law outlawing such youthful excursions would have received overwhelming support.

So, too, the elimination of body wastes is no longer tolerated as a public activity. In fact, in the United States there seems to be some tendency to confine it entirely to the home. As Edward T. Hall has noted:

The distribution of public toilets in America reflects our tendency to deny the existence of urgency even with normal physiological needs. I know of no other place in the world where anyone leaving home or office is put to periodic torture because great pains have been taken to hide the location of rest rooms. Yet Americans are the people who judge the advancement of others by their plumbing. (Hall, 1959:138)

The exception to this, of course, is the gas station where rest rooms are prominently located and often advertised. Apparently the designers of public facilities are of the opinion that the only Americans who ever have to "go" are those in automobiles. At present, the public elimination activity of the few remaining nonhuman animals in the city— mostly dogs and cats—is still grudgingly tolerated. But the controversies that have emerged in the 1970s in a number of cities over how to handle the "dog mess" problem suggest that even that may eventually be banished.[4]

Nor are the public areas of the city enlivened any longer by punishments and executions. Gone are the whipping post, the gibbet, the stake, the pillory, and the stocks—those artifacts of urban life in "the good old days." The "humanitarian movements" that accompanied industrialization in both England and the United States apparently operated on the motto "out of sight, out of mind," and through their efforts a whole spectrum of man's inhumanities to man moved indoors, behind walls and out of sight.[5]

Other activities which added to the hubbub of the public space of the preindustrial city have simply been rendered unnecessary by modern technology: water collection, garbage and waste disposal, and, in large measure, the distribution and collection of news. The struggle over the use of certain public space for advertising purposes continues, however, as when conservationists and "city beautiful" groups battle mightily with business interests over outdoor billboards and signs.

This is not to suggest that nothing is supposed to go on in the modern city's public space. A great many things are deemed appropriate. There is, however, a tendency to assign certain activities to certain spaces, thus avoiding the "pile-up" that was characteristic of the preindustrial city. Some of the more interesting struggles that go on in the contemporary urban settlement have their basis in this tendency toward the avoidance of pile-up. In many cities, for example, the populace has been unable to decide whether streets (as distinct from sidewalks) should be reserved exclusively for pedestrians or exclusively for transportation vehicles. The utopian visions of city planners—with their overground malls and underground streets, or their underground malls and overground streets, or their overground streets and above-ground malls—illustrate clearly this preference for separation.

So, too, soliciting by prostitutes in many cities is tolerated only so long as it can be contained. Having set aside certain public areas for certain activities, city fathers and populace alike look askance at any spill-over. One can be certain that the following newspaper item did not go unattended in city hall:

Hookers are now soliciting on Muni [cipal] buses! Explained one to Lenore Cautrelle: "Well, you see, I can't afford a car." (Herb Caen, *San Francisco Chronicle*, April 22, 1970)

But if city hall fails to take the initiative, citizen groups may feel compelled to do so:

A group of actors and actresses, including Joan Hackett, Lee Grant and Peter Falk, yesterday asked Mayor John V. Lindsay to establish a "Red Light" district outside the Times Square area [of New York City] to rid it of *prostitutes and other undesirables.*

In a letter to the Mayor signed by Miss Hackett, the group said, "Quite simply stated, we propose cleaning up the Broadway area now, and when legislation permits, establishing a 'Red Light' district in New York *out of any business area,* but especially [out of] the most exciting theater area in the world." (" 'Red Light' District Requested," *San Francisco Chronicle,* June 20, 1972, p. 54; emphasis added)

Frequently, activity pile-up is controlled by means of licenses and permits. While retail buying and selling remains very much a public activity, it has largely been moved indoors, off the streets and walkways. Certainly much of this movement is due to technological innovations, economic pressures, and the general rationalization of business, but the practice of licensing, and thereby controlling the numbers of street vendors, was undoubtedly of some import as well.[6]

In many cities, entertainment, ceremonials and pageants, religious expressions, and political meetings and debates are thought to be most appropriately undertaken in the public areas set aside specifically for such purposes: nightclubs, auditoriums, arenas, churches, meeting halls, and so forth. The spilling-over of these activities into streets, parks, playgrounds, and squares is allowed, but controlled by permit. The situation in Detroit, described below, is typical of most modern cities:

> You had a story about a bongo drummer getting arrested at Belle Isle beach for playing a musical instrument in a public park. Does that mean I could get ticketed for playing my harmonica in Palmer Park?
>
> D. N.

> Yep, also for preaching or speechmaking without a permit. You get pinched if you draw large crowds, disturb others using the park. Penalty is up to $100 fine or 30 days in jail. You will be safe with your harmonica playing if you keep it to yourself. The bongo player didn't. Some 35,000 people were near the beach; hundreds gathered around him. Then gawking motorists created a traffic hazard. As for speechmaking, five parks allow it if you have a permit. If you can't get one, take your soapbox to the front of the Old County Building. You need no permit there, mostly because passersby seldom stop to listen. (Action Line, *Detroit Free Press*, July 2, 1966)

Much additional activity that cluttered the public areas of the preindustrial city has, in the modern city, been "controlled" by the simple expedient of making it completely illegal (Stinchcombe, 1963). In one medium-sized American community, for example, among the many acts that are prohibited in public places are the following:

> Beg in any public place;
> Utter vile, profane or obscene language in any public place;
> Engage in any indecent, insulting, immoral or obscene conduct in any public place;
> Make any immoral exhibition or indecent exposure of his or her person;
> Improperly, lewdly or wrongfully accost, ogle, insult, annoy, follow, pursue, lay hands on, or by any gesture, movement of body or otherwise wrongfully molest any person in any public place or public vehicle;

Engage in any disturbance, fight or quarrel in a public place;

Collect or stand in crowds, or arrange, encourage or abet the collection of persons in crowds for illegal or mischievous purposes in any public place;

Jostle or roughly crowd persons in any street, alley, park or public building;

Loiter on any street or sidewalk or in any park or public building or conduct himself in any public place so as to obstruct the free and uninterrupted passage of the public;

Disturb the public peace and quiet by loud, boisterous, or vulgar conduct. (Ann Arbor, Michigan Ordinance Code, Ann Arbor: Municipal Codification Service, Inc., 1957, chap. 108, paragraph 9:62)

Ordinances like these, of course, with their usefully vague wordings can be and are enforced quite selectively. In many instances they probably only legalize practices of spatial segregation which developed independently of the law and which subsequently came to be seen as proper. Thus the fact that these ordinances (and others like them) can be used to control such preindustrial city pastimes as hanging about, begging, or socializing and playing in the street, does not gainsay the fact that the original reduction of these activities was undoubtedly the consequence of forces having nothing at all to do with law.

One of the characteristics of an industrially developed and technologically advanced society is that it tends to keep a rather large proportion of its population tied up in organizationally controlled work and play. The old floating populations, so characteristic of preindustrial and early industrial cities, are, in the modern city, largely eliminated. When enough people are pulled into schools and jobs, and when their few free hours are devoted to home and family or organized recreation, then very little time and very few people are left for hanging about. Nevertheless, this trend toward affiliating the entire population is hardly complete, not even in the United States. Where floating populations still exist, and where hanging about is a standard activity, municipal ordinances can and do come into play.[7] Ordinances against loitering and blocking the streets have long been used against young black males (see, for example, Werthman and Piliavin, 1967), and in recent years they have been used against young people more generally. When the existing laws are not deemed sufficient to control newly emergent floaters, emergency measures can always be rushed through:

The anti-hippie "keep-off-the-grass" law in Carmel's [California] public parks is legal the State Court of Appeal said yesterday.

The 2-year-old law has been challenged as discriminatory and as an unconstitutional abridgement of freedom of assembly.

The Carmel City Council passed the law as an "emergency ordinance," in the summer of 1968. It prohibits climbing in trees or lounging on lawns in the parks.

The declaration of emergency left little doubt what the City Council thought it was: "[We] have observed an extraordinary influx of undesirable and unsanitary visitors to the city, sometimes known as 'hippies,' and find that unless proper regulations are adopted immediately, the use and enjoyment of public property will be jeopardized, if not entirely eliminated."

"The public parks and beaches are, in many cases, rendered unfit for normal public use by the unregulated and uncontrolled conduct of the new transients," the declaration said. (*San Francisco Chronicle*, March 28, 1970)

This same municipality apparently felt, however, that laws, in and of themselves, were insufficient to the danger:

Carmel "welcomes" visitors with a heart-warming pamphlet that tells them what they CAN'T do. For instance, no camping, no sleeping on beaches, no sitting or lying on the grass in Devendorf Park, no panhandling, no vending without a license, no standing around rapping, no staying out after 10:30 p.m. if you're under 18. And if you were planning to hurl the pamphlet away in disgust, don't. No littering. (Herb Caen, *San Francisco Chronicle*, July 30, 1970)

Begging is another activity that in most modern cities has been declared illegal. But like hanging about, its reduction (and in some cities, complete disappearance) has probably been the consequence of extralegal forces. The distribution of affluence made possible by industrialization, the development of a welfare state to care for the remaining indigent, and the efforts of the humanitarian, labor, and reform movements during the nineteenth and twentieth centuries were undoubtedly major factors in its demise. The fact that it has emerged again among the young tells us less, I think, about the economic conditions of industrialized nation states than it does about the joys that humans can find in "conning" one another. These youthful beggars may merely be reviving an old preindustrial city tradition—as we shall see in Chapter Eight.

Adults still socialize in the public space of the modern city (see Part 2, especially Chapter Six). And children still play. But both do so to a far lesser degree than did their urban ancestors. Neither activity is actually illegal, but both can be discouraged and controlled by the application of various ordinances—for example, against crowds collecting or against blocking a sidewalk or street. Again, however, other forces are at work. The modern urbanite—even the poorest—is simply far more adequately housed than was the average city dweller in times past. When he or she wants to visit with friends, the living room is as comfortable as the street or corner tavern. Many urban homes have areas specifically designed for adult and child recreation (playrooms, yards). These are made possible not only by improvements in building techniques but by the areal expansion of the city as well—the latter having made available a greater allotment of space per family. These private resources are supplemented by public ones—parks and playgrounds—another example of the modern city's propensity to relegate special activities to specialized space.[8]

Finally, some note should be made of the reduced necessity for walking in the modern city. This particular activity remains legal, but the extent to which it is approved is questionable. Like other historic necessities (for example, cooking over fire), it has, in the modern world, become largely a recreational activity, indulged in by masochistic cultists. Those people who still indulge in it *for a living*, such as mail carriers, beat-policemen and night watchmen, are frequently punished with low status, poor pay and the continual threat of attack by unfriendly dogs and people. Who or what are killing walking is a complex matter. The mass-produced automobile is usually assigned the major responsibility, but it is surely being aided and abetted by the areal expansion of the city (making possible wider, straighter streets, and itself engendered by the railroad and trolley), the telegraph, the telephone, and the establishment of relatively reliable government postal systems. As an aside, it might be mentioned that one of the more fascinating characteristics of the automobile is its ability to surround its occupants in a cocoon of privacy as they move through the public space of the city. As we shall see in Chapter Six, it thereby enables them to avoid for long stretches of time any necessity to confront the world of strangers.

The Spatial Segregation of Persons. Given the tendency of the modern city to segregate activities, it is hardly surprising that persons should be segregated as well. Yet the segregation of the latter is even more extensive than the discussion in the preceding section has implied. For the sake of simplicity and brevity, we shall here consider person-separation only in terms of class/caste/ethnicity, age, and moral categories, although these hardly exhaust the dimensions which modern urban humans use to spatially separate themselves from one another. In later chapters, when we consider such phenomena as "colonization" and "home territories," the full complexities of this separating tendency should become more apparent.

To paraphrase the old adage, to segregate is human, to integrate, divine. Even in the preindustrial city, where many forces conspired to "mix" the populace, there were strains toward flocking together among the similarly feathered birds.[9] By the eighteenth century, neighborhood segregation by class was already apparent, for example, in London (George, 1965; Chancellor, 1907), and as the city moved outward during the nineteenth and twentieth centuries, residential class homogenization intensified.[10] In all the emerging modern cities, wherever economic status was compounded by ethnicity or wherever caste lines were drawn, different "kinds" of neighborhoods multiplied: Chinatowns and rich Jewish areas; black ghettoes with middle class and poor districts (Drake and Cayton, 1962); working class suburbs (B. Berger, 1960) and enclaves of WASP affluence; Italian "villages" (Gans, 1962) and California developments of white southern immigrants on their way up.[11]

The contributors to this *class/caste/ethnicity* residential segregation, so characteristic of the modern city, are many and varied; too much so to consider here more than superficially. The areal expansion of the city, combined with a variety of technological innovations, made such segregation possible. And as I suggested in Chapter Three, the desire of the emerging middle class to separate itself from the "dangerous classes" provided a motivational impetus. Developers did their bit, creating district after district of similarly valued homes, and then "protecting" those values through "covenants" and "gentlemen's agreements." Zoning, at least in the United States, has been one of the more interesting instruments of segregation. It has had a major responsibility in banning mixed land use, that is, in separating place of residence from place of work. Since work places tend necessarily to be integrated, the banning of mixed land use must be considered a separatist stroke of genius (see Schnore, 1967; Toll, 1969). Zoning has helped, too, to ensure that residential areas, once developed on single-class lines, would evermore remain so.[12] And in recent years, urban renewal, despite its humanitarian guise, has operated largely to remove the black and the poor from areas impinging too closely on white middle and upper class residential and commercial territory.[13]

Commercial areas, even within the city's central business district, may be segregated as well. San Francisco, for example, a city so dense and compact that it is almost preindustrial in its spatial mix, is nevertheless very much characteristic of the modern city in its central schizophrenia:

The image-conscious San Franciscan nervously warns the visitor: "Stay off Market. It's no more San Francisco than Broadway is New York." A specious argument. Might as well say Post Street is no more San Francisco than Fifth Avenue is New York. Market is mucho San Francisco—our main drag, and don't linger overlong on the second word. It's a drag only if you can't face the fact that San Francisco isn't all bankers at Jack's, Dolly Fritz at Trader Vic's—and No. 263 off the Golden Gate Bridge. . . .

Market is old men spitting on the sidewalk and blowing their noses in the gutters. Women too broad of beam to wear slacks, but wearing them anyway, tucked into pointy boots. Girls with hair tossed a mile high over pouty faces filled with chewing gum. Old ladies smoking cigarettes and flipping them away expertly. Greasy-haired boys wearing pants so tight they must have been painted on, standing in silent knots, icy glance on passing girls. Young men in shiny leather jackets trying to look insolent and dangerous, which they could very well be. Slim-hipped boy-girls piloting motorcycles with frigid efficiency, returning your stare with contemptuous flick of dead eyes.

Market is rock'n'roll blaring out of little record shops, $9.95 shoes and $19.95 dresses, the smell of hot dogs, men spooning crab cocktails into faces hidden inside upturned collars, schoolgirls eating ice cream sandwiches, dirty magazines with their pages scotchtaped so you can't get a free peek, pinball games flashing their obscene lights, and bums in World War II overcoats who take your quarter without the thanks you didn't want anyway. . . . (Herb Caen, *San Francisco Chronicle*, June 14, 1964)

Perhaps it is not too outlandish to suggest that the fact that Market and Post are within minutes of one another may have something to do with municipal plans to turn the former into San Francisco's "Fifth Avenue."

Commercial segregation along class lines, of course, didn't just happen, anymore than residential segregation just happened. It too is the result of multitudinous forces, one of the more important of which, again, was zoning. In 1916, for example, zoning laws "saved" New York's Fifth Avenue:

They [the Fifth Avenue Merchants Association] wanted the garment industry to get out of Fifth Avenue, or at the very least, they wanted it literally held down. They wanted this because the things which were the essences of the garment industry—the strange tongues, the outlandish ap-

pearance and the very smell of its immigrant laborers, its relentless drive to
follow the retail trade wherever it went, its great concentrations of plants
and people—violated the ambience in which luxury retailing thrives. It
demands insulation from gross forms of work and workers, the symbols of
wealth and good living and sidewalks inviting the stroll, the pause, the purchase.

A representative of the association summed it up.

> The high-class retail business for which Fifth Avenue is so well
> known is the most sensitive and delicate organism imaginable,
> depending, first, on the exclusiveness of the neighborhood; sec-
> ond, on its nearness to the homes of the rich and the large ho-
> tels; and, third, on its lack of congestion, especially on sidewalks,
> so that the customers may not be crowded or jammed in a hur-
> lyburly crowd on their way to and from the different shops.
> . . . The loft buildings have already invaded the side streets
> with their hordes of factory employees. If an adequate move
> were made restricting the occupancy of the buildings so that no
> manufacturing could be done either on Fifth Avenue or from
> Madison Avenue over to Sixth Avenue, the matter would be
> solved. The employees from these loft buildings cannot be con-
> trolled. They spend their time—lunch hour and before
> business—on the avenue, congregating in crowds that are
> doing more than any other thing to destroy the exclusiveness
> and desirability of Fifth Avenue. If the exclusiveness and desir-
> ability of Fifth Avenue are destroyed, the value of real estate on
> Fifth Avenue will depreciate immediately. (Toll, 1969:158–59)

Given the eloquence of the Association's plea, it is not surprising that
the desired building-occupancy restrictions became law, thus protecting the inalienable right of the well-to-do to spend their money without having to rub shoulders with the "dangerous classes."

Age is another category along which the spatial segregation of persons in the modern city proceeds. Children were one of the first groups
to be contained. In the United States, for example, child labor laws,
compulsory schooling, and measures designed to control "juvenile
delinquents"—all nineteenth and early twentieth century innovations
—moved children out of the work place and off the streets, at least during major portions of the day. With the development of specialized public and private play space, it was possible to keep them relatively segregated for even more hours. The separation of work and residence helped
too, reducing any necessity for them to mix with working adults. Nur-
sery schools for preschool children and colleges for postschool youth
have extended the duration of their segregation from the adult world,
and, at least for the college-aged, have intensified it:

Relative to age in American technological society, we may note that the coincidence between it and territory is proceeding apace and is most spectacular in the host communities of the ever-expanding multiversities. Into many of these communities in recent years, there have thronged literally tens of thousands of what we might call "youth"—human animals ranging in age from late teens to middle twenties. Because the political powers have opted for the model of a few large educational institutions, rather than many small ones, "cities of youth" are being created. (J. Lofland, 1968:127)

Age segregation, however, is not limited to children:

Indeed, there would seem to be evolving a pattern wherein an age-sex unit of early adults establishes itself in an early-adult neighborhood, its members spawn their offspring and then, at the appropriate age, move to a middle-adult territory. In this way, age-sex units are always able to be with their "own kind," territorily protected from the contamination of contact with many other age categories. . . .

Although all of this is only a tendency at present, it would seem to be a growing tendency and one which assumes additional significance in the light of the already more pronounced territorial segregation of late adults. We are all well aware that persons of sixty and over—often described with polite euphemisms such as "senior citizens"—have begun to assemble in special buildings in cities, in special neighborhoods within suburbs, and, indeed, in special areas of the nation. (J. Lofland, 1968:129)

As with all forms of spatial segregation within the modern city, many forces are at work here also. The relationship between buying power and position in the life cycle, combined with the single-value character of many housing areas, almost guarantees age segregation. If these forces are insufficient, housing developers can help the trend along. Thus, an ad for a newly developed California subdivision, outside San Jose, assures potential buyers that they will have

Nice People for Neighbors

What kind of people are these who seek out country living . . . and then add their own special flair? To begin with, by requirement, one member of each family must be at least 45 years old. This puts the general population beyond child raising and ready for new rewards in life.

By actual survey, these same people are successful, well educated, friendly, and respectful of another's privacy. Many are working professionals—teachers, engineers, lawyers. There are several sales representatives, a fireman, a carpenter, even a former locomotive engineer! Virtually all residents are the kind of people with a high respect for tradition. (*San Francisco Sunday Examiner and Chronicle*, July 26, 1970)

Perhaps, from the point of view of the developers, the delights of age segregation (including, apparently, political homogenization) will compensate for the fact that buyers are going to have to enjoy their "country living" in the midst of one of the most urbanized sections of the United States (*Newsweek*, September 14, 1970).

As is rather clearly implied in the above advertisement, segregation of persons in the modern city also involves *moral* categories. Those humans deemed "beyond the pale" are set apart from "respectable citizens." Every city, for example, has its vice section and its skid row (road)—areas where the modern world's outcastes can be contained.[14] But sometimes, in some cities, containment is thought to be insufficient and more innovative segregating tactics are called for, tactics which may even conflict with political convention, economic necessity, or aesthetic values.

In Nice, France:

Mayor Jacques Medecin is convinced that tourism can be saved on the French Riviera if the federal government will permit him to open "maisons de tolerance," better known as legal bordellos.

According to the mayor, houses of prostitution will clear the jammed streets of their most disorderly traffic "and will solve a lot of other problems, too. . . ."

If he has his way, he will house Nice's prostitutes in a vast ensemble of comfortable buildings where they may receive guests in their own studio apartments "and practice their jobs as professionals."

"They will stay off the sidewalks to the great satisfaction of shopkeepers, restauteurs and hotelmen," promised the French politician. . . . (Ferris Hartman, "French Way to Keep Girls Honest," *San Francisco Chronicle*, April 10, 1970)

In South Africa, where to be black is a "mortal sin," new segregation plans fly in the face of the demands of urban economics:

South Africa's latest plans for the country's 15 million Africans and colored is to keep them out of sight.

If the proposed new national government legislation is implemented, Africans working in white areas will be restricted to the back rooms and out of town warehouses, out of sight of the five million whites. . . .

Despite the stubborn record of the government, few businessmen really believe that the government can carry through the new plans without totally wrecking the country's economy.

African jobs prohibited under the new legislation would be shop assistants, salesmen, reception clerks, telephonists, typists, cashiers, and clerks. . . . (*San Francisco Sunday Examiner and Chronicle*, August 9, 1970)

And in the United States, even aesthetic considerations must give way before the necessities of moral separation:

The grandeur of a 40-foot-wide staircase descending to the mezzanine level of the Powell street subway station may have to be abandoned, [San Francisco's] Transit Task Force reported yesterday.

Director Jack Barron said merchants in the area . . . are increasingly afraid that such a broad stairway might be a gathering place for militants or hippies. . . . (*San Francisco Chronicle*, July 21, 1970) [15]

Other sorts of morally devalued categories are simply put away altogether. The "feeble-minded" and "insane," who used to roam the streets of the preindustrial city, now have their own institutions. Many of the lamed and maimed now live out their lives in hospitals and nursing homes.[16] Both groups are the recipients of nineteenth and twentieth century "reforms." So is the contemporary lawbreaker. In fact, to anticipate a bit, the transformation from appearential to spatial ordering is perhaps most clearly expressed in the fact that in the modern city, lawbreakers are not mutilated, they are segregated.

MASKED HETEROGENEITY OF POPULACE

There is certainly no question but that the residents of the modern city are a heterogeneous lot. Of course, there are differences *among* cities in this regard—Des Moines is undoubtedly no match for New York or London—but these differences appear rather minor when we compare the city to the small town or isolated settlement. In fact, given the ease of modern travel and worldwide migratory tendencies, the modern city is probably a good deal more heterogeneous than was the preindustrial. What is particularly interesting about this modern heterogeneity, however, is the extent to which it tends to be masked.

As we have just seen, lawbreakers are no longer mutilated. That is, body markings no longer provide clues to the strange other's moral categories.[17] And while language (should we hear the other speak) may be of some help in identifying his or her ethnicity, home region, or class (Ellis, 1967), universal schooling, status mobility, and movies, radio, and television have done much to limit its reliability.

That leaves costuming. Surely in the dress and hair styles of the city's populace, there are reliable clues to identities. To a degree, of course, this is true. Sociologists have made much of the outward display of "status symbolism" in the anonymity of the city.[18] But what I suggest here is that they have made much out of very little. I do not suggest that city dwellers all look alike. They certainly do not. I have no brief with those who complain about the drab conformity of modern humans. To walk down the street of any modern city is to encounter the most marvelous array of get-ups and garbs. Nor am I suggesting that there are *no* structural links between costume and category. What I *am* saying is that these various costumes, in the main, provide rather unreliable clues to the "identities" of their wearers.

Many factors have contributed to this state of affairs. As mentioned in Chapter Three, the mass production of clothing has blurred the overt expression of buying power. The trained eye can probably easily distinguish between a $400 original and a $30 copy, but most of us have rather illiterate eyes. The general westernization of clothing is another factor—for example, the Russian traveler in Constantinople (Istanbul) today is likely to be wearing a business suit. In addition, in their search for new ideas, fashion designers have borrowed freely from the dress styles of many countries. Thus, the New Delhi housewife may wear a sleeveless shift, while the Omaha housewife may go to a cocktail party in a sari. The spread of affluence, particularly in the West, makes it possible for large numbers of persons to choose among the abundant variety of clothing styles available. And the absence of legal support for dress regulations allows them to do so freely.

This last mentioned factor—the absence of legal support for dress regulations—is perhaps one of the most crucial factors. Given this absence, costuming becomes not a matter of law—written or unwritten—but a matter of fashion, that is, a matter of fad. *And it is the essence of fad to be copied.*

Let us consider as one example the rather widespread adoption by the American young (as well as by some of their elders) during the late 1960s of longer hair, rather "casual" dress, and—at least by the males—facial hair. To certain segments of the American public, this particular form of costuming was a clear indication that the wearer espoused a dangerous, revolutionary, and negative philosophy (usually referred to as hippie-radical, an interesting contradiction in terms) which was inimical to the interests of upstanding, respectable, and patriotic Americans. Among this same segment of the public, it was also accepted as fact that wearers of "the costume" did not bathe, were usually unemployed, plotted revolution, engaged in free love, opposed war, and, most horrible of all, used drugs other than alcohol. Among other segments of the populace, the negative aspects of the above assessment might be absent, but the belief that "the costume" was a reliable indicator remained.

The fact of the matter is, however, that the reliability of the costume (or of any of its parts) as an identity indicator was (and continues to be) highly variable. In some conservative cities of the American Midwest or South, it might have been a fairly good one. In the more faddish climates of the east and west coasts, however, it discriminated rather poorly.

When it first emerged, during the early 1960s, the costume was probably a very good indicator. It was adopted then as an identity badge by young people, largely of middle class origin, who were rejecting the world of their parents and were turning inward in their search for peace (hippies) or turning outward in their search for change (radicals). These young people, however, unlike the elites of old, had no access to laws or the machinery of their enforcement to keep their identity badge undefiled. They could not prevent its adoption by apolitical and aphilosophical working class youth; they could not prevent its co-optation by the "hipper" elements of the American mainstream; and they could not prevent its mass production by manufacturers anxious to get in on the "latest thing."[19] The general result was chaos. Department stores did a marvelous business in men's wigs, catering to the desires of swinging, bearded, but short-haired conservative males to be even more swinging after working hours. Wedding pictures of the aristocratic young appearing on the "society" pages of major metropolitan newspapers were magnificent studies in incongruity. Standing amidst the symbols of wealth, power, and tradition were the bride and groom—she in her granny glasses and "Salvation Army store" dress; he in his beard, beads, and jeans. The picture was further complicated by the fact that the viewer could not be sure whether these wedding outfits were purchased in a second-hand store or at some very chic and expensive boutique. Even national entertainment figures could not be counted on to "be" what they "appeared," as the following illustrates:

Johnny Cash is no hippie, though his hair is almost long enough and his box back coat is acceptable both to his hippie audience and to his natural Oklahoma hill fans. Johnny Cash played Madison Square Garden this winter and upset his younger audience by endorsing the United States presence in Vietnam in a simplistic patriotic way. (Ralph J. Gleason, "Trains, Prisons and Some History," *San Francisco Chronicle*, March 9, 1970)

The entire situation was made even more chaotic by the fact that, simultaneously, forces were also operating in the other direction. That is, a good many persons were far less "straight" than they appeared. Dress regulations could be and were enforced in both school and work settings (although they were constantly being challenged in the courts), such that many persons who might wish to express a more "hip" identity were prevented from doing so—at least for part of the day.[20] In addition, many of the politically-oriented young—radical, liberal, and moderate—knowing that their usual appearance was offensive to the people they wished to influence, adopted what were thought to be more uncommittal styles.

What I have said here regarding the hippie-radical costume might be said about any other sort of costume. There is simply very little in the modern industrialized world to prevent persons from dressing up, down or across their "appropriate" social categories. If the young wish to dress like the old, and the old like the young; if the poor wish to dress like the rich, and the rich like the poor; if the males want to "feminize" their dress, and the females "masculinize" theirs; if the lawyer wants to look like a seaman, and the seaman like a lawyer; if the Nigerian wishes to dress like an Englishman, and the American wishes to dress like a Nigerian, who is to stop them? And since there is no one to stop them, and there is a giant worldwide fashion industry to encourage them, it is hardly surprising that in the modern city, the linking of identity to costume is a very problematic activity indeed.

Identifying Strangers in the Modern City

THE DOMINANCE OF SPATIAL ORDERING

The modern urbanite, then, in contrast to his preindustrial counterpart, primarily uses location rather than appearance to identify the strange others who surround him. In the preindustrial city, space was chaotic, appearances were ordered. In the modern city, appearances are chaotic, space is ordered. In the preindustrial city, a man was what he wore. In the modern city, a man is where he stands.[21]

A homosexual male is a man in a homosexual bar and not necessarily a man in a pink ruffled shirt. A prostitute is a woman standing alone in the "Tenderloin," and not necessarily a woman in a revealing costume.[22] Elites are persons who can be found in the stores and restaurants which cater to their incredible buying power and not necessarily the persons who wear silk. The poor are persons who live in a certain section of town and not necessarily the people who wear the most tattered clothes. A "middle American" is someone who goes to the Elk's Club, and don't let that moustache fool you. A sales clerk is someone who is to be found behind the counter, never mind that he is indistinguishable from his customers. A university professor is someone who stands facing the students in a university classroom. And the fact that he may look like his students, like a Wall Street lawyer, or like a skid row bum should not be allowed to obscure this simple truth.

The modern city dweller's penchant for linking "who" to "where" turned up again and again in my interviews with various residents of San Francisco and its surrounding suburbs. Ask them if they're ever afraid in the city, and they will tell you that it depends on where in the city they happen to be. Ask them if they ever talk to strangers and they tell you about a bar they know of where everybody talks to everybody else. Ask them about people and their responses are brief. Ask them about places and they cite chapter and verse:

Q: How do you feel when you're in a public place? Any public place.
A: That depends on the kinds, on the type of public place you're in at the time. It would vary as to the type of place you're in whether you feel comfortable or whether you don't.
Q: How about "making contact" with strangers?
A: I think that the way a person presents himself, through his dress, through his walk, his mannerisms can either help or hinder making contacts with other persons. A hippie on *Montgomery Street* [San Francisco's financial district] is very unlikely to make contact because *the Montgomery Street people* in *their area* are likely to alienate him [sic] just by the way he dresses. But in another situation, the idea would be reversed. I find that for me, one of the best ways to make contact, say I'm going to a strange place, is to know something about the way the people *in that place* handle themselves, the way they dress, the way they walk, and the speech and mannerisms and everything, cause that can really help making contacts—if you have to make contacts. If you prefer to remain anonymous, the best thing to do is just the opposite, cause nobody's going to want to make contacts with you. [Emphasis added]

Note that in the above quotes, the major reference is to place and *its identity*, or, to put it more accurately, *its ambience*. The first informant does not say—as the preindustrial city dweller might have— "That depends on how the people look who are present." Instead she says, "That depends on the kinds, on the type of public place." The second informant does not get specific about "appropriate dress, speech, and mannerisms," but she does get specific about place. She does not tell us that it would be hard for a hippie to talk to a short-haired beardless man in a business suit. But she does tell us that the hippie would have a hard time "making contact" on Montgomery Street. As we shall see in the next section and in Chapter Five, and as is clear from the above example, the modern urbanite does, of course, use appearance to help him identify strange others. But for him, *appearance is most reliable as an indicator when it is linked with location.*

The following segment of the summary of an interview with a San Francisco woman in her late thirties, suggests just how important the spatial order of the modern city can come to be in the life of its residents:

The city to her is made up of many districts and to know where someone lives is to be able to judge him. Thus, with regard to her daughter, she can tell a lot about people her daughter meets by the school they go to, for the school they attend tells one the neighborhood they live in, and the neighborhood they live in tells one something about the kind of people they are. She notes that busing [of school children] would make such judgments impossible and she feels that this is one of the reasons she is opposed to it.

In Chapter Five, when we explore the acquisition of urban meanings, we shall consider the intricate knowledge of place possessed by city dwellers in more detail. For now, it is sufficient simply to understand how crucial a part such knowledge plays when one is maneuvering in the world of strangers.

THE LIMITED USE OF APPEARENTIAL ORDERING

Just as the preindustrial city contained within it elements of the spatial order that would eventually dominate, so does the modern city contain within it elements of the appearential order that once dominated. Just as the preindustrial urbanite was helped along by spatial clues, so the modern urbanite is helped along by appearential clues. And when combined with location, these clues increase the probability that a "correct" identification will be made.

In the late 1950s in New York City, for example, one might have been able to make some assessment of a strange male other's class standing on the basis of such clues as the following:

1. *Upper-Middle and Upper Class:* well-groomed, clean, latest style clothes (especially suits and ties), subdued colored clothes which are neatly

pressed, of good quality, not worn and are of matching colors (using as criteria the present men's fashion advertisements).

II. *Lower-Middle Class:* less well-groomed, clean, wearing suits and ties but of out-dated style, colors not so subdued, clothes showing some wear, fair to poor quality, less well pressed, articles of "clashing" colors.

III. *Working Class:* not so well-groomed, clean wash trousers, no suit coat (a waist jacket usually), no ties, "clashing" colors.

IV. *Derelict:* poorly groomed, dirty, dirty wash pants, suit coat (usually out of style, worn, unpressed, dirty). (J. Lofland and Lejeune, 1960:105–6)

These little *appearential portraits* were developed by two sociologists in a study of Alcoholics Anonymous, as a means of "standardizing" observer judgments of participants' class standing. The very fact that they felt it necessary to codify in order to standardize suggests something about the less than clear-cut character of appearance as an identity indicator in the modern city. I suspect that in the preindustrial city, an intelligent and knowledgeable observer would no more have required codification of class indicators than a contemporary adult requires written instructions to distinguish between a Volkswagen and a Cadillac. In any case, portraits such as these are utilized. As we shall see later, however, the particularly skilled urbanite uses them cautiously.

Of somewhat greater reliability are the appearential clues provided by those hangovers from the preindustrial city—*uniforms.* These are not much worn in the modern city, but where they are they are of immeasurable assistance in making identifications. Most frequently they signal occupation, and since in the industrialized state, occupation is so closely tied to class, they signal the latter as well. Some of them make identification possible without any reference to location. The garb of a priest or the traditional habit of a nun are two examples. The outfits of some policemen are another example—although in a few communities, the traditional uniform is being replaced with slacks and blazer, a community relations move designed to "humanize" the force. While such a change may very well make policemen more lovable, it also makes them a good deal less identifiable—removing yet another appearential clue from the modern city's small supply of clues.[23] Many other uniforms currently in use are somewhat more tied to location. A hotel doorman, for example, is only unmistakably a hotel doorman when he is standing in front of a hotel door. A nurse (minus her cap) outside the hospital might be taken for a beautician, a waitress, a lab technician, or any one of a variety of "women in white."

As an aside, it might be noted that one of the more interesting aspects of uniforms is their capacity for signaling identity so quickly that, even in interaction, the uniformed other may be relegated to the status of nonperson, to use Goffman's term (1959:151). This is well illustrated in the common complaint of nuns that no one ever looks at their faces, or in the ability of a uniformed workman to enter a woman's restroom without attracting any notice; or, even more explicitly, in the following account:

A cat may not everywhere look at a king, nor does a person of position always look at a person of none. I was once a party to a practical joke, the point of which was to see whether a certain lady would recognize her own son were he to attend us, her guests, as a valet. She did not, as she never looked at his face.[24]

Finally, there are still in the modern city, as there were in the preindustrial city, what we might call *unmaskable diversities*. Skin color is perhaps the clearest example, although there are others: facial structure, age and sex (although both of these latter depend to a considerable degree on costuming), and highly visible deformities. To the degree that such physical attributes are thought to have *social* significance, they become important appearential clues. The situation of the black man or woman in the United States hardly requires elaboration here, although note might be made of the fact that until recently, skin color has operated rather like a uniform in rendering its "wearer" a nonperson. The underlying similarity between the complaint of the nun that no one ever looks at her face and the assertion of whites that "all Negroes look alike" is unmistakable.

Visible deformities as appearential clues often appear to have a rather different effect. As a number of sociologists have pointed out, some persons in America appear to feel that a handicap renders its bearer totally incompetent.[25] As such, they feel no hesitation in approaching total strangers to offer unneeded help or to express unwanted curiosity. This willingness on the part of "normals" to intrude themselves into the affairs of the "stigmatized" (unless the latter is viewed as threatening, a condition we shall consider in a later chapter) most certainly adds to the burden of an already burdensome life as the following incident clearly demonstrates:

A male, middle aged, is wandering about the bus depot. He is blind, or at least partially blind and has with him a mutt who apparently serves as his guide dog. The dog is wearing a special harness to aid in the signaling that must go on between them. A middle aged woman has been watching him for some time. He is now standing in front of the lunch counter, apparently preparatory to taking a seat. As he is standing there, the woman approaches, introduces herself and begins telling him about some people she knows who are blind and what was done for them and so forth. He listens politely for a few moments, then turns and begins to maneuver himself onto a lunch counter seat. The woman, noting this, desires to be helpful and she tries to assist him in getting up to the counter and on to a stool. In doing so, she bumps into the dog several times, changes positions and then gets herself, the dog and the man tangled up in the leash. During all this she keeps reaching down to pat the dog who is becoming more confused and excited all the time. Finally she leaves, the man orders coffee, finishes drinking it and leaves unaided; a far smoother departure than arrival.

The Tenuous Nature of Spatial Order

I suggested in Chapter Two that under the assault of human intractability, all systems of order are continually in the process of breaking down. The order of urban public space is certainly no exception. In the preindustrial city, persons were continually dressing themselves in "inappropriate" costumes. In the modern city, they are continually showing up in "inappropriate" places, doing "inappropriate" things.

We have already seen a good deal of this in the foregoing pages: prostitutes who desert their "assigned" district and solicit aboard municipal buses; young people who leave the confines of cities of youth and harass the residents of adult enclaves. This latter phenomenon, in fact, would appear to have recently become a cause célèbre among the guardians of order in many modern cities. The city of Carmel, California, as we saw, faced the "danger" squarely and passed some emergency ordinances. So did the European city of Amsterdam:

New ordinances to discourage young people from hanging around Dam Square in Amsterdam went into effect yesterday, touching off disturbances that left three persons wounded by police gunfire.

The new ordinances were intended to keep "hippies" from loitering in the square opposite the Royal Palace, and from sleeping there at night. . . . (*San Francisco Chronicle*, August 25, 1970)

In San Francisco, no new laws were enacted, but there was no dearth of moanings and groanings over the "terribleness" of the situation. In the spring and summer of 1970, local newspapers carried a series of stories predicting that most horrible of consequences—a slump in the tourist business—if things were not "cleaned up." In February, for example, the Sunday paper ran an almost full-page story with the intriguing headline: "Why Vital Conventions are Deserting the City." The factors contributing to this disaster turned out to be numerous, but among them was "the hippie situation":

"I'd hate to see San Francisco lose its image of being a friendly, courteous city," he [Robert K. Sullivan, general manager of the Convention and Visitors Bureau] added. "But the kids are pan-handling—and selling matter like the *Berkeley Barb* on *Union Square.*

"The conventions are not bothered by it, but the families don't want their children exposed to it."

The bureau manager said the individual tourist is getting pretty jumpy about San Francisco.

"We get more and more indications that the hippie thing is not an attraction—it is not like the flower children *in the Haight-Ashbury several years ago.*" (*San Francisco Sunday Examiner and Chronicle*, February 1, 1970, italics added)

Note that the objection is not to "hippies" per se. They were considered a tourist attraction during the late 1960s when they remained in their out-of-the-way Haight-Ashbury district. The objection is to "hippies" in Union Square, located in the middle of the city's commercial and hotel area.

In June, 1970, another news headline suggested that the worst had already happened: "Tourist Slump in S.F.—'Poor Image' Blamed." Within the story—a coverage of a local Convention and Visitors Bureau annual membership brunch—a number of remedies were suggested, among them:

"Let's also clean out the reputation that San Francisco or the Bay Area has been a haven of yippies, hippies, the birthplace of disorderly demonstrations, and dope."

He [one of the meeting speakers] warned that without vigorous action a serious "economic void" would result and threaten the business of the bureau members. (*San Francisco Chronicle*, June 11, 1970)

Whether there was any connection between this warning and the events of a month later, recounted below, is, of course, difficult to say:

Union Square Drug Arrests

The Tactical Unit arrested eight persons—four of them juveniles—on narcotics charges in Union Square in an afternoon swoop yesterday.

There was no violence and none of those arrested offered any resistance.

Sergeant Edward Epting said the arrests were made as a result of continuing surveillance of the Union Square area and "because we have had a lot of complaints from citizens" . . . (*San Francisco Chronicle*, July 30, 1970)

In paying so much attention to youthful assaults on the spatial order, I do not mean to imply that they are the only persons who ever get "out of place." The movements of one group into another's neighborhood or school are also seen as troublesome by municipal authorities (even when they sponsor it). Vagrants, drifters, and "skid row bums" are another source of difficulty. As Caleb Foote has so nicely demonstrated in his article on "Vagrancy-type Law and Its Administration" (1969), eternal vigilance would appear to be the price of spatial order. Sometimes offenders merely step outside their proper districts:

In discharging defendants with out-of-the-central-city addresses, the magistrate made comments such as the following:

"You stay out in West Philadelphia."
"Stay up in the fifteenth ward; I'll take care of you up there."
"What are you doing in this part of town? You stay where you belong; we've got enough bums down here without you."
(Foote, 1969:297)

But others have the effrontery to leave their own city:

Magistrate: Where do you live?
Defendant: Norfolk.
Magistrate: What are you doing in Philadelphia?
Defendant: Well, I didn't have any work down there, so I came up here to see if I could find. . . .
Magistrate (who had been shaking his head): That story's not good enough for me. I'm going to have you investigated. You're a vagrant. Three months in the House of Correction.[26]

Eternal vigilance must be maintained not only against "vagrants and bums," but against straying young black males, as well.

Gang members report that the boundaries of neighborhoods are patrolled with great seriousness and severity. The police are seen as very hard on "suspicious looking" adolescents who have strayed from home territory.

(Do you guys stay mostly at Hunters Point or do you travel into other districts?) If we go someplace, they tell us to go on home. Because every time we go somewhere we mostly go in big groups and they don't want us. One time we was walking on Steiner Street. So a cop drove up and he say, "Hey! Hanky and Panky! Come here!" And he say, "You all out of bounds, get back on the other side of Steiner Street." Steiner Street is supposed to be out of bounds. (What's on the other side of Steiner?) Nothin' but houses. (Werthman and Piliavin, 1967:77)

Things don't change. Like day before yesterday. We were sitting down on the steps talking with Joe and them. So here comes the police, coming down there messing with people.
"Where do you live?" they say.
"Up on the Hill."
He say, "Where do you eat at?"
"Up on the Hill."
"Where do you sleep at?"
"Up on the Hill."
He say, "Where you get your mail at?"
I say, "Up on the Hill."
He say, "Well don't you think you ought to be getting up the Hill right now!"
So we went up the Hill. (Werthman and Piliavin, 1967:98)

In Chapter Three, I suggested, rather tentatively, that the spatial order of the modern city was to some degree a creation of the middle class—anxious in the early industrial city to separate themselves, physically and socially, from the encroaching "dangerous classes." Here, I want to suggest, again quite tentatively, that the spatial order in the modern city is importantly maintained by this same group. I want to suggest, that is, that the instruments for the creation and maintenance of the segregation of persons and activities in urban public space—the underpinning of spatial order—are largely in their control. We have met these instruments over and over again in the preceding pages: zoning regulations—past and present; municipal ordinances—past and present; housing developments—past and present; laws and practices inspired by humanitarian and reform groups—past and present; and, those maintenance men par excellence, the modern police.

In a fascinating paper, "On the Demand for Order in Civil Society" (1967), Allan Silver has pointed out that the modern police organization goes back only to the middle of the nineteenth century. Prior to that time, police functions were generally handled by "ordinary, respectable citizens," or, for purposes of internal peace-keeping, by the military. With increasing concentration of large populations in small areas, neither proved very efficient. But with the creation of the police, it became possible to exercise potentially violent supervision over the population by bureaucratic means widely diffused throughout civil society in small and discretionary operations that [were] capable of rapid concentration. (Silver, 1967:8)

We have seen repeated examples in the preceding pages of these "small and discretionary operations" at work. And were it not for the police, the effects of many of the other instruments of spatial order maintenance would be largely vitiated.[27]

Behind the police, of course, stands the middle class. It is they who control the means to keep the spatial order intact in the face of repeated assault. It is they—however unwitting they may be of the full consequences—who perform or have performed at their direction the "dirty work" (Hughes, 1964) of sustaining predictability in a world continually threatened with unpredictability. But all urbanites, including those against whom the instruments of segregation are used, rely on this order, on this predictability, in making their way among strangers.

And a city's populace does more than simply "buy" bourgeois-produced order. Through their beliefs and understandings and through their actions, however unwitting, they reinforce and sustain it. It is to a consideration of those beliefs and understandings and actions that we now turn.

2

Urban
Public Behavior:
City Dwellers
in Action

The ordering of urban public space—whether appearential or spatial—is by no means a total solution to the problem engendered by the fact that the city is a world of strangers. Ordering merely makes it possible for the city dweller to operate within a relatively predictable milieu. It merely gives him a stable basis for making relatively accurate identifications of the strangers who surround him. It merely makes possible a basis for action. It certainly does not ensure that he will have either the *knowledge* to identify or the *skills* to act. In Chapter Five, then, we shall be concerned with how such urban learning is acquired; with the ways, that is, in which the city dweller cognitively masters the enormously complex physical and social environment that is his home.

Chapters Six and Seven, in contrast, explore some of the devices that city dwellers utilize to reduce the complexity of their environment and thereby reduce, to a greater or lesser degree, for a greater or lesser period of time, their need for urban learning. Our concern in these chapters will be with "avoiding" the city, in the sense of avoiding the occasions for, or the risks inherent in, stranger contact. We shall be watching urbanites as they literally or symbolically transform the city's public space—the locus of the world of strangers—into private or semiprivate space. We shall be watching, in various forms, one of the great miracles of city life.

Finally, in Chapter Eight, we shall be looking at some of the activities of highly skilled and highly knowledgeable urbanites when they are seeking not security but adventure, not avoidance but encounters, not transformation but utilization. In this chapter, we turn from activities that serve to deny the city as a world of strangers to activities that serve to confirm and celebrate it.

These four chapters, of course, hardly exhaust the topic of urban public behavior. In fact, they barely scratch the surface. They are perhaps most fruitfully read as mere glimpses behind the curtain of disattention that familiarity has raised before the human drama which is daily acted out in urban public space.

CHAPTER FIVE

URBAN LEARNING
The Acquisition of City Meanings and Skills

If we are to begin to come to grips with the process of urban learning, the process of acquiring the requisite knowledge and skills for acting in a world of strangers, it seems advisable to spend a few moments at the outset reviewing and bringing together some of the ideas that have been sprinkled here and there in the foregoing pages. In Chapter One, we were concerned, in part, with just what kind of creature the human being is, anyway. At that time, it was suggested, in so many words, that it is the sort of creature who likes to "do right," who likes to keep its best "face" forward, as it were. Having, as it does, a rather fragile self, it prefers not to expose this self to ridicule or embarrassment or other degrading experiences. It likes, that is, to have as many humans as possible (but particularly those for whom it cares) consider it a fine fellow. Being considered a fine fellow, however, turns out to be something less than a lead-pipe cinch, since the possibilities for doing the wrong thing in the wrong place at the wrong time are rampant.

It was further suggested that if this poor creature were to keep its self relatively unbruised, it needed three things:

(1) the rules for "coding" or defining the objects and situations in its world;

(2) accompanying behavioral repertoires which are thought to be appropriate to the coded objects and situations; and

(3) enough information about the object or situation to be able to activate the coding rules.

Part 1 was largely about arrangements which provide relatively reliable insurance that those human creatures living in the city will have available, on the basis of sight alone, "enough" information about the strangers who surround them to make it possible for them to activate the coding rules. As we saw, in the preindustrial city the best single source of information on the strange other's identity was his appearance. In the modern city, the best single source of information is his location. But, to reiterate and emphasize a point made earlier, in all urban settlements, the skilled city dweller utilizes appearential *and* locational *and* behavioral clues to make identifications—each piece of information reinforcing, correcting, or adding to the other.

Unfortunately, having enough information structurally available and knowing what to do with it are different matters. The city dweller (like all humans) needs more than raw data. He needs also to know what the raw data mean; that is, he needs to know how to code them. And he needs to know how to act under varying circumstances and with varying goals in mind vis-à-vis the coded objects; that is, he must be able to utilize the most appropriate behavioral repertoires.

This situation, already complex, becomes even more so when we realize that the city dweller (or any human, but our concern is only with urban ones) is not only picking up information about the other, coding it, and acting upon it; he is simultaneously and interrelatedly giving off information about himself which the other codes and acts upon. That is, he needs to know how to code the other and what behavior to expect from him. But he also needs the skills to apply the coding scheme to himself and to bring off his own "part" without a flaw.

In Chapter One, I suggested that the coding schemes and behavioral repertoires applied to self and other are largely provided by the culture in which the human participates. Allowing of course for individual innovation and rapid social change, this is largely true. But this does not gainsay the fact that such cultural know-how must be learned. We are concerned here, then, with some of the ways in which this learning occurs. We shall look first at the *acquisition of meanings,* at how the city dweller learns to code another's appearance, location, and behavior. Then we shall consider the *acquisition of skills,* the acquisition of personal know-how regarding how to dress, where to go, and how to act. The two sections are, of course, massively interrelated and are separated only for analytic purposes. Most of our attention will be concentrated on the modern city dweller, as most of the available materials pertain to him. Wherever possible, however, we shall explore the learning process among preindustrial and early industrial urbanites as well.

The Acquisition of Meanings

How does the city dweller know what the information he gathers as he moves through urban public space means? How does he learn to connect certain appearances, locations, or behavior with certain categories of being? The answer is both simple and profound. Like all humans, he is taught. From the moment of birth, he is bombarded with instructions. Breasts mean food. Little girls wear dresses. Big people are adults. Black people are poor (or happy or revolutionaries, or whatever). White people are rich (or dishonest or bosses, or whatever). Nice people don't go *there*. Nice girls don't do *that*. Only the *best people* come to this place. And so forth and so on. Some of this instruction is quite explicitly given; a good deal more is merely "picked up." Through his own experience, the individual not only adds to his knowledge of meanings, he also discovers that while some of his learned associations are fairly accurate, some others require minor modifications, and some are just plain wrong. This process of learning, retaining, modifying, and discarding is lifelong—although under conditions of rapid change there is probably more new learning, modifying, and discarding than there is retaining.

But this is familiar stuff. It is the standard menu for courses and books on child development, socialization, race relations, and so forth. And it is applicable to all human learning about all kinds of things.[1] Because it is such "familiar stuff," and because it is so widely applicable, in this and the following section, it will merely be assumed. Rather than tracing the full intricacies of the learning process, we shall focus only on certain small parts of it—parts that are particularly interesting and particularly relevant to the world of strangers.

CODING APPEARANCE

One of the more entertaining ways that city dwellers learn to attach meanings to the appearances of surrounding strangers is through the theater or its equivalent. We saw in Chapter Two how the Elizabethan theater used costuming to communicate status or rank, occupation, and nationality of the characters being portrayed, and it was suggested at that time that in doing so it merely reflected "real-life" practices. While this is true, more than reflection was certainly involved. At the same time that it was expressing its era's appearential customs, the Elizabethan theater was *also providing instruction in them.* The play-goer who had never seen a Florentine nobleman, for example, could leave a performance in which such a personage had been portrayed, armed with one more identity portrait to add to his already well-stocked mental gallery.

In its function as teacher, the Elizabethan theater was certainly not unique. During the Hellenistic period, the Carthaginian merchant was a widely known social type. When he appeared on the stage

wearing ear-rings, but no cloak, and followed by his aged slaves, bent double under bundles of trashy wares . . . the audience . . . rock[ed] with laughter. (G. and C. Charles-Picard, 1961:165)

The comic value of such a character certainly depended on his recognition by many members of the audience. But those who were not familiar with him before the play surely were afterwards.

The theater is particularly useful in teaching city-goers how to identify newly emergent types. Thus, in nineteenth century Boston, when the "bum" or "vagrant" was first appearing in great numbers on the American scene (one part of early industrialism's floating population), notice of his existence and instructions in his typical appearance were provided, in part, through his characterization on the Boston stage (Lane, 1967:193–94).

In the modern city, as we have seen, appearance is less reliable as an identity indicator than it was in times past. Nevertheless, the contemporary theater (along with its technological equivalents, movies and television) continues to provide instructions in "who looks like what." Sometimes, of course, these prove to be less than helpful—as with television's recent responsibility for teaching that the "hippie-radical costume" was a sure clue to its wearer's identity. Yet despite such instances of oversimplification, many of the appearential meanings provided by the legitimate theater, movies, and television are sufficiently accurate to prove useful, especially if not depended upon too exclusively. A number of my informants, who had been raised in rural areas or small towns, reported that they were "prepared" for the people they met in the city through years of Saturday afternoon movies and evening television shows.

Less visual means may also be used to instruct city dwellers in the meaning of appearance. In twelfth century Europe, the *goliards*, a "somewhat disreputable branch of the scholastic fraternity" who

" 'roam [ed] from city to city . . . in Paris, seeking the liberal arts, in Orleans, classics, at Salerno, medicine, at Toledo, magic—but nowhere manners or morals,' " were made known to the populace not only by personal encounters but by the poetry and songs which the *goliards* composed describing themselves (Rowling, 1968:153). In the contemporary world, newspapers and magazines perform a similar function. Again, much of what they teach is of dubious reliability, but on occasion, the printed word may help to correct inaccurate stereotypes which are stalking the land. Thus, through one of its standard features—the "Question Man"—one major metropolitan daily recently suggested to its readers that man should not be judged by hair-length or facial hair alone. The question was asked, "Do you judge all long-haired people alike?" Among the responses which the paper printed, two were particularly instructive:

S. B., computer operator: No, but most people do. I don't have long hair but I have a beard. Right now I'm looking for an apartment and I have found many people are prejudiced because I have a beard.

S. P., bail bond project girl: No. Long hair is such a popular fad, such an accepted fashion, that it doesn't really mean anything anymore. (*San Francisco Chronicle*, June 29, 1970)

Systems for coding the meaning of appearance may not be known or even available to all city dwellers. Subgroups within the city may develop portraits of certain social types which are only known by, and meaningful to, them. Thus, for example, cabdrivers have developed

an extensive typology of cab-users, the attributes imputed to each type having a certain predictive value, particularly as regards tipping. (F. Davis, 1967:268)

Some of the indicators used by the cabdrivers to "place" any given customer are behavioral and locational, but appearance is equally important. The "Blowhard," for example:

is a false Sport. Although *often wearing the outer mantle of the Sport* [a good tipper], he lacks the real Sport's casualness, assured manners and comfortable style. . . . (F. Davis, 1967:268 italics added)

Or, the "Lady Shopper":

Although almost as numerous as businessmen, Lady Shoppers are not nearly as well thought of by cabdrivers. The stereotype is a middle-aged woman, fashionably though unattractively dressed, sitting somewhat stiffly at the edge of her seat and wearing a fixed glare which bespeaks her conviction that she is being "taken for a ride." Her major delinquency, however, is undertipping; her preferred coin is a dime, no more or less, regardless of how long or arduous the trip. A forever repeated story is of the annoyed driver, who, after a grueling trip with a Lady Shopper, hands the coin back, telling her, "Lady, keep your lousy dime. You need it more than I do." (F. Davis, 1967:268–69)

Restricted coding schemes such as this one are available to only a few people, not only because their usefulness to a wider populace is limited, but also because they are created and perpetuated by word of mouth among networks of persons who know one another personally. Unless learned by someone who has a reason and the means to publicize them more widely (as in this case), they remain the exclusive property of whatever little world gave them birth.

CODING LOCATION

Just as the city dweller learns to code appearance through a lifelong and complex process involving explicit and implicit teaching and personal experience, so does he learn about the meanings of locations, about what is expected to go on where and who is to be expected to be doing it. The location in question may, of course, be as big as an entire city or as small as a cubby-hole bar, for it is as important for the urbanite to know what to expect in the little public spaces as in the large ones.

In the communication of spatial meanings, word-of-mouth instruction, at least in the modern city and at least for some people, appears to play a crucial part. My informants, for example, reported again and again that much of their understanding of the city depended on being told about this or that location or type of location by this or that family member, friend, or acquaintance. As noted in Chapter Four, these same people exhibited a startlingly underdeveloped vocabulary for describing how people looked, but a well-developed vocabulary for describing locations and whom one might expect to find in them. To the degree that they are at all typical of modern city dwellers, we might surmise that a good deal of locational talk passes back and forth among urbanites.

Such "talk" begins for the individual in childhood. Watch a parent and child as they move through a city's public spaces. By example, admonitions, and tongue-lashings, the parent is teaching the child such crucial matters as these: that a grocery store is a place to shop, not to play (have you ever seen a mother after a wandering child has unloaded one entire supermarket shelf onto the floor?); that playgrounds are places to play, not to eliminate waste materials; that libraries are places to read, not to engage in shouting matches; and that one must learn to distinguish such places from one another. Locational socialization is not limited to such gross "type" delineations, of course. Instructions may become quite specific, as when the child is warned that he may go into this particular candy store but not into that one because "bad people" hang out in the latter; or that in this restaurant he may eat with his hands but in the one next door he must use utensils. He learns that the children on this street are acceptable playmates, while those who live three streets over are not; that certain benches in the park are reserved for old people; and that while bars are appropriate only for adults, certain bars are appropriate only for certain kinds of adults (for example, homosexuals, escorted females, people who live in the surrounding neighborhood, and so on). Naturally some of what the child learns will later have to be discarded, as in the following:

My mother is so fearful of the city. She's fearful of the Italian section because the Italians live over there and she's fearful of the taxi cab drivers because everybody knows . . . [laugh]. She's all for these myths built up and yet she's lived in a city all her life. She was always fearful of having my sister and I go into the downtown area, because everybody knows that young girls are carried away into white slavery [laughter]. . . . I always wanted to break away because they held on to me more tightly. And because I wanted to break away, I was always doing what they didn't want me to do. And so I tried to experience it for myself. I was once in the downtown area by myself and nobody, never once was I carried off into white slavery.

But much of it will undoubtedly stand him in good stead. This is not to say that the individual continues to follow childhood instructions. He may, once free of parental control, decide to patronize the forbidden candy store, or others like it. The important point—assuming there has not been too much change—is that if he does so, he knows what to expect.[2]

As I have said, such word-of-mouth instruction continues through adulthood. A young male reports that he would not walk through the Tenderloin district of San Francisco alone at night because he has a friend who was robbed there. A woman started going to a certain restaurant because someone told her that unescorted females would not be bothered. And another woman learns what the people are like in a certain section of the city through a new neighbor who has just "escaped" the horrors of that area's schools.

Learning about entire cities may also take place in this way. The following conversation is fictional rather than actual; its time is nineteenth century rather than twentieth. But it is a conversation that has probably been repeated over and over again by very real people in the contemporary world:

> "So you were never in London before?" said Mr. Wemmick to me.
> "No," said I.
> "I was new here once," said Mr. Wemmick. "Rum to think of now."
> "You are well acquainted with it now?"
> "Why yes," said Mr. Wemmick. "I know the moves of it."
> "Is it a very wicked place?" I asked, more for the sake of saying something than for information.
> "You may get cheated, robbed and murdered in London. But there are plenty of people anywhere, who'd do that for you."
> "If there is bad blood between you and them" said I, to soften it off a little.
> "Oh, I don't know about bad blood," returned Mr. Wemmick. "There's not much bad blood about. They'll do it, if there's anything to be got by it."
> "That makes it worse."
> "You think so?" returned Mr. Wemmick. "Much about the same, I should say." (Dickens, 1964:183)

In the modern city, the mass media also serve as teachers of locational meanings—both general and specific. A reader of *The New York Times Magazine* in 1966, for example, could learn not only about a new type of city bar—a "social club" providing a neutral meeting ground for young, unattached males and females (in San Francisco these are now called "body-exchange" bars)—he could even learn the names and locations of a few of them: "Fridays" on New York's upper east side; "The Store" in Chicago's Near North side; "The Camelot" in San Francisco's Pacific Heights (H. F. Waters, "The Disenchanted: Girls in the City," *The New York Times Magazine*, February 6, 1966:34). And the reader of the December 15, 1969 *San Francisco Chronicle* could discover that there was a street in his city that he would do well to avoid:

There is a street in our town where people sit at night behind drawn shades, with doors and windows well bolted, closing their eyes and ignoring the message of their ears, while crime and violence and jungle brutality surge in the darkness outside.

The 1400 block of Waller Street—in the heart of the Haight-Ashbury —has earned the name of "Terror Terrace" among many of its older habitues. . . .

The block, and its immediate environs, has during the past year been the scene of: three murders, seven violent assaults, five burglaries, four hold-ups, six instances of forcible rape, three purse snatchings, eleven narcotics raids, or arrests.

Nightly screams and the sounds of physical assault are heard by a diminishing number of tenants and homeowners left over from the period when this neighborhood was a wholesome middle class bailiwick. (R. Patterson, "Violence Stalks a Street Called Terror Terrace," *San Francisco Examiner*, December 15, 1969)

It might be noted that the general accuracy of teachings such as this one is, in many respects, irrelevant. It might be, for example, that one could gather an equally impressive list of crimes in the same period for other areas of the city which are not thought to be dangerous. It might be that looked at more closely, the crimes here reported would turn out to be less ominous than the story suggests (for example, the violence largely occurred between people who knew one another). The point is, that when an area is designated dangerous, urbanites lose little by believing the designation and acting on the basis of it, that is, by avoiding the area. It simply doesn't matter whether it is true or not.[3] *But*, the opposite situation does not obtain. If an area is designated as safe or pleasant, or whatever, and it turns out not to be, then the individual who has acted on the basis of the designation and gone to the area may be in for an unpleasant, embarrassing, or even dangerous experience. As a general principle, then, one might say that for the city dweller, accentuating the negative is always the better part of valor.[4]

Television, motion pictures, and radio all play their part in teaching urbanites how to code various locations. So do those little-appreciated artifacts—guide books. Supposedly designed for visitors and tourists, they nevertheless turn up in the hands of city dwellers—newcomers and oldtimers alike. When read and interpreted carefully, they offer detailed insights into the appropriate meanings of this or that place, area, or city.[5]

Q: What's so important about those little [guide] books in choosing a restaurant?

A: They tell you about the food and the size and the kind of people that are running it. . . . You can make implications and generalizations from those little books, and from looking at the place on the outside. Like you can imply that say a Greek restaurant is going to be fairly noisy and crowded and lively. And a French restaurant or something else is going to be more quiet and sedate. You know, you can almost make big generalizations from past experiences and from what you know of ethnic groups.

The urbanite is not merely the passive recipient of meaning messages, however. He or she is also self-taught. Personal experience may reinforce or correct the teachings of others, but it may also be the source of new learning. Thus, the individual who actually goes to a certain location, not only knows about it in the future but knows about other locations of its type as well, both in his or her home city and in those which he or she is visiting:

Q: If you were a complete stranger in a city and had several hours to kill, say between trains or buses, what would you do with yourself?
A: I really have found myself in that situation quite frequently. One place, of course, is the coffee shop in the train station. However, if you do have time, I was caught in Boston once and I went to the public library. And Philadelphia once, I happened to go to a museum, the Ben Franklin museum which was right in that area where I was stranded for a couple of hours.
Q: Did you know it was there?
A: No, there was a, *usually in the train station areas in the city, there's a tourist information place* and usually I look up those and find whatever's free, and available. So that's usually what I have done. (Emphasis added.)

Note that in this excerpt from an interview, the informant is telling us that she knows what to expect not only in train stations but also in museums and public libraries. She knows from prior experiences (as well as from what she has been taught) that she can go to a library or museum for free, that she can hang around in them for a period of time without being thought odd and that she, a woman alone, is unlikely there to be either bothered or molested. In this excerpt, also, we see the interrelatedness of acquired meanings and acquired skills. Having learned the former, the individual utilizes them to grasp his city *and* to guide his movements; to grasp the city's populace *and* to direct his interaction.[6]

CODING BEHAVIOR

I have not up to this point said anything about the fact that city dwellers use the observed *behavior* of others as well as their appearance or location to "identify" them. I have not done so for several reasons. First, because appearential and locational clues are more quickly grasped than are behavioral ones, and are therefore primary. Second, because the meaning of any behavior is often dependent upon the "identity" of the person doing it; that is, the same action can have different meanings if performed by different persons. And third, because relatively reliable readings of another's behavior are often dependent on personal—even intimate—knowing, as in the following description of a "typical scene":

When a husband comes home from the office, takes off his hat, hangs up his coat and says "Hi," to his wife, the way in which he says "Hi" re-inforced by the manner in which he sheds his overcoat, summarizes his feelings about the way things went at the office. If his wife wants the details she may have to listen for awhile, yet she grasps in an instant the significant message for her; namely, what kind of an evening they are going to spend and how she is going to have to cope with it. (Hall, 1959:94)

Nevertheless, there are occasions and situations in which the urbanite is called upon to code the other's behavior as a means of identifying him. Sometimes, for example, the appearential and/or locational clues are incomplete or indistinct and take on certainty only with the addition of behavioral ones, as is often the case when one is attempting to identify the clerks in a retail store. Or, if the other is not acting in the manner which his appearance and location clearly predicted he would, then the primary clues may have to be discarded entirely and an identification made on the basis of behavior alone. Suppose, for example, that a young heterosexual male were to strike up a conversation with another very "straight" looking male in a bar frequented by heterosexual businessmen. The young man has every reason to believe, under these circumstances, that no homosexual overtures will be made. On the other hand, should such an overture be the second male's intent, the young man would do well to read the subtle behavioral signs early so as to be able to direct his own actions. That is, his ability to code behavior would enable him to correct his initial erroneous identification. Depending on his own preferences, then, he could either terminate the encounter or let it continue, but in either case he would "know the ropes."

We shall see in the next chapters some of the ways in which humans use their knowledge of behavioral meanings as they move through urban public space. For now, I want only to emphasize three points. First, as I have said, such meanings tend to be identity-specific. That is, one can best code another's behavior (verbal as well as nonverbal) if one knows "who" he or she is. The more one knows about the other, the better one is able to assess his or her actions. The most accurate readings are of those known personally. Therefore, in the world of strangers, behavioral clues are frequently most useful after an identification has been made, *not before*.

Second, many behavioral meanings tend also to be culture-specific. They do not travel well and are probably the source of most of the culture-shock that urbanites experience in their interaction —even with city dwellers—in countries other than their own. As an example:

In Latin America the interaction distance is much less than it is in the United States. Indeed, people cannot talk comfortably with one another unless they are very close to the distance that evokes either sexual or hostile feelings in the North American. The result is that when they move close, we withdraw and back away. As a consequence, they think we are distant or cold, withdrawn and unfriendly. We, on the other hand, are constantly accusing them of breathing down our necks, crowding us, and spraying our faces.

Americans who have spent some time in Latin America without learning these space considerations make other adaptations, like barricading themselves behind their desks, using chairs and typewriter tables to keep the Latin American at what is to us a comfortable distance. The result is that the Latin American may even climb over the obstacles until he has achieved a distance at which he can comfortably talk. (Hall, 1959:164)

Third, while there is some explicit teaching of the meaning of behavior to adults (see the next section), much teaching of behavioral meanings occurs outside the awareness of both teacher and student, primarily in the course of childhood socialization. This is particularly the case with "body language"—those nonverbal gestures and movements which humans use to help them communicate with one another. One is often able to read such "language" quite accurately (theatrical productions depend on this ability as do many humans seeking privacy in public, as we shall see in Chapter Seven), but one is frequently not aware *how* one *learned* to do so; often not aware *how* one *did* so; and sometimes not aware *that* one did so.[7]

The Acquisition of Skills

It is quite certain that he who has not learned how to code appearances, locations, and behavior will not have the skill to utilize these understandings in guiding his own actions. Even a highly skilled linguist cannot speak a language he has never learned. On the other hand, having the former does not guarantee the latter. Persons do vary in the extent to which they actually put into practice their acquired meanings and thus polish their skills. To try to operate in the city without either is undoubtedly to ask for trouble, but at least, for a time, the individual may be protected by his own ignorance regarding what he doesn't know. On the other hand, to understand, without the skill to do, may be quite discomforting; on occasion, terrifying.[8] Our concern here, however, is not primarily with accounting for individual variation in urban skills—although this is a fascinating topic in itself—but with looking at some of the ways in which such skills are acquired.

LEARNING HOW TO DRESS

Having learned the meanings attached to appearances—in terms of both separate items (for example, granny glasses) and total presentations—the city dweller is in a position to apply these understandings to himself or herself. In the preindustrial city, as we have seen, this is relatively unproblematic. The poor, for example, by and large, had available to them only a limited stock from which to choose, and whatever they chose was quite certain to advertise their economic status. As we have seen also, much dress was specified by law or tradition. One simply wore what one was expected to wear. (For the limited exceptions to this, see Chapter Eight.) In the modern city, however, the situation is quite different. Except for those few whose employment requires the wearing of uniforms, most persons are free to pick and choose among a great abundance of different styles, materials, and accessories. And herein lies the difficulty. The individual may be able to code the appearances of others quite well, but be uncertain exactly what combination of elements has created the overall presentation. In applying his or her coding knowledge to self, then, there is always the possibility for error. Thus, a male struggling to appear every inch the upper–middle class businessman may destroy the impression by wearing white socks.

There are, "fortunately," in America, experts who can assist the less adept to "come on" correctly; that is, in the way they wish to. Most newspapers, for example, carry columns of advice regarding what to wear with what, and these are useful for those persons who wish to adhere to upper–middle class standards. Fashion magazines perform a similar service, particularly through their advertisements, since these can be cut out and studied. And if all this fails, there is still the clothing store clerk to advise that spike heels are not part of the fashion scene this year. To be able to use the store clerk successfully, however, the individual also requires an understanding of locational meanings. That is, he or she must know which store is likely to be of the most service vis-á-vis the desired identity. To come on as a weekend swinger, it's no good shopping at a store which specializes in suits for matrons. Nor is the Macy's clerk likely to be able to assist one in creating the studied casualness of the upper class.[9]

Certain widely understood caricatures can also be helpful in teaching the individual what to avoid. Thus, the imagery of the American tourist in a European city, with his checkered shirt, baseball cap, four cameras, and three guide books is an object lesson in how not to come on as a world-weary traveler. So too, the dumb-blonde social type, so insightfully portrayed by such women as Marilyn Monroe and Jayne Mansfield, can be read for hints as to clothing styles and hair colors to avoid if one wishes to be taken seriously and not simply to bed.

Most city dwellers, however, probably do not need extra help in learning how to dress. Their grasp of appearential meanings is sufficient for relatively successful self-application. And if they do make a mistake, and then recognize it, they have added to the sophistication of their understanding and increased their skills. Most city dwellers, like Shirley Jackson's [Greenwich] "villager," know very well how to transform identification into presentation, especially with the help of the right setting:

She went into Whelan's and sat at the counter, putting her copy of the *Villager* down on the counter next to her pocketbook and *The Charterhouse of Parma* which she had read enthusiastically up to page fifty and carried now only for effect. (Jackson, 1960b:40)

LEARNING WHERE TO GO

The trick in using one's know-how regarding locational meanings as a guide to movement in the modern city involves the capacity to gauge one's own presentational and interactional abilities. Of course, if what I know leads me to avoid a location, there's no problem. Nothing ventured, nothing lost. But if I am actually considering going somewhere, knowing what to expect will not necessarily tell me whether I can operate in the setting as well as I might wish. Thus, an individual may know about pool rooms, know who is to be found there, and so on, and still doubt his ability to fit in:

If I went to a pool room, I would feel uncomfortable cause I don't know how I'm supposed to act or what I'm supposed to tell the guy at the desk and how I'm supposed to set up things and I would feel terribly uncomfortable.

So, too, every city dweller knows that there may be exceptions to his generalized understandings; that he may sometime go to a place that is something other than what he expected. To learn where to go, then, he must learn to judge how well he can handle the unanticipated. If he does not handle it well, he may be in for a very uncomfortable time, as was the young man who related the following:

There's one restaurant that I'll never go back to. Good food, excellent service. In Fisherman's Wharf. Now in Fisherman's Wharf, most of the time it's very informal dress. You can wear what you want. We went into this one restaurant in informal dress and I walked in and before I could even ask whether you should have a tie and coat on, a coat was draped around me and a clip-on tie attached to my shirt.

The coat was about five sizes too large. I was just escorted to the table and sat down. Now I looked positively ridiculous. Now after that I didn't really enjoy the meal. And got out as soon as possible. . . .

. . . They have a kind of lobby which is on a raised platform and the restaurant is situated below it. And there's a screen between them and the restaurant itself. You know I could have simply taken it off and said, sorry, thank you and walked out. But just the situation, I was so dumbfounded.

And as I think back on it and picture it in my mind, an awful lot had to do with because it was dark in there. For some reason it just kind of . . . I was in a semistate of shock anyway and then this darkness. I couldn't orient myself. I couldn't get myself into this kind of groove that would tell me, now listen, this is not what I want, get out of here.

On the other hand, if the individual is at ease with the relatively unexpected, the exact same situation may turn out to be quite enjoyable:

I was at the same place I think. [Both these excerpts are from a group interview.] I walked in and I had on a shirt and tie, but I had on a sweater instead of a jacket. And I walked in and the guy stopped me at the door, the maitre d'. "I'm afraid you can't go in like that but we do have some jackets over here." Immediately I was on the defensive. I said, "Well how much is that going to cost me?" I thought I was going to have to rent a jacket. And he turned around and he looked at me and he said, "Sir, I can't charge you; I can't accept money because they're watching me." So I put on this ridiculous gray jacket, covered with soup stains. I kept picking up forks and knives with the sleeves. But I think it was the same place as this and I really felt better after I put him on the defensive. After that I was able to relax and enjoy the meal.

But how does the individual learn to gauge his own abilities without risk? And how does he even develop them without going to new places where he may feel uncomfortable? The answer seems to be that he does not, and this is perhaps one of the greatest ironies of city living. It is possible, of course, as we shall see in the next chapter, simply to stick, to a greater or lesser degree, to the "safe" places. In doing so, however, one increases one's vulnerability to disorganization in the face of change. Or, one can take risks, rushing headlong into new places, new people, and new situations, thereby increasing one's self-knowledge and one's skills and, in the long run, finding the city not to be risky at all (see Chapter Eight). Most urbanites probably combine the two approaches in learning where to go. Much of their time they stick to the safe places; occasionally they venture forth into those locales they always "heard of but never tried."

What I am saying then is simply this. Once the individual has learned to code urban locations, once he knows who and what to expect in them, he does not require any further instructions on this topic to make his way through the world of stangers. What he requires, rather, is knowledge of himself.

LEARNING HOW TO ACT

Assuming an urbanite is in the "right" place at the "right" time in the "right" costume, how does he know what to do? How does he know what actions are appropriate, given the identity he wishes to project to the human object or objects he has identified? As I have suggested earlier, he calls on his knowledge of behavioral repertoires. He uses his understanding of the links between identities and behavior to guide his own actions. In the preceding section, we noted that there are likely to be individual variations in versatility; that it does not necessarily follow that because one knows what to do, one will be able to do it. Nevertheless, most humans are exceptionally good actors. Through a subtle and complex socialization process, they learn not only how to interpret behavior but how to "perform" it.[10] It is probably only under conditions of rapid change that large numbers of people are likely to find themselves in situations where they do not know what to do.

In the relative social stability of the *preindustrial* city, individuals learned about the manners appropriate to their category vis-à-vis other categories simply as a matter of course. Many of these were traditionally prescribed, and deviation (especially on the part of lower-status persons) was likely to be swiftly sanctioned (Sjoberg, 1960:125–26). In Tibetan cities in the past, as an example, "whenever the high political leaders mount or dismount from their horses, '. . . riders are to climb down and salute. Pedestrians should stand aside with their hats in their hands and their tongues hanging out' " (Sjoberg, 1960:126). This is not to suggest, of course, that humans always behaved precisely as the elites thought they should. If they had, there would have been no need for the two policemen who typically sat in niches in the proscenium of the Roman theatre, "facing the audience when a play was in progress, and when necessary, admonish [ing] the unruly with the long staff that each carried" (Tanzer, 1939:68). Nor would it have been necessary for a Pompeian restaurant owner to paint messages on his walls urging his customers to "practice moderation and good behavior" (Tanzer, 1939:48).

Learning what was traditional and being sanctioned if one did otherwise were not, however, always sufficient, even in the preindustrial city. New situations might occur, new groups might emerge, for which tradition provided no guidelines. How, then, was a person to know what to do? Well, one solution was to read a book. Given the low levels of literacy, this was probably not very helpful to very many people, but for those who could read, guidance in how to act was there to be found.

One English gentleman, for example, during the fifteenth century, wrote a book describing various journeys of his around Europe as well as to the Holy Land. In it, he provided some quite explicit instructions for those pilgrims who might follow him:

When you come to haven towns, if you shall tarry there three days, go betimes to land to secure lodging ahead of the others, for it will be taken quickly, and if there is any good food, get it before the others arrive. On arriving at Jaffa, the port for Jerusalem, the same haste must be observed so as to secure one of the best asses. You shall pay no more for the best than for the worst. . . . Take good heed of your knives and other small things for the Saracens will talk with you and make you good cheer but they will steal from you what you have if they can. (Quoted in Rowling, 1968:99)

In the fourteenth century, literate Frenchwomen of the emerging urban-based bourgeois might learn what behavior was appropriate for them by reading the Menagier de Paris' instructions to his young wife:

When you go to town or to church go suitably accompanied by honour-able women according to your estate, and flee suspicious company, never al-lowing any ill famed women to be seen in your presence. And as you go bear your head upright and your eyelids low and without fluttering, and look straight in front of you and about four rods ahead, without looking round at any man or woman to the right or to the left, nor looking up, nor glancing from place to place, nor stopping to speak to anyone on the road. (Quoted in Power, 1955:106)

There were, additionally, some situations in which urban humans found themselves confronting entirely new physical objects, and in at least one case, the government itself took responsibility for teaching them how to act:

In 1643, the House of Commons ordered "that the officers and soldiers at the courts of guard be required not to permit any to cut down trees or wood in Hyde Park, and not to suffer any such persons as go out to the works to cut wood in the park, or to bring any from thence but by war-rant from the committee appointed for that ordinance." . . . Again, it was ordered "that no soldier or other person whatsoever, shall presume to pull down or take away any of the pales belonging to the said Park, nor kill or destroy any deer therein, nor cut, sell or carry away any wood growing in or about the said Park or mounds thereof, etc." (Quoted in Larwood, 1881:24–25)

As discussed earlier, the *modern* city does provide many opportuni-ties for getting involved in situations where one does not know how to act. It is such a hodgepodge of persons, worlds, and life-styles that no one's childhood socialization could possibly be adequate to every situa-tion. Nevertheless, as we have seen, this built-in infirmity may largely be neutralized by the simple expedient of avoiding those places for which one is unprepared. And should there be some perceived change in the overall city situation, the modern urbanite can be pretty sure that there will be plenty of people around telling him what to do now.

Thus the recent panic over "crime in the city" has resulted in books of instruction (for example, Ellison, 1968); newspaper dos and don'ts:

Don't carry much money in your purse. If someone grabs it, let him have it. . . . If you have to wait in the car for a friend, take the key out of the ignition. If a criminal manages to get in the car beside you, and forces you to start the car, try to kill the engine by giving it too much gas. . . .
Don't let strangers pick you up. That nice guy you had a drink with at the bar may not be so nice alone with you. . . . (Merla Zellerbach, "You and the Sex Criminal," *San Francisco Chronicle*, June 8, 1970)

and even hotel-room signs:

Keep door locked when in room. Do not display valuables in room. Place them in hotel safe deposit box. Close room doors by hand when leaving hotel. Never admit persons with unsolicited deliveries. Do not leave luggage unattended when checking out. Do not reveal name of hotel or room number to strangers. Deposit key with desk clerk upon leaving. Never admit repairman to room without checking with the manager. Never discuss plans for staying away from hotel with strangers. (Quoted in Herb Caen, *San Francisco Chronicle*, July 8, 1970)

In neither the preindustrial nor the modern city, then, is the matter of how to act terribly problematic for great numbers of persons. Rather it is the early industrial city, with the appearential order breaking down and the spatial order only beginning to emerge; it is the early industrial city, with its massive hordes of rural peasants becoming urbanites overnight; it is the early industrial city that is the setting for the massive and explicit teaching of city ways.

Sometimes the teaching was done privately, as when early twentieth century Polish immigrants to Chicago wrote to those back home who were preparing to make the same journey and instructed them in how to get along in a world of strangers:

In another letter I will tell you everything, how it ought to be and how you ought to behave on the way, but now I only inform you that the ship tickets are sent. (Thomas and Znaniecki, 1918:213)

Dear brother-in-law, when you leave if you have any baggage, I mean any large trunk or large bag, you can give it up, but don't give it into anybody's hands without a receipt. If you have a receipt the baggage will not be lost. . . . And give everywhere the same names that there may not be any trouble about names. (Thomas and Znaniecki, 1918:213–14)

Mr. Wisniewski, if they ask you during the journey about anything say only this, that you bring children to their parents. That is all; you don't need any other explanations. And now again, if God leads you happily through the water perhaps they will require somebody mother or father to come and meet you in New York; then they will ask "Is it your father or mother?" Let them [the children] say "It is our mother or father." And say Mr. Wisniewski is my brother. Then all will be well, only don't give any other explanation than such as we request you to give. (Thomas and Znaniecki, 1918:218)

The extent to which such private tutoring occurred is impossible to say. Few individuals were as interested as Thomas and Znaniecki in saving the private correspondence of the "nobodies" for posterity. It is possible to say with more assurance, however, that a considerable amount of public instruction was taking place. Much of this appeared to be aimed toward, and probably swallowed by, members of the emerging nonelite bourgeois who longed to behave like citified "gentlemen and ladies." Or, if they did not long to, there were members of their group who longed to have them long to. Thus, in Cincinnati, as early as 1830, theater owners were urging their patrons to develop more elegant public manners. One provided them with a poster, delineating exactly how they were expected to behave:

I. Gentlemen will be particular in not disturbing the audience by loud talking in the Bar-Room, nor by personal altercations in any part of the house.

II. Gentlemen in the boxes and in the pit are expected not to wear their hats nor to stand nor sit on the railing during the performance; as they will thereby prevent the company behind, and in the lobby, from seeing the stage. Those in the side boxes will endeavor to avoid leaning forward as, from the construction of the house, the projection of one person's head must interrupt the view of several others on the same line of seats.

III. The practice of cracking nuts, now abandoned in all well regulated theatres, should be entirely avoided during the time the curtain is up; as it must necessarily interfere with the pleasure of those who feel disposed to attend to the performance.

IV. Persons in the upper Boxes and Gallery will be careful to avoid the uncourteous habit of throwing nutshells, apples, etc., into the Pit; and those in the Pit are cautioned against clambering over the balustrade into the Boxes, either during or at the end of the Performance.

V. Persons in the Gallery are requested not to disturb the harmony of the House by boisterous conduct, either in language or by striking with sticks on the seats or bannisters. . . . (Quoted in Trollope, 1960:133, Editor's note 5)

In the United States, at least, a good deal of the public teaching was done by those self-appointed experts on "how to act": the authors of etiquette books. A casual purview of such books from 1881 to 1962 reveals both a concentration on explicit instructions for public behavior during the period when the early industrial city in the United States was at its most confusing, and a gradually decreasing concern with these matters as the modern city came into its own.

Published in 1881, for example, a little book entitled, *Our Deportment*, or "The Manners, Conduct and Dress of the Most Refined Society," contains four chapters devoted to "correct" public behavior: Chapter XII, "Etiquette of the Street"; Chapter XIII, "Etiquette of Public Places"; Chapter XIV, "Etiquette of Travelling"; and Chapter XXIII, "General Rules of Conduct." The reader of these chapters was provided with such explicit admonitions as:

No gentleman is ever guilty of the offense of standing on street corners and the steps of hotels or other public places and boldly scrutinizing every lady who passes.

Never speak to your acquaintance from one side of the street to the other. Shouting is a certain sign of vulgarity. First approach, then make your communication to your acquaintance or friends in a moderately loud tone of voice.

Never turn a corner at full speed or you may find yourself knocked down, or may knock down another by the violent contact. Always look in the way you are going or you may chance to meet some awkward collision. (J. Young, 1881:151,155)

By 1892, such single-minded concern with public behavior had abated somewhat. A section of *The Housekeeper's Helper*, entitled "Polite Deportment," devoted only about seven paragraphs to instructing its readers in the intricate manners of public space. However, what instructions it did provide were no less explicit than those of its predecessor:

Should you tread upon or stumble against anyone, do not fail to make immediate apology. Of course, you will not stare at nor point to people, nor carry umbrella or cane horizontally under your arm. (*The Housekeeper's Helper*, 1892:560)

Standard Etiquette, published in 1925, contains a general discussion of proper behavior in traveling and business but limits its explicit instructions to two pages of brief don'ts:

Don't talk in a loud voice or act in an eccentric manner, both make one conspicuous.

Don't appear to notice blunders in service when others are around.

Don't give exhibitions of anger, fear, hatred, embarrassment, ardor or undue hilarity in public—it is embarrassing for others and in bad taste. (Brant, 1925:115–16)

By the 1940s, the etiquette books were suggesting little more than that the individual in a public setting should make himself as inconspicuous as possible:

Do nothing in company that calls attention to the body or its functions.

Inconspicuousness is the keynote to well-bred behavior in public. (Boykin, 1940:20, 211)

Go your way quietly, taking your place in the crowd unobtrusively, attracting no attention to yourself.

Conduct yourself quietly and unobtrusively. Do not attract attention to yourself and a companion by talking loudly, laughing uproariously, whistling, singing or humming. (Sprackling, 1944:219,232)

And the 1962 edition of Amy Vanderbilt's *New Complete Book of Etiquette* contains not a single reference to proper behavior in the world of strangers.

In this chapter, we have been concerned, somewhat superficially, with how the city dweller "learns the ropes" of urban living. In the next two chapters, we shall take a look at what he does with all this know-how, and with how he sometimes manages to avoid ever acquiring it in the first place.

CHAPTER SIX

PRIVATIZING PUBLIC SPACE
Locational Transformations

In this and the following chapter, we shall be concerned with some of the things that humans do in the city which function to reduce, to a greater or lesser degree, the complexities of living in a world of strangers. We shall be concerned, in particular, with a number of ways in which ostensibly public space is *transformed* into a kind of private or semiprivate space.[1] Three methods of privatizing public space involving an actual transformation in the character of a location will be considered: (1) the creation of *home territories;* (2) the creation of *urban villages*, both *concentrated* and *dispersed;* and (3) the creation of temporary mobile "homes" by means of the *traveling pack*.[2] Despite the unity of their consequences, these transforming devices[3] vary among themselves rather extensively: in terms of the size of the space involved, in terms of the form and permanency of the transformation, in terms of the degree of privatization obtained, in terms of the urban know-how required, and so forth. Additionally, any one device may be used with greater or lesser success depending upon the character of the surrounding environment (physical and social) and depending upon what else is happening in that environment. All of this will become clearer as I proceed. At this point, I wish only to emphasize that the phenomena we shall consider are of a shifting, moving, fluid character. To try to capture them with the written word is to freeze them —to make them more solid, more static, more permanent than they are. To write about them is, thus, more or less to distort them.

Creating Home Territories

The city is a world of strangers simply because its population is so large that anyone living in it cannot possibly know personally everyone else living in it. Even the individual who works very hard at acquiring acquaintances will never succeed in getting to know more than a minuscule proportion of the city's total population. Nevertheless, urbanites can and do arrange things such that their encounters with the personally-unknown when they are out in public are minimized and their encounters with the personally-known are maximized.[4] One such arrangement involves the creation of home territories. By a home territory, I refer to a relatively small piece of public space which is taken over—either by individuals acting independently or by an already formed group acting in concert—and turned into "a home away from home." To understand how this is done, we need to consider variations in the knowledge that one can have about, and thus in the relationship that one can have to, any piece of public space. We need to consider the matter of *casual, familiar,* and *intimate* knowledge and the establishment of *customer, patron,* and *resident* relationships.

CASUAL KNOWLEDGE AND CUSTOMERS

In the preceding chapter, where we were interested in how urbanites come to acquire urban learning, note was made of the fact that persons know various public spaces in a variety of ways. It is possible, for example, to know of a place only in the sense that one knows about places or areas of that "type." It is possible also to know about a specific locale, but never to have actually experienced it; that is, to have never gone there oneself. And finally, it is possible to know a place on the basis of actually having been there.[5] We might call this latter sort of knowing personal knowing, as distinct from categoric or hearsay knowing,[6] and it is this which concerns us here. Personal knowledge also varies—it may be more or less detailed, more or less complete, more or less certain—the reasons for its variance being numerous: individual differences in learning capacity, differences in rates of change, openness of the space itself to surveillance, and so forth. Our interest, however, is only in knowledge variations which result from differences in the *amount of time* the individual (alone or as part of a group) spends in the setting.

The least complete, detailed, and certain knowledge may be said to be casual and it is in the possession of the customer, who acquires it through short-term usage on intermittent, infrequent occasions.

Knowledge of this sort tends to be limited to a general conception of the physical layout of the public space in question. The customer is unlikely to know, except in the most superficial sense, any of the people with whom he is sharing the space. He may, for example, recognize a long-term employee if there is one, but he will not know that person's name, nor will he and the employee have established the minimal relationship requisite for an exchange of pleasantries.

It seems likely that most of the personal knowledge of small public spaces that city dwellers possess is of this character, since its acquisition is neither time-consuming nor inconvenient. It is picked up quite casually, as one moves about one's daily round. What it lacks in detail, completeness, or certainty, it makes up for in generalized usefulness. When one is out and about in the city, it is very helpful to know that there is a public restroom here, a telephone there, a newspaper stand across the street. Armed with knowledge such as this, the individual is able to go directly to whatever he may be looking for and is not required to seek the assistance of strangers—which he may consider risky—in reaching his goal.

FAMILIAR KNOWLEDGE AND PATRONS

Of a somewhat higher "quality" is the familiar information possessed by patrons. The patron gains his knowledge through regular rather than irregular usage, but the duration of his stay on any one occasion is likely to be relatively brief. His knowledge of the physical features of the setting is on a par with that of the customer, but unlike the latter, the patron is certain to "know" some of the people who share the space with him. Thus, for example, long-term patrons of coffee shops, restaurants, and bars often come not only to know the local bartenders or waitresses but to develop a nodding or speaking acquaintance with other regular users as well. Similarly, the file clerk who passes an intersection each morning on his way to work is likely to wave in recognition to the traffic cop or news-dealer stationed there; he may even develop the habit of stopping to share a few words with one or the other before hurrying on his way. Or, the regular commuter may establish a friendly relationship with the porter of the depot in which he waits, and may even know the depot manager and share an occasional cup of coffee with him.

Wherever one has established a patron relationship, one can, to a limited degree, find relief from the challenging anonymity of much urban public space. This is not to say that a good deal of urban know-how isn't needed to acquire familiar information in the first place. It most certainly is. But having become a patron, one can begin to relax a bit, to feel at ease, to find pleasure in the development of one's space-bound friendships—and perhaps, in memory at least, to surround the patronized premises with an aura of romance:

It was perhaps in the smaller, more secluded establishments [pubs, in nineteenth century London] that the essence of Cockney friendliness seemed enshrined. Such a place was well described by W. W. Jacobs when he wrote, "A little pub in the turning off the Mile End Road—clean as a new pin, and as quiet and respectable as a front parlour. Everybody calling the landlady 'Ma,' and the landlady calling most of them by their Christian names and asking after their families. There were two poll parrots in cages, with not a bad word between them—except once when a man played the cornet outside—and a canary that sang its heart out." In these places (as in so much of London) the best things—the company, the glowing coal fire, the highly polished mugs and glasses, the cozy nooks were thrown in free. The habitues of the public-house have been well described by a survivor from those days. "Cronies as we were none of us knew anything of one another's lives. We knew one another only by nick-names and where each went after leaving for the night was known only to the individual. We had not curiosity in the matter. We met simply to be ourselves for a short time, to throw off the trappings that we necessarily had to wear in civilized society, to discuss affairs of the day, sometimes to be very rude to one another, and for a time we all glowed in the fascinating light of human individuality." [7]

The patron, however, has more to gain than simply a reduction in anonymity and an increase in short-term pleasure. By reason of having established semipersonal relationships with the setting's employees, the patron is in a position to gain acquiescence, even assistance, in utilizing the setting for purposes other than those for which it is overtly intended. He may, for example, be able to take a respite from his busy rounds on the comfortable bar stool of his favorite bar without being required to buy a drink. He may use the corner newsstand as a shelter from a sudden downpour. He may receive his phone calls at the local delicatessen. Or, as in the taverns of Colonial America, he may use the setting as a meeting place where he and his friends can plot revolution. [8]

In the modern city at least, such extraneous doings run counter to the contemporary penchant for segregating activities. But at the same time, patron relationships also contribute to and reinforce the spatial segregation of persons—an interesting paradox that will rise again when we consider the more extensive extraneous doings of those persons to whom we now turn—the real creators of home territories, residents.[9]

INTIMATE KNOWLEDGE AND RESIDENTS

As the knowledge one has about any particular public space increases in detail, completeness, and certainty, a peculiar alteration begins to take place in the character of the space itself. As the individual increases his knowledge, he transforms what were initially strangers into personally-known others. As he does this, he increases his ability to use the setting for his own private purposes. The more knowledge he possesses, the less the setting is an alien place full of strangers, the more it begins to seem like home. And when his knowledge approaches maximum, in detail, completeness, and certainty, the setting ceases to be, for him, for all practical purposes, an urban public locale at all. It becomes, in effect, semiprivate space; it becomes a home territory.

The alteration is never complete, of course, as long as the setting continues to be legally defined as a place open to the public. Nevertheless, the extent to which small public spaces can come to be viewed as home territories, as well as the degree to which those who hold this view can come to behave as if it were true, is one of the more remarkable chapters in the story of the city dweller's struggle to reduce the complexity of the world in which he lives.

Despite the cozy relationship which the patron may establish with a familiarly known locale, he cannot truly be said to have created a home territory. That distinction belongs to the resident, who, by dint of not only using the locale regularly but using it on most occasions for long periods of time, acquires for himself an intimate knowledge of all there is to know and a set of privileges that goes with such mastery.

The resident's knowledge of the physical features of his home territory is detailed, not only with regard to available facilities but in terms of ebb and flow of usage as well. He not only knows where everything is, he also knows when the locale will be full, when empty; when certain of its facilities will be most in demand, when ignored. In addition, he is fully aware of all other users of the setting and is likely to be able to determine who is the first-timer, who the irregular customer, who the regular patron, or who the fellow resident. Members of the latter two categories are known to him personally. Of customers and first-timers, of course, he has only simple categoric knowledge, but he is so "at home" in the setting that in any interaction with them, he proceeds from a position of strength.

Becoming a resident is a time-consuming process. It requires that the individual hang about some public space for long and regular periods. Dropping in now and then may do for the customer, stopping by briefly three times a week may do for the patron, but becoming and remaining a resident is almost a full-time job. In fact, for some people, it *is* a full-time job and they constitute one type of resident: the public space *employee*. The other type of resident achieves his status avocationally rather than vocationally; these are the colonizers. As might be expected, given the long hours required, colonizers tend primarily to be drawn from the ranks of our old acquaintances: the organizationally unaffiliated floaters. In Imperial Rome, for example, young male dandies—rich and poor—with time on their hands, "took over" any number of barbershops:

Idlers went frequently and dawdled there [in the barbershop]. If we consider the time they spent and the anxieties which obsessed them, it is perhaps hardly fair to call "idlers" men who were continually busy dividing their attention between the comb and the mirror. . . . The crowd which assembled from dawn to the eighth hour was so great that the *tonstrina* became a rendezvous, a club, a gossip shop, an inexhaustible dispensary of information, a place for arranging interviews and the like. (Carcopino, 1940:157)

In eighteenth century London, the unemployed might make themselves at home in some small section of a park:

There [in Hyde Park], whilst the unthinking part of mankind were discussing their eating and drinking for the support of their own private persons, without any regard for the public, this worthy upholsterer and his friends discussed the affairs of Europe and grieved over the numerous mistakes committed by the powers that were. So profound was this politician, so great attention did he pay to the interests of Europe, that he entirely neglected his own, and soon found himself a bankrupt. Then he became a *habitué* of the park, for not only was he always sure to find there gentlemen who, like himself, knew what was "going on in the capitol," but there also he was out of the reach of the tipstaffs, catchpoles and bailiffs. (Larwood, 1881:380–81)

And in the modern city, old people "take over" bus depots, young people appropriate plazas and squares, and skid row males or vagrants feel right at home in the bars of their choice.

All residents—employees and colonizers alike—tend to exhibit, to a greater or lesser degree, three characteristics. First, as already noted, they tend to use the locale for their own private purposes. Second, they tend to indulge in what Erving Goffman has called, "the backstage language of behavior":

Throughout Western society there tends to be one informal or backstage language of behavior, and another language of behavior for occasions when a performance is being presented. The backstage language consists of reciprocal first-naming, cooperative decision-making, profanity, open sexual remarks, elaborate griping, smoking, rough informal dress, "sloppy" sitting and standing posture, use of dialect or sub-standard speech, mumbling and shouting, playful aggressivity and "kidding," inconsiderateness for the other in minor but potentially symbolic acts, minor physical self-involvements such as humming, whistling, chewing, nibbling, belching and flatulence. (Goffman, 1959:128)

And third, they tend to hold an attitude of proprietary rights toward the setting, similar to that which an individual might have toward his own home.

Whether one, two, or all three of these characteristics are exhibited to a greater or lesser degree, depends on a number of additional factors. These include such matters as whether the resident is an employee or a colonizer; whether he becomes a resident entirely on his own, or as part of a group; and whether the exhibition of the characteristic depends upon the support or tacit approval of others—residents, patrons, customers, or first-timers. Some of the ways in which these factors affect exhibition will be noted as each characteristic is discussed in turn.

There is nothing startling in the assertion that employees utilize their places of employment for *private purposes*—whether that place of employment happens to be a public setting or not. Work places are commonly locales in which romances bloom and friendships form; in which troubles are aired and counsel is given, and in which personal letters are written and personal phone calls are received. The extent to which any place of employment may be used for such purposes varies, of course, depending upon the type of work site, attitude of employer, amount of slack time, and so on. One thing is clear, however: employees in public settings (the only work site of concern here) are considerably more restricted in their pursuit of private purposes than are colonizers. The young woman stationed in an airport-terminal insurance booth may be able to devote herself to knitting or socializing with the guard during slack periods, but when customers are numerous, she must switch her devotion to work requirements or risk losing her job. The manager of a bus depot may spend a good deal of his day drinking coffee with acquaintances, but he is expected to spend sufficient time at work to keep the depot running at least at a minimal level of efficiency.

In contrast, colonizers are, almost by definition, devoting the major portion of their time to the pursuit of private purposes. They have no other reason for hanging around. In contemporary American cities, for example, it is not unusual for bus depots to be heavily populated by aged pensioners who have no intention of taking a bus. Instead, the depot is used as a home-away-from-home; its colonizers arriving early in the morning, coming and going throughout the day and leaving only at night. Within its confines, the pensioners are quite busy: they meet and visit with their fellow residents (employees and colonizers), read their papers, make plans for outings. Friends and relatives may "call on" them here, as in one case I observed where an aged gentleman was visited one afternoon by his equally aged fiancée who had come to discuss their impending marriage and Social Security difficulties; or, as in another case, when another aged gentleman met his daughter at noon for a brown-bag lunch. But frequently, no such "calling" is required; the people they care about are colonizers like themselves:

Some old people come and go [from the New York Port Authority bus terminal near Times Square] like characters in a dream, having fixed roles to play. Two are known as "the lovers." They come in separately, meet, sit and hold hands a while, then leave.

Romeo is in his early 70's, a tall spare man with bony shoulders that seem like pipes under his jacket. Juliet is in her late 60's, short, round-faced.

"You would think they were 16 years old and just in love," a woman said. "She always wears a veil on her hair. He wears a little cap, a couple of sizes too small, and they sit and hold hands." (McCandlish Phillips, "The Waiting Room for Death," *San Francisco Sunday Examiner and Chronicle*, June 21, 1970)

Colonization of this sort, of course, would be impossible without the at least tacit consent of employees or whoever else might have responsibility for the setting. One has only to read that "at times the bus travelers cannot get a seat because so many of 'the regulars' are there. . . ." [10] or to observe a group of pensioners loitering all day under a sign which reads, "Loitering Prohibited—Violators Will Be Prose-cuted," to understand that this is the case.

Other types of colonization are equally dependent upon the tacit approval of others. Bars which serve as homosexual meeting places could not do so for long if the managers wished otherwise.[11] A laundromat, situated close to a university campus, could not serve as a substitute coffee house for male students without at least a grudging willingness on the part of the owner.

The necessity for this tacit approval is most clearly seen in cases where having once been granted, it is withdrawn, or where having been granted, the colonization is soon halted. One example of the former situation is the following. A small park, located just off the business section of a midwestern city had been used for years by skid row alcoholics as a combined meeting place, hotel, restaurant, and bar. However, after several citizens complained of the spectacle thus created, police saw to it that the park was cleared of its residents. In cases where approval has never been granted, discovery of the colonization often leads to its elimination. Thus, for example, when it came to the attention of officials in another midwestern area that certain highway rest stops were being used as homosexual meeting places, measures were immediately taken to bring such "misuse" to a halt.[12]

Continuing colonization *is* possible without the tacit consent of those responsible for the setting, but in such cases, camouflage becomes essential. However, it seems unlikely that any *large* numbers of persons can successfully colonize without tacit approval. (Certainly unapproved colonizers may be part of a group and learn the ways of colonization through the group; but if they are to be successful, they cannot appear in the setting with large numbers of their fellows.) Camouflaged colonization also greatly restricts the exhibition of the other characteristics of residents, particularly *backstage language*.

In a delightful book, *Subways Are For Sleeping*, Edmund G. Love tells of the numerous uses to which public settings are put by persons who live in New York without money. The book is replete with examples of the necessity for camouflage if such persons are to be successful. Witness the following excerpts:

I know of two men who have been living in Grand Central station for almost ten years. They have learned to vary their routine enough to maintain the anonymity necessary for such a project. . . .

Shelby says that it is always advisable to carry something when sleeping in a lobby. House officers are apt to respect a man's privacy if he has an umbrella or brief case lying in his lap.

After seven-thirty in the evening, in order to read a book in Grand Central or Penn Station, a person either has to wear hornrimmed glasses or look exceptionally prosperous. Anyone else is apt to come under surveillance. On the other hand, newspaper readers never seem to attract attention and even the seediest vagrant can sit in Grand Central all night without being molested if he continues to read a paper. . . .

Most men in his [penniless] condition who visit the Public Library go to the reading rooms. Either they have never heard of the microfilm room or they underestimate its possibilities. Consequently, the attendants there have never met a real vagrant face to face. They assume that anyone who has heard of microfilm and wishes to use it is in search of learning. They check the film out to the applicant and never follow up. Moreover, the accommodations are very comfortable. The room is warm, and the upright film-display stands give a man an excellent place to rest his head. (Love, 1957:7, 18, 20–21, 23)

In each of these instances, the individual, lacking the tacit approval of those in charge, was required to act in such a way as to suggest that his use of the setting was a legitimate one—he was required to act, in effect, as if he were in a public place.

In contrast, colonizers blessed with approval need be prepared for no such performances. They are free, rather, to behave (at least within limits) as if they were in the privacy of their own homes. Thus, some pensioners in bus depots make no pretense of being there to take a bus. They carry nothing to suggest that they might be traveling and move about the depot in an easygoing, unhurried way. No one watching could possibly assume their presence was in any way related to the hurry-up business of travel. They make no bones about the fact that they know one another, often hailing each other by first name across the room. When a pensioner sits down to take a nap, he does so purposefully, settling himself as comfortably as possible, making no attempt to suggest that the resulting nap is accidental. Their dress is casual, often sloppy, usually wrinkled, although most generally clean. A few do affect a suit and tie, sometimes even a hat, but the various items of apparel seldom match, and no one would be likely to take them for traveling businessmen.

Of course, such backstage language is limited. The resident colonizer may relax his behavior a good deal, but the fact remains, he *is* in a public place, and if he is to retain approval for his colonization, such relaxation must be controlled. Thus, while a pensioner may feel suffi-

ciently at ease in the setting to wait until after leaving the rest room to
finish zipping his trousers, he is well advised to make certain such casualness results in no "exposure." And while he may have no com-
punction about relieving a genital itch while seated in the midst of the
waiting area, he must make at least a passing effort at covering such
action with his free hand.

Employees, too, are restricted in the extent to which they may display backstage language. Should the setting be dominated by sympa-
thetic and supportive patrons and residents, the restrictions may be
minimal. A young barmaid may, if the setting is filled with people she
knows well, lounge behind the counter, freely discuss her sex life, even
loudly ask a patron or resident to take over while she goes to the rest
room. But should a newcomer or customer appear, she will be constrained to present herself in a more businesslike manner. A depot manager, in shirt sleeves with tie askew, may sit with his feet on the desk
of his glass-paneled office as long as the depot contains no one who
will take offense. But when a business associate is due for an appoint-
ment, he will sit up, put on his jacket, straighten his tie, and generally
prepare to show himself in a more professional light.

Just as there is great variation in the extent to which residents may
use a public setting for private purposes or indulge in backstage language, so, too, there is great variation in the extent and type of *proprietary rights* or attitudes which may be displayed. Camouflaged colonizers, such as the vagrants described by Love, are greatly restricted in
this regard. Since they are present without approval in the first place,
it ill behooves them to call attention to themselves by acting as if the
setting were their own.

Proprietary attitudes among approved residents take a variety of
forms, "acting the host" being the mildest and probably the most common. Among resident employees, of course, this is not only tolerated
but expected. Such tasks as giving directions and offering assistance are
part of the employee's job. But acting the host is not restricted to employees; colonizers commonly take on such a role. Among bus depot
pensioners, the host attitude displays itself as a willingness, even eager-
ness, to assist confused travelers, as the following incident illustrates:

A young man is seated at a bench near the front of the depot. Nearby, a
raincoated pensioner, who has been in this location most of the morning, is
reading his paper. An unintelligible announcement comes over the loud-
speaker. The young man rises as if to leave, then hesitates, uncertain. He
turns to the pensioner, asks for clarification as to the announcement. The

pensioner replies that the Kalamazoo, not the Flint bus was called. He asks the young man what time his bus was supposed to leave. The reply is 11:15. The pensioner nods, puts down his paper, pulls out a schedule and looks at it. Then he informs the young man that both Greyhound and Short Line have changed their schedules within the last few days and as a result, everything is very confused. He suggests being patient, assuring him that the Flint bus will be along soon.

The schedule which the pensioner consulted was only one among many carried in his pocket. Later, after the young man had departed, he pulled out the entire stack and began going over them one by one with great concentration. The adequate host, apparently, must have his information straight.

A somewhat stronger proprietary attitude has to do with the resident's treatment of property items found in the setting. Pensioners, for example, claim any newspaper not in the hands of another as their own and, having read it, take the owner's prerogative of passing it on to someone else. In fact, if conditions allow, the resident may even take on the owner's prerogative of selling the item to someone else. Thus, for example, in one American city, early in 1970, a number of males took over a public dump for fun and profit. The municipal practice was to charge an admission fee to citizens wishing either to dispose of their excess possessions or to acquire more by choosing from what others had left. Unbeknownst to the authorities, however, a group of men went into business for themselves, picking over the piles of salvageable items and then setting up little second-hand stores around their trucks. Visitors to the dump were told that it was "too dangerous" to climb on the piles, and were "encouraged" to purchase any items they might want from the already established "stores." It might be noted too, that the oft-reported tendency of employees to steal from their work places may have less to do with "bureaucratic distance" than with a strong sense of proprietary rights.

But the strongest expression of proprietary rights involves an attempt to restrict access to the home territory. Such attempts are rarely successful. When they are, of course, the home territory ceases to be located in public space at all. In most situations, any attempts at restriction are resisted by those in charge of the setting. Thus aircraft maintenance crews may feel they have a claim to certain tables in the airport cafeteria, but were they to insist that customers seated at tables move elsewhere, management sanctions would be speedily applied. Attempts by adolescent gangs to stake out certain streets as "turf" and then control traffic flow within the area are met with strong disapproval and resistance by city authorities.[13] Nevertheless, such attempts may, for awhile, be successful, particularly if the gang is large. No such even short-term success would be expected by a lone colonizer. He can too easily be overcome by a superior force.

However, with the support, or at least neutrality, of those in charge, colonizers may display their proprietary rights to such an extent that the space in question can be said to be public only in the most technical sense. Sherri Cavan has described one such locale:

Inasmuch as the Hangout is defined first as a public drinking place and only alternatively as a home territory for homosexuals, the degree to which the invasion of outsiders can be curtailed by the indigenous population is limited. The interest of the owner in maintaining the bar as a profitable establishment tends to set the limits on the degree to which the bar can be converted into a private territory. In this sense, then, no outsider can be forceably removed from the area unless he can be categorized as a public nuisance. But on the part of the indigenous population, the difference between legitimate customers and public nuisances is often vague and in general almost all outsiders are classified somewhere in between, as objects which can be officially treated in improper ways. (Cavan, 1963:24–25)

The indigenous population of the Hangout defended its territory by "bending, abridging and breaking the interaction rules of polite society" (Cavan, 1963:21). Any stranger entering the bar became the focus of attention, the object of public comment, the butt of repeated jokes. His masculinity was questioned, his female companion (if any) was insulted. While such defensive measures did not completely restrict outsider access (which would not have been tolerated by the owner), it most certainly did succeed in limiting it. Having undergone such an experience on one occasion, many persons probably chose never to return.[14]

A final and more general aspect of proprietary attitudes toward home territories may now be stated. To the extent that such attitudes are held by a sufficiently large number in any given locale and to the extent that they do not preclude hospitality to outsiders, they may be highly functional for the maintenance of public safety. Jane Jacobs has suggested that if city sidewalks are to be safe places

there should be, in the brains behind the eyes on the street, an almost unconscious assumption of general street support when the chips are down. (Jacobs, 1963:56)

Residents may help to make such assumptions tenable relative to all sorts of public space. The resident is, after all, on home ground and the integrity of a human's home is rarely violated with impunity. We should, then, not be surprised to read that:

You can take a midnight stroll through Bhendi Bazaar [in Bombay] without any fear. Sidewalk dwellers sleeping on their rickety rope cots will guarantee your safety from hoodlums. (Rukmini Devi, "Hello Young Lovers, You're Under Attack," *San Francisco Chronicle*, January 21, 1970)

HOME TERRITORIES AND SPATIAL ORDER

Some pages back, I suggested that the development of patron relationships to small pieces of public space result in an interesting paradox. Such relationships tend to work both for and against the dominant spatial order of the modern city. This paradox is even more apparent relative to residents, particularly resident colonizers. On the one hand, the establishment of home territories contributes greatly to the spatial segregation of persons. This bar is taken over by homosexuals, that cafeteria by elderly ladies, this hot dog stand by motorcycle buffs, that section of the park by mothers with small children, and so forth. Through the unplanned, uncoordinated actions of all these individuals and groups, the pervasive ethic of the modern city that there is a place for everyone (and everything) and that everyone (and everything) should be in its place is strengthened. On the other hand, however, colonization at the same time works against the spatial order and adds even more complexity to an already complex environment. It does this in several ways. First, to the degree that colonized settings are deemed appropriate for persons other than those doing the colonizing, the urban scheme for who is expected to be found where is challenged. Thus, for example, bus depots are expected to house persons waiting to take a bus. They are not expected to serve as second homes for elderly men and women. When they do so, the urbanite must revise his mental map. Second, to the degree that colonizers engage in activities other than those for which the setting is intended, their home territories become the scenes for "doings" that are quite unexpected to the first-timer who happens in. Again, his carefully learned set of urban meanings requires revision. Third, the process of creating home territories is continual; so is the process of abandoning them. Thus the urbanite's mental map is relatively unstable. The "bar where we always used to go after the football game had turned into a gay bar, it was very embarrassing." First-timers and customers are particularly vulnerable to unexpected and rapid takeovers since they either have never been in the setting before or go only infrequently, and are therefore likely not to be present as the change is occurring. But even patrons may be caught with their expectations down, as it were. Who is present and what is happening in any small piece of public space can literally change overnight, as when a large group decides, as a body, to "hang-out" in this or that place.

In sum then, the process of colonization, of creating home territories, makes the urban world "safer" and easier for those doing the colonizing. It even contributes to the overall spatial order on which the modern ur-banite depends. But at the same time that it is making the city more pre-dictable, it is also making it more unpredictable, thus increasing the difficulty of operating in a world of strangers.

Creating Urban Villages

An urban village is a home territory writ large. It differs from the lat-ter in one crucial respect, however.[15] In the urban village, the entire round of life may, for some people, be encompassed within its limits. This is not true of the home territory which, as we have seen, tends primarily to be restricted to persons who either work in it or hang about in it. Both the employee and the colonizer have to go home sometime. And yet, residents of home territories and those of urban vil-lages have much in common: they have both created personal worlds in the midst of urban anonymity. They have both succeeded in turn-ing public space into semiprivate enclaves. Given their similarities, it is not surprising that a perceptive author should have likened the one to the other:

The little unknown people who inhabited the Reeves Building corridors—elevator-runners, starter, engineers, superintendent, and the doubtful looking lame man who conducted the news and cigar stand— were in no way city dwellers. They were rustics, living in a constricted valley, interested only in one another and in The Building. Their Main Street was the entrance hall with its stone floor, severe marble ceiling and the inner windows of the shops. The liveliest place on the street was the Reeves Building Barber Shop but this was also Babbitt's one embarrass-ment. Himself, he patronized the glittering Pompeian Barber Shop in the Hotel Thornleigh, and every time he passed the Reeves shop—ten times a day, a hundred times—he felt untrue to his own village. (Sinclair Lewis, 1961:358; the quote is from *Babbitt*)

Lewis is here describing what I have called resident employees, but he has captured, I think, the essence of both residents and villagers. In the midst of the city, they recreate the small town, the village, the tribe. Secure in personal networks, they treat the intruding stranger like "tribal" humans have always treated him: he is ogled, gossiped about, interrogated, put through "rites of passage," driven away, or incorporated into the tribe. To venture into a home territory or an urban village, is, in some sense, to take a step into another world.

In this section, we shall be concerned with two types of urban villages. The one, the spatially concentrated neighborhood, is relatively familiar. It is frequently described both in fiction and in the writings of social scientists. The second type—the territorially dispersed village—is perhaps not so familiar, for it is a modern invention, depending heavily for its integrity on the automobile. Let us consider the traditional before delving into the innovative.

CONCENTRATED VILLAGES:
THE WORLD IS THE NEIGHBORHOOD

In its "ideal" form, the concentrated urban village is a small settlement, set intact in the middle of a large city. All its inhabitants know one another personally, their relationships are long-lasting—from birth to grave—and whatever one knows, the others are likely to know too. The ideal neighborhood village neither needs nor requires the intrusion of "outside" organizations. It polices itself, it cares for itself, it plans for itself:

"Consider," he stated, "that you were observed smoking under the stairway, not only by your father but by all the neighborhood. You were loved and protected by your neighborhood, although you thought it was filled with enemies. But the truth is, let a thief enter, let a man be lewd, or molest a child, let a man assault, and the neighborhood will rise and crush him, then or now or anytime or anywhere, the neighborhood defends itself. The police are few, the residents are many, the neighborhood is its own department, it cures or mends, it regulates itself. . . ." (Harris, 1968:453)

But the "ideal" neighborhood village, like the passage just quoted, is a fiction. A village in a city is not really the same as a village set apart. The rest of the city is overwhelmingly evident; it intrudes, and it often must be invaded. Given the propensity for work–home separation in the modern city, many villagers must leave their home town to earn a living. And the representatives of the larger city are difficult to exclude. How can the police, the social workers, the street repairmen, the tourists, the casual visitors be kept from cluttering the streets of the village? How can the village be a thing apart when it depends for its very life on the world outside itself? [16] No, the urban village is not really a village. And yet, despite the difficulties, it can often manage to give a pretty good imitation of one.

In the contemporary United States, those which do the best imitations appear to be ethnic neighborhoods. Initially established to provide mutual assistance and support among immigrants who knew neither the language nor the ways of their adopted land, these little enclaves have survived the assaults of the years. Despite mobility, despite the move to the suburbs, despite urban renewal, despite invasion by other groups, here and there they can still be found, weakened, bleeding, perhaps dying, and yet, still intact.[17] To the degree that they are successful in maintaining both their existence and their integrity, village neighborhoods make it possible for at least some of their inhabitants not only to avoid the world of strangers, but to avoid even learning how to operate in a world of strangers. For these protected few (most usually, women and those able to work and live within the boundaries), to know another is still to know him personally.[18]

In contemporary Britain, perhaps because of its relative ethnic homogeneity and its more rigid class structure, working class rather than ethnic neighborhoods appear to most closely approach the ideal. London's Bethnal Green, for example:

The function of the kindred can be understood only when it is realized that long standing residence is the usual thing. Fifty-three percent of the people in the general sample were born in Bethnal Green, and over half those not born locally had lived in the borough for more than fifteen years. Most people have therefore had time to get to know plenty of other local inhabitants. They share the same background. The people they see when they go out for a walk are people they played with as children. "I've always known Frank and Barney," said Mr. Sykes. "We was kids together. We knew each other from so high. We were all in the same street." They are the people they went to school with. "It's friendly here," according to Mrs. Warner. "You can't hardly ever go out without meeting someone you know. Often its someone you were at school with." They are the people they knew at the youth club, fellow-members of a teen-age gang, or boxing opponents. They have the associations of a lifetime in common. If they are brought up from childhood with someone they may not necessarily like him, they certainly "know" him. If they live in the same street for long they cannot help getting to know people whom they see every day, talk to and hear about in endless conversation. . . . The Bethnal Greener is therefore surrounded not only by his own relatives and their acquaintances, but also by his own acquaintances and their relatives.[19]

Most urban neighborhoods are, of course, not so *gemeinschaftlich* as those I have been describing. But neither are they all as anonymous and unconnected as popular imageries of the city might lead one to expect. Wherever there is a fair amount of residential stability, combined with stability among the area's commercial establishments, some approximation of the urban village may be achieved. People will perhaps not know all their neighbors, but they will know some of them. And they will know about a good many more. They may be connected to one another through certain core people, a long-time inhabitant of the area, for example, who makes it her business to know and know about everybody else. Or, a merchant may serve as well. In the city, owners of neighborhood grocery stores often act as the cement that holds the inhabitants together—introducing them to one another, providing a locale where they can meet, circulating the gossip. If the owners of commercial establishments also live in the area, so much more does the neighborhood approach a village.[20]

That the city is not entirely a network of urban villages whose public sectors have a kind of semiprivate character is merely testimony to the strength of forces which operate to destroy them when they are established, or to prevent them from being established in the first place. The restless mobility of the urban population is probably the key factor. Urbanites have so many reasons for moving on, so few reasons for staying put, that many potential urban villages die almost before they are born. San Francisco's Haight-Ashbury is a case in point. Given enough years, it might have become a village; the flower children might have grown old together, finding some kind of satisfaction out of creating an oasis of personalism in the desert of impersonality. But they too found more reasons to go than to stay.[21] Despite the modern city's penchant for spatially segregating persons, despite the fact that urban villages contribute to and reinforce this tendency, the city is not kind to the neighborhood villager. But then, why should it be? He is after all, an anachronism—a "tribal" human in a cosmopolitan world, a parochial, a traditionalist. He has not yet learned, as have his more innovative counterparts, that technology is the key to successfully creating and maintaining a village in the midst of the city.

DISPERSED VILLAGES: RESTRICTIVE ROUTES

There is more than one way to create a village. In a century characterized by technological gadgetry, why must a village be concentrated in one place? The answer is, of course, that it need not be. And it need not be because of that most "wondrous" of all technological gadgets, the automobile.

The automobile has a particularly interesting and significant characteristic: it allows its passengers to move through the public sectors of the city encased in a cocoon of private space. It makes it possible for one to encounter the city at the same time one is avoiding it. And it makes possible a linking of widely dispersed urban spaces to such a degree that, for all practical purposes, they are spatially contiguous.

What I am suggesting here is that the urbanite, by using the automobile, can guide himself about the city, can restrict his routing about the city, in such a way that *he almost never has to enter any truly public space*. He can go from his home to the homes of his friends, from his home to his place of work, from his place of work to a home territory, from a home territory back to where he lives; and he can do all this without ever encountering for more than a few brief seconds the world of strangers. He moves entirely in a world of personally-known others, through space that is either private or semiprivate, creating out of these people and these spaces a settlement that has escaped the traditional boundaries while leaving intact the personal knowing that is the essential core of village life.[22]

The extent to which modern city dwellers create for themselves dispersed villages is impossible to estimate. Cleveland Amory tells us of one group that has done so: "Generally speaking, so restricted is the Proper Boston Woman's patronage that to her Boston might well be a town of a few thousand people instead of a city of a million" (Amory, 1950:113). And among the people I interviewed, there appeared to be at least two or three who had created or who were in the process of creating such a village. When such persons spoke of "knowing" the city, they spoke primarily of "knowing how to get around by car"— of knowing how to drive from their homes to a friend's house, or how to get back and forth from work with minimal difficulty. This knowledge is likely to be quite detailed, as the following excerpt from an interview summary suggests:

He especially knows the traffic patterns in these areas [areas of the city just described as being most familiar with]. He can tell by how someone is driving whether or not they know the area and if they do not he can usually predict errors they are going to make. For example, like whether someone is trying to get on————during the rush hour at the wrong intersection, or whether people know where————splits and know to get into the correct lane. He knows where the buses go in these areas, which buses go where, where the stop signs and stop lights are, which are the quickest routes from his apartment to frequent destinations, where there are pot holes in the streets and so forth.

It is, of course, true that any urbanite who owns and drives an automobile about the city develops this kind of knowledge. What is peculiar about the inhabitants of dispersed villages is the exclusivity of this sort of knowledge. When asked about public space generally, they reply *only* in terms of city streets which are traversed by automobile and which provide access to the various little private and semiprivate spaces that make up their world.

Ironically, inhabitants of dispersed urban villages often appear to conceive of themselves as cosmopolitans; as very much city people; as brave adventurers seeking out the thrills and dangers of urban public space. "Why would anyone want to live in San Francisco?" one such self-defined "cosmopolitan" asked me in disdain. "Why here in Berkeley we can go right from home to the bookstores and record shops and little boutiques and back again, and it's all very convenient. We hardly ever have to leave the car."

Creating Mobile "Homes": The Traveling Pack

The disadvantage of home territories and urban villages—both concentrated and dispersed—is that they are fixed. One can, and often has to, move outside them. For those wishing to avoid the world of strangers, this poses something of a problem. But, as I have said, urbanites are an ingenious lot. If one cannot stay within the protective privacy of the home territory or village, the solution is to take that privacy along with one. This can be accomplished by the simple expedient of "traveling in packs." It would seem that in the city, as in much of life, there is safety in numbers:

Q: Are there [public] places in the city where you feel especially comfortable?

A: It depends on who you're with. I used to go to the city with a group of friends, a big group of friends and we just brought our own culture wherever we went and when we went anywhere, we were involved in what was going on and laughing and it didn't matter, you know, we brought everything with us. You were with people you could trust.

As the above passage suggests, in any particular public space when a group is sufficiently large, there is created for the individuals who make it up an area of private space. That is, a sufficiently large group provides for its members a kind of mobile "home territory" which they may move about with them from setting to setting. This is possible because a group is (by definition) made up of persons who know one another well and who identify with one another and who thus reciprocally ensure mutual protection and self-confirmation.

Any need for concern with establishing one's identity to strangers or with ascertaining the identity of strangers is eliminated. Just as the rural villager, secure in his own territory and surrounded by his own people, may care nothing for the good opinions of persons in surrounding villages (and in fact, may even view a lack of approval on their part as indicative of the superiority of his own group), so too the member of a group in a public setting may be unconcerned about the responses which his behavior elicits from surrounding strangers. The group itself provides all the reassurance and support necessary.

What constitutes "sufficiently large," however, will vary depending upon a number of other factors such as the size of other groups also present, the dimensions of the space itself, or the amount of leeway allowed by the setting in what is considered acceptable behavior.

For example, if the others in the setting form a group larger than the one of which the individual is a member, his own group may have little success in shielding him. Thus, I once observed a group of seven military prisoners, handcuffed together in subgroups of two or three, enter an airport terminal, suffering from acute embarrassment and humiliation. Heads were lowered, eyes were averted from others in the setting, faces were pale and strained, despite an obvious attempt to act unconcerned. When their three military guards ordered them to sit, all adjusted their postures so as to blot out any view of the handcuffs from all but the nearest or most attentive observers. While the size of the prisoner group was fairly large, the fact that they were quite obviously prisoners pushed all others in the setting into a group of nonprisoners. The size of the latter group thus greatly exceeded seven. But in a setting where prisoners greatly outnumber nonprisoners, it seems likely that they could successfully support one another and protect themselves from any discomfort. A visitor to a penitentiary, passing among large numbers of prisoners, is apt to feel a good deal more threatened than do they.

Whether a group is "sufficiently large" may also be determined by the actual size or dimensions of the particular space into which it enters. A group of five may have a much greater sense of insulation from others if the dimensions are small than if they are large. A giant room tends to shrink even a good-sized group into insignificance, as many a hostess has learned to her sorrow. Thus, for example, groups of three or four, lost in a spacious air terminal, behave a good deal more like lone individuals (that is, speak more softly, move about less freely, and so on; see next chapter), than do groups of the same size in the more cozy confines of a small bus depot.

Finally, the range of behavior thought to be permissible in the setting may also affect how large a group is required to create a sense of being in home territory. Only a very large group, for example, would risk loud talk and laughter in a church, while a much smaller group would feel quite free to exhibit similar behavior on a city bus.

Whatever the requisites for sufficient size, when a group reaches the necessary numbers, its members begin to act in a way that is in stark contrast to the actions of those others in the same locale who are alone or with one or two others. Members of groups, in fact, tend to exhibit behavior similar to that of residents. They use public space with abandon, in such a way that, for example, a group of adolescents can choose to play running games in an air terminal. They feel free to indulge in backstage behavior, calling each other by name, yelling at one another across the expanse of the setting, using obscene language and laughing loudly at private jokes. And they express proprietary attitudes. If their numbers are plentiful enough, they may even force others to depart, as when the overflow from a convention invades a city's nightspots.

Traveling in packs, then, is an additional method for avoiding the city while living in it. It is certainly a highly effective device, but it probably has only limited usefulness. After all, who but adolescents could find, or even want to find, six or seven or more friends to accompany one everywhere one went. Most urbanites, on the contrary, when they venture out into public space, must do so alone, or at most with one or two others. And it is to these "loners" and their methods that we now turn.

CHAPTER SEVEN

PRIVATIZING PUBLIC SPACE
Symbolic Transformation

The various methods of locational transformation are limited in their usefulness. They all require the immediate presence of a smaller or larger group of personally-known others. Or, to phrase the situation more "sociologically," they all require that the individual either stay where his primary group is or take his primary group with him. It is, in fact, this cooperative presence of others that allows the transformation in the character of the *location* itself to occur.

Yet city dwellers often have occasion to venture out alone (or, with one or two others, but we shall concentrate mainly on the loner) into the world of strangers—into the public space of the urban settlement. Surely, if there is any urbanite who cannot "avoid" the city, who is incapable of privatizing its public space, it is this lone individual. But no, even in this situation, there are things that can be done. (In fact, most of the instructing in "how to act" in the city, discussed in Chapter Five, is precisely instructing in how to act under these circumstances.) The lone individual cannot transform the character of public space. He can, however, transform the character of his *social psychological relationship* to that space. By utilizing body management—by controlling gestures, facial expressions, movements, and so on—the individual can create around himself a symbolic shield of privacy. He can, that is, move through public space in such a way as to make himself as inconspicuous as possible, while simultaneously communicating to anyone who might happen to look that he is definitely *not* open to interaction.

Body management is probably the most widely used of all the various creative devices for privatizing public space. It is probably largely responsible for the insistence among many observers of the urban scene that disattention is the *sine qua non* of city interaction.[1] It is probably also responsible for the innumerable characterizations of the city—at least of the modern city—as cold, unfriendly, cruel, inhospitable, and so forth. One cannot help but think how ironic it is that a device for "avoiding" the city should come to be seen as capturing its very essence.[2]

Practicing Symbolic Transformation

THE ENTRANCE SEQUENCE

Let us begin by watching city dwellers in what would appear to be a relatively simple set of actions. The task is to move from one kind of public space (for example, a sidewalk) to another kind of public space (for example, an enclosed setting). But the trick is to do it without making an ass of oneself—to do it and remain inconspicuous, to do it and to give no one a reason to have anything at all to say about the matter. This particular action sequence may be broken down into three phases. The first involves checking for readiness, the second, taking a reading, and the third, reaching a position. We shall consider each in turn.

Checking for Readiness. During the very few seconds immediately before and immediately after entering the setting, the individual takes some precautions to insure a flawless approach. He checks out and, if necessary, rearranges his body presentation to make certain nothing in his appearance is other than he might wish. And, should such be required, he takes care of any last-minute physical needs. That is, he spends a few seconds on backstage behavior so as to be prepared for the ensuing on-stage situation.

Very often body presentation checks and repairs involve no more than making certain one's hair is appropriately arranged, as in the following examples:

A young male approaches the door. He carries a briefcase in one hand; the other hangs free. As he nears the door he uses his free hand to brush the hair back from his forehead, then opens the door with that hand and enters.

Two girls come toward the entrance. About three yards from the door, each begins to pass her hand over her hair, as though brushing it. They continue this until they reach the door. Apparently unfinished, they stop for a few seconds in front of the door while continuing the process.

Men often do little more than pat their heads, as though assuring themselves that no wayward hairs will be standing straight up.

When, as is often the case, the setting entrance contains a plate glass door, the door forms a mirror which may then be used to check parts of the body not otherwise visible. Thus:

A young woman nears the door. When she reaches it she stops for a moment, lowers her head, raising her eyes so that the top of her head is visible to her in the glass. She examines this view for a second, then raises her head again and moves inside.

On occasion, the individual may feel a more thorough check and repair is in order, as apparently did the two young men described below:

A young male is coming down the path toward the door. He is carrying nothing; both arms swing freely at his sides. As he comes within a few yards of the door, he puts one hand up to his shirt pocket, rearranging the pencils which he carries within. Then with both hands he pulls at his belt. Finally, just before entering, he uses one hand to wipe quickly at his hair.

A young male is almost to the door. He stops, grabs at the center of his belt with both hands and pulls up on his trousers, glances down briefly in the direction of his zipper and just as he passes through the entrance, he pushes on the bridge of his glasses with one finger.

Last minute physical needs are also satisfied during these few seconds. Thus persons may be observed coughing, yawning, sniffling, blowing, and scratching just before coming into the full view of the occupants of the setting.[3]

Taking a Reading. Either at the same time or immediately after the check for readiness, the individual takes the next step in his approach. He takes a reading of the setting. That is, he familiarizes himself with its physical layout. This is important, for it makes possible the final step of the sequence: reaching a position.

Coming into a setting with which one is unfamiliar is confusing. The individual is barraged by a sudden mass of visual and audial stimuli. If he is to take a position within the setting without creating a scene, he must avoid such errors as walking into walls, tripping over furniture, or opening broom-closet doors. And to avoid such errors, he must somehow organize the barrage of incoming stimuli into a fairly clear picture of the arrangement of the setting.

Anyone who has been in the setting on a previous occasion, of course, has an advantage in this phase of the sequence. He or she already knows its physical features. Nevertheless, such persons are not entirely free of the necessity to take a reading. Arrangements do change: furniture is moved, facilities are relocated, and, in depots and terminals, luggage may litter the floor space—the exact placement of which no one can know beforehand.

Americans seem to feel constrained to take readings as quickly as possible and to do so in such a way as to suggest that they are not doing so. One might think that under the barrage of masses of new stimuli, the most sensible procedure would be to pause for a few moments just inside the setting in order to most adequately and efficiently assess the physical layout. But such frank, unabashed assessments are rarely observed. To prolong the period in which one is in view of all those already settled within the setting is to prolong the period of disadvantage. The approach sequence is difficult enough (since during it the individual is "in the spotlight," as it were) even at its briefest; to prolong it is to prolong a period where the slightest error is visible to the largest number.[4]

The most common reading style observed is also the quickest. The individual enters and moves rapidly into the setting without a pause, but during his first few seconds within the setting, moves his eyes rapidly, covering everything within range. Sometimes this is done without moving his head. The entire body, head included, is fully directed into the setting, as though the individual were following a tunnel running right through the middle of the setting. Only the eyes move, darting quickly from side to side, then straight ahead, then to the side. More often, the body remains straight, but the head is allowed to turn. Even here, the movement is swift. Once the eye has focused and taken in an object or area, it loses focus almost immediately and darts in another direction. The head cannot move as quickly as the eye, but within a few seconds after the eye has unfocused, it too shifts position.[5] Only rarely does the entire body move from side to side, following the head and eyes; and when it does, the movement is very slight.

A second reading style is somewhat slower, utilizing as it does a kind of "delaying tactic." This involves a minute pause, necessitated by some small task in which the individual engages himself, the pause providing a few additional seconds within which to assess surroundings. Thus we may observe persons pausing briefly, just inside an entrance, to remove gloves, reach for a cigarette, take off sunglasses, transfer a purse from one arm to another, retrieve change from a pocket, or, if the outside weather is chill, shiver for a moment as though to shake off the cold. This is not to suggest that such delaying tactics are necessarily deliberate. It is quite understandable that for purposes of physical comfort one might wish to remove one's gloves upon entering an indoor setting. But whether deliberate or not, such acts do result in a delay in the approach process and thus in an opportunity to take a fairly complete reading.

A third style involves stimuli restriction. Rather than trying to take in the entire setting at one time, the individual restricts himself to only one section of the approach area, guiding himself through this section until he has reached a position. Sometimes this involves taking a reading only of the floor area. In this case, the head and eyes are cast down from the moment of entrance, the individual sees the setting only as floor space, legs and shoes, and makes his way toward a position ignoring all other aspects of the setting. More often, stimuli restriction involves concentration on one side of a setting. Here the individual takes a reading only of the area which adjoins the wall or rim of the setting. The opposite side of the depot, store, or whatever, is ignored until he has reached a position. Thus an individual using this reading style may enter a bus depot, immediately look to the left, take in the booths and lunch counter contained in that section, and, never averting his eyes to glance at the area to his right, follow the lunch counter section all the way through the approach area.

There is, finally, a fourth possibility: the individual may avoid taking a reading at all. This may be accomplished in a variety of ways. First, if there are two persons entering together, one ahead of the other, the second in line may rely on his companion to assess the situation and simply follow wherever he goes. When this occurs, one may observe a kind of "follow the leader" dance, with the second person repeating the body movements of the first in an almost stylized fashion. Second, the individual may avoid a reading by simply keeping his head turned in the direction from which he came, rather than in the direction toward which he is going. This would seem to be a rather dangerous ploy, because by not looking where he is going, the individual risks flawing his approach with bumps, stumbles, and trips. On the other hand, it does allow one to avoid taking note of whether one is being watched. Perhaps the gain is thought to override the risk. Perhaps the individual assumes that anyone watching will assume that a person behaving in such extraordinary fashion must surely be engrossed in something of legitimate interest and importance. As such, any awkward slips should be readily discounted. This is a relatively common ploy when three persons are entering together. The lead person turns at the moment of entrance so as to face his companions and literally backs into the setting. Presumably in such situations, one's companions, who are looking forward, can be relied upon to provide warnings of any imminent disasters. However, it is not unusual to observe a lone individual employ the same tactic, maintaining his gaze from the moment of entrance until he is well within the setting of the area he has just passed through.

Reaching a Position. The final phase involves reaching a position, securing a stopping place, or attaining a goal. Thus, the sequence may be said to be complete when the individual takes a seat in a booth, reaches a ticket window, stops in front of a cigarette machine, and so on.

Persons who avoid taking a reading at all may be said to have reached a position whenever they come to a halt, or, in the case of those backing in, whenever they turn around. They are by this time far enough into the setting so that they may simply stop and stand without being conspicuous. The spotlight is off once the approach has been completed, although the length of the approach area will vary from setting to setting.

Those who take a restricted reading may reach a position simply by following the area they have chosen to observe, as we have seen above. The initial reading, although limited, yields enough information to enable them to move toward a position with relative ease.

For persons taking a full reading, whether quickly or by utilizing a delaying tactic, there are a number of alternative methods by which a position may be reached. They may, after seeing the various alternatives, opt for the restricted tactic noted above and simply follow one side of the setting until they have reached a satisfactory stopping place. When the setting is a particularly complex one, involving a jumble of people and/or objects, this is probably one of the least difficult and least dangerous methods.

However, the individual may have spotted the exact position site he wishes to take during the initial reading—quite possible if the setting is not too large, complex, or crowded. In such a case, he may use what may be called a "beeline tactic." With eyes focused on the desired site, he moves straight toward it, rapidly, purposefully, turning neither his body, head nor eyes in any other direction. Presumably, such single-minded concentration eases some of the difficulties of the approach, in much the same way that the restricted and back-in tactics do. First, the individual cuts off some of the incoming stimuli, thus avoiding confusing distractions and reaches his position in record time. Second, by focusing continually on the position site, he prevents himself from taking much notice of those around him and avoids any full realization of the numbers of strangers who may or may not be looking at him.

Similar to the beeline tactic (and possessed of the same advantages) is the "object-concentration tactic." Here, during the initial reading, the individual ascertains the general direction or the exact location of the position he wishes to attain. But rather than focusing on that spot, he chooses some object in the general direction of his destination and lavishes his attention on that. Thus a large wall clock, just above and to the side of a door toward which he is headed, may receive his gaze all the way through the approach. This is a particularly useful method if the setting is not excessively crowded so that one does not have to be so careful about keeping an eye on the path ahead. When the setting is large, and the distance to the position great, the object of focus may change. During the first lap of the journey, a display board may serve; once that is passed, the gaze may shift to a wall mural, then finally to a row of chairs.

In some situations, both the beeline and object-concentration tactics may be modified. If the desired position is somewhat beyond the approach area, as is often the case when large numbers of people are present, the riveted gaze may be relaxed somewhat after one has achieved a more crowded (and thus less exposed) section of the setting. Here, there is an alternating of gaze from the object or site to one side, then the other. But even here the side looks are brief; the first focus of attention continues to be the main one.

As the reader has probably already noted, to utilize body management as a device for avoiding the city, the urbanite is required to call upon a considerable amount of city know-how. He must not only understand the meanings of various body movements, positions, and so forth; he must have the skills to apply this understanding to his own behavior. That all this skill should be put to such a negative use is perhaps one of the great ironies of city life.

WAITING STYLES

Let us now consider another situation. The city dweller has entered some particular public space—a bus depot or airport, let's say—and finds that he or she has to wait a while. *Now* the trick is to *sustain* one's inconspicuousness and to *continue* to make very clear that one is not open for interaction. We shall look at only three of the many styles that might be assumed to bring off this task with distinction: "*The Sweet Young Thing*," "*The Nester*," *and* "*The Investigator*.*"* I should point out that while the latter two may appear to the reader to be less inconspicuous than the former, this difference is more apparent than real. In the locales in which I have observed them being "acted out" (bus depots and air terminals), they blend in very nicely with the overall tone of the setting.

The Sweet Young Thing. As the name suggests, this is a style most commonly assumed by "respectable" young women who are extremely anxious to remain that way. This is not the style of the "liberated" woman, but of the woman who truly believes all the propaganda she's heard that "nice girls don't."

The style of the Sweet Young Thing involves very little movement. Having once taken a position inside the setting, usually a seated one, she rarely leaves it. Her posture is straight, potentially suggestive or revealing "slouching" is not dared. She crosses her legs or her ankles but takes great care to see that no more of her is showing than current standards of good taste allow.

She inevitably has a book or magazine in her possession, which is drawn from her coat or handbag the moment she has settled herself in a position. The book or magazine is never closely read; to become engrossed is to risk losing awareness and control of one's posture. In addition, it is essential to be on a constant look-out for any approaching danger. But while reading material receives little close attention, it is always conspicuously present, either lying on the lap or held out from the body with one hand, about midway between the lap and the face. Such a prop serves to demonstrate that she is tending to her own affairs, not on the prowl for strange males and not the type of young lady who would invite attention by boldly staring about. While she does gaze at her surroundings, her glances are usually short and casual, risking no eye contact. On the occasions when she allows herself to simply stare, she makes certain her eyes are turned toward the floor, chair, wall, potted plant, or any other inanimate object.

Should the occasion arise when she must leave her position and move to another location, she does so purposefully, in a businesslike, no-nonsense way. She does not "stroll" from one part of the setting to another. Having first carefully planned her move, she proceeds with all deliberate speed to her new destination.

The Nester. The Nester style derives its name from the main activity engaged in by those who use it. Having once established a position, such persons busy themselves with arranging and rearranging "props," much in the manner of a bird building and occupying a nest. The following anecdote is an apt illustration and makes clear what I mean by "props":

Mrs. B. of our church parish always came to Mass with an incredible number of small items in her possession. We seemed always to be seated in the pew just behind her so that before services began we had a very clear view of her activity. Having entered the pew, she first knelt for a few minutes in prayer, then sat back, opened her purse and began pulling out various items. First came the missal which she looked over carefully, opened and marked for the day's services, and then laid to one side. Next came her rosary, carefully taken from its tiny box and placed in a convenient pocket for later use. Then the collection envelope was drawn forth, examined closely and finally placed between the pages of the missal. If it were a warm day, she would remove her coat, taking great care to fold it just so and place it next to her. Her hat needed rearranging quite often too, and she spent quite a bit of time removing and replacing pins. She invariably went to the altar to light a candle, necessitating an inspection of her change purse and often a bit of housekeeping in the handbag itself. When she had lit the candle and returned to her pew, she seemed always to find that things had been disarranged or were not as propitiously placed as she might wish, and the whole process would begin again. It was said in our parish that Mass could not begin until Mrs. B. had finished building her nest.

Like Mrs. B., Nesters in public settings are possessed of an amazing number of items of personal property and they spend most of their time in the setting caring for them.

Nesters seem primarily to be young men and middle-aged women. Whatever sex, they are always very neat in appearance. They are somewhat less restricted in their movements than is the Sweet Young Thing, although like her, having once secured a position, they rarely leave it. Indeed, they are really much too busy to do so. However, unlike the Sweet Young Thing, Nesters are not confined to one rigid posture. In fact, their duties require that they have considerable freedom of body movement within the confines of their positions.

Sometimes the Nester's possessions, though numerous, are small in size, as is the case with the young man described below who was able to carry them all in his pocket, a small briefcase, and a paper sack:

A young man, mid-twenties, sits down on one of the benches in the bus depot. He places a briefcase, which he had carried under his arm, on his lap and opens it. He withdraws several small pieces of paper, examining each with some intensity, then returns them to the case. He stands up slightly so as to pull some coins from his pants pocket, then sits again and counts the money several times before returning it to the pocket. Now he takes a checkbook from the briefcase and spends a few minutes bringing the check register up to date. The checkbook is returned to the case, and a spiral notebook is withdrawn. He begins writing, but this too lasts only a few minutes. Then the notebook is replaced, the briefcase closed, and a paper sack is set neatly on top of it. In a few seconds, the paper sack is removed, the briefcase reopened, and a packet of letter-size paper is withdrawn. He glances through these, returns them, and then in rapid succession, pulls out and returns a newspaper, book, brochure, and letter-size envelope.

On other occasions, the Nester may be kept busy looking after items of a much bulkier nature. In such cases, there is a good deal more standing up and sitting down, lifting and juggling, than in the situation illustrated above. Witness the activity of a middle class woman in her late forties or early fifties:

A yellow convertible stops outside the bus depot and a woman emerges. She makes several trips from the car to the locker area, finally places a number of items in one of the lockers and leaves. About a half hour later she returns, her arms laden with additional packages. She sets them on a bench, goes to the lockers, retrieves what has been placed inside and brings these things to the bench as well. Her possessions now include two dress boxes, a hat box, a suitcase, a purse, a paper sack, and a raincoat on a hangar, protected by a plastic cover. She sits down next to this stack and begins to arrange them. The suitcase is placed on the floor, dress boxes on top; the raincoat is laid across the back of the bench. Her purse and the paper sack are placed next to her. She surveys this handiwork and, apparently dissatisfied, begins to rearrange it. This arranging and rearranging continues for fifteen minutes until a bus is called, and she transports all her gear, in several trips, out to the loading area.

Should Nesters be required to forsake their positions temporarily, they do so only after making certain that everything is in place (if they cannot take it all with them). Even if they must leave some things behind, they do not move to their new destination empty-handed, but carry along some item, such as a briefcase. During the passage, they continue their work, looking through or tidying up whatever item they were able to bring along. Once returned to the initial position, they inevitably find that the props left behind need to be rearranged once more.

Note that this absorption with props functions to keep the eyes occupied so that one does not have to be concerned with eye contact (a type of contact which body-management users take great pains to avoid). And the busyness suggests to those about that here is a person who has many important things to do and is therefore not a person with whom one should attempt any interaction.

The Investigator. Less confining in body movement than either of the previous styles, the Investigator stance nevertheless protects those who utilize it from eye contact and undesired interaction. Investigators (primarily mature—late thirties or older—males) are quite as absorbed and thus unapproachable as Nesters. But unlike Nesters, the objects of their absorption are not personal props but the various facilities of the setting itself.

Having first reached a position within the setting, the Investigator surveys his surroundings with some care. Then, having done this, he leaves his position to begin a minute investigation of every inanimate object in sight. Occasionally he returns to his initial position or establishes a new one, but most of his time is spent moving about. The Investigator is at his best, of course, if the setting is large and complex and presents a wide array of items for him to look at. But if the setting contains no such "lush growth," he remains undaunted. A truly skilled Investigator can spend five minutes gazing at a sign which contains only three words. Let us follow one Investigator as he moves about a small but well-supplied bus depot:

A middle or lower–middle class male, early forties, is wandering about. He spends a few moments standing in front of a small gift vending machine, looking at the display of available items, then sits down on the bench across from the machine to continue his investigation. He rises, goes up the stairs to the rest room, stopping en route to look at the various signs which adorn the walls. Leaving the rest room, he moves to the front of the depot, taking note of the menus on the wall behind the lunch counter. Now he comes further into the depot again, stops in front of a medal-making machine and proceeds to read all the instructions printed on it. He comes back even further, now gazes at a sign urging travelers to tag their luggage. Leaving this spot, he moves to a Diners Club display—a desklike arrangement with a sign asking people to fill out applications for a Diners Club card. There is a place on the desk apparently designed to hold applications, but it is empty. He remains in front of the desk for about three minutes, then goes back to the gift machine which once again receives his studied attention. Now he goes out the side exit and looks at the buses parked in the runway, comes back in, stands gazing out the window to the runway. Leaving this location, he goes to the rear exit, looks out at the parking lot for some five minutes. Coming back into the middle of the depot, he examines a coke machine and the photo booth situated next to it, then sits down at the bench facing these two items and continues his examination. He rises after a few minutes and goes over to the phone booths, spends about four minutes looking through the telephone directory.

The Investigator continues this kind of movement during the entire time he is in the setting. When he leaves, he has given a few moments of undivided attention to every machine, phone booth, sign, clock, window, door, chair, ash tray, water fountain, and newspaper stand in the place.

Principles of Symbolic Transformation

We have been looking at some specific examples of persons using body management under particular circumstances to create for themselves a symbolic shield of privacy. It is useful now to consider some more general principles of this device.

FIRST PRINCIPLE: MINIMIZE EXPRESSIVITY

Keep one's facial expression impassive. Look neither happy nor sad, angry nor peaceful. Avoid laughter and tears (unless called for by the setting, as in a movie theater). Singing or talking to oneself is taboo. This impassivity should also be expressed in one's dress, which should not stand out as odd or different vis-à-vis the dress of others in the setting. If one is with one or two other persons, conversation should be conducted in a quiet tone, kept, if possible, inaudible to strange others in the setting.[6]

SECOND PRINCIPLE: MINIMIZE BODY CONTACT

Keep oneself to oneself. Avoid bumping into, brushing past, stepping on, or colliding with any strange persons.[7] Keep alert to the speed with which, and direction in which, these persons are moving, so as to guide one's own actions appropriately. Follow the rule of generally staying to the right, but do not assume that others will do the same. A description of two incidents shows the concrete operation of this principle:

The scene is a large airport terminal. Man #1 is in the process of moving from the waiting area, across the open passageway and toward the entrance to the dining room. Man #2 is proceeding down the passageway. Their movements are such that they appear to be headed for a collision. Just short of the point where the collision would occur, man #1 pauses for a fraction of a second, turning his head in the direction of the display case (position of pause marked *P* on Figure 1). He then proceeds, passing just behind man #2.

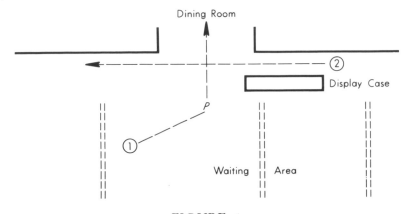

FIGURE 1

The scene of the second incident (Figure 2) is a city street. Woman *A* is in the process of crossing the street and is moving along the sidewalk in a straight line. Woman *B* is approaching the corner at right angles to woman *A*. As in the preceding episode, their movements are such that they appear on a collision course. As woman *A* nears the point of collision (the side-walk corner), her movements slow down, almost imperceptibly with no actual break in stride. At the same time, woman *B*'s movements speed up, so that rather than colliding, *A* passes directly behind *B*.

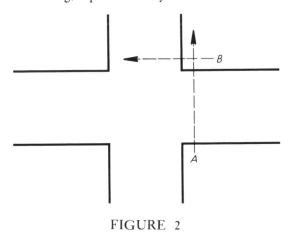

FIGURE 2

THIRD PRINCIPLE: LOOK BEFORE YOU SIT

Keep oneself apart. Avoid seating oneself in such a way as to suggest to a strange other that one wishes to interact. In making one's decision, bear in mind that the distance which signals a desire for interaction will vary according to such simultaneously operating factors as the following. (1) How much seating there is to choose from: If a lunch counter is crowded, one may sit anywhere. If it has only one customer, do not sit next to that person but choose a seat some distance away. (2) One's own sex and the sex of the person one will sit next to: It appears to be the case that whenever the age and sex of two strangers are such that one might appear sexually attractive to the other, the distance required to ensure that no interaction signal is given is greater than if no sexual attraction potential obtains. (3) Whether the person one will sit next to is alone or with others: If the person is part of a group, one may sit closer than if the person is alone. However, if the area is generally empty, sitting close to the group may still be interpreted as "horning in." Factor number (1) must be kept in mind at all times. (4) The use to which the particular public space is put: In a highly task-oriented setting like a library, one may sit closer to another with impunity than in the more sociable atmosphere of a bar.[8] (5) The physical arrangement of the setting and the potential this holds for eye contact: Some settings are arranged so that to sit in a given spot is to be placed in the position of having to look at the person seated opposite. Unless one has some personal prop such as a book or magazine which can be used to cut off the line of vision, such positions should be avoided.[9] The following example suggests the interrelation between one's seating decision and the potential for eye contact:

Four middle class women are seated in the waiting area of a bus depot as indicated in Figure 3. Women *A, B,* and *C* had been present first, and *A* had been avoiding any possibilities of eye contact with *B* and *C* by turning her head to her right in such a way as to look toward the front of the depot. Woman *D* then arrived, placing some packages in the empty end seat and sitting down next to *A.* Now the problem of eye contact for *A* has been complicated. To look straight ahead is to look directly at *B* or *C,* or at least to appear to be doing so. To look toward the front of the depot is to look directly at *D* or to strain her neck so as to look either in front of or behind *D*'s head. To look to the rear of the depot requires considerable strain and also involves looking in the direction of persons seated to her left. For several minutes, *A* attempts to continue looking to the front, straining so as to direct her gaze either in front of or behind *D*, or occasionally alternating or looking directly at *B* or *C*. That she is straining is evident by the rapid shifts in the direction of her gaze and by an almost continual rubbing of the neck. Finally, apparently finding the strain too much, she leaves, goes to the front of the depot, and returns minutes later to take a different seat.

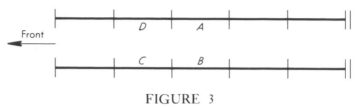

FIGURE 3

Keep one's eyes to oneself.[10] Avoid even accidental contact. The following techniques are useful for this purpose. (1) If in a seated or waiting situation, have some prop to look at such as a book or magazine or letter. (2) Concentrate one's gaze on inanimate objects. (3) If one wishes to gaze about, glance at surrounding persons only below the neck. (4) Utilize the "middle distance stare." This is particularly effective in situations which are either so crowded or so arranged that no matter where one looks, one is looking at someone. The middle distance stare requires that one look out into the setting, but do so without focusing *on* anything. Its effectiveness lies in the ability of other humans to determine whether or not someone is actually looking at them (that is, whether the eye gazing in their direction is focused. See above, note 5). (5) Wear sunglasses. One can then look people right in the eye without their being aware that one is doing so.[11]

FIFTH PRINCIPLE: WHEN IN DOUBT, FLEE

Keep oneself protected. Avoid coming close to anyone who either looks or behaves "oddly." Such persons are unpredictable, may accost one despite one's precautions, and may involve one in conspicuous interaction. Two incidents described below will illustrate:

I had an experience in a bus depot in Sacramento. I was way across the room and there was an old man sitting there and he must have started to have an epileptic fit or withdrawal symptoms or something and people just sort of—shooooh—like he was a magnetic force that was driving them away. There was about a 100 yard radius around him, there was just nobody. He was completely by himself. And I wondered whether I should go over there or not, but I thought I'd better not cause I don't know what I'm going to be doing if I go over there.

A large group is gathered in a hall connecting two University buildings to listen to and argue with the anti-Vietnam War speakers. There are heated exchanges and as the voices grow louder, more people join the crowd. A young man, a spastic, has just entered the hall and is standing quietly, listening to the speaker. Suddenly he becomes animated, rushes forward, losing more and more control of his limbs as he does so. He flails his arms, trying to attract the attention of the main speaker. He begins to talk, he is angry, but the words come out slurred and indistinct. He struggles to make himself understood, but succeeds only in becoming more excited and more uncontrolled. His head rolls against his shoulders, his legs bow, his arms move in all directions, his eyes dart to and fro. The crowd, so noisy before, is hushed. Eyes turn from him and people begin to leave, slowly at first, then with increasing momentum until only a few persons remain. Newcomers stop for a moment to listen, but unlike those before them, do not remain for more than a few seconds. He watches the crowd disperse, pleads for them to listen, lurches toward those nearest him as though to prevent their leaving. Finally, after completing his argument with the speaker, he himself leaves. A young co-ed greets an incoming friend a moment later, tells her of the incident and expresses her view that the entire episode was vulgar and grotesque.

SIXTH PRINCIPLE: WHEN IN DOUBT, DISATTEND

Keep oneself aloof. Avoid attending (unless one can do so from a safe distance) to anyone who either looks or behaves "oddly." When fleeing is not possible, act as if nothing peculiar were going on. Do nothing to suggest to the person in question that he or she is not quite "normal." Behave generally as the city dwellers do in the following incident:

We entered the coffee shop about 11:00 P.M. and sat in booths along one side. I was sitting so that I could see everyone in the booths ahead of us, all the way up to the door. We had not been there very long when a man of about fifty came in and sat himself down about three booths ahead, facing in my direction. He ordered, and for awhile I did not pay much attention to him; that is, until a murmur of conversation and a slight blur of movement made me look again in his direction. There he sat, eating his dinner, and quite clearly carrying on an animated conversation with someone who, also quite clearly, was not there. This invisible companion to judge by the man's actions, was apparently seated on the other side of the table. As time passed, the conversation became more audible, and the man began to gesture more boldly, apparently involved in some very intense conversation. His invisible companion carried on his part in the interchange, for every few minutes the man would stop, cock his head, hold his fork suspended, and listen in rapt attention to what his companion had to say. There were not very many people in the coffee shop, and those who were present were going out of their way to pretend they hadn't noticed. There was a young couple sitting in a booth right across the aisle from him and they were taking great pains to keep from looking at him and to stifle any laughter that might threaten to arise. I could see the employees every once in a while duck into the kitchen area to laugh quietly among themselves, or at least comment on the behavior, but I noted that the waitress who served the old gentleman did so with great calm, waiting patiently should he be in the midst of conversation, until he had finished before asking if he wanted anything else. Incidentally, the invisible companion apparently was not hungry, for no food was ordered for him. I'm not quite certain what would have happened had an order for two been placed, but I rather suspect that it would have been served without comment.

We have been looking at a variety of devices—home territories, urban villages, traveling packs, and body management—which city dwellers use to avoid the world of strangers, to create, as it were, larger or smaller pieces of private or semiprivate space out of the public spaces of their urban environment. It is time now to turn to a contrasting aspect of city life and city behavior—that having to do with adventure. Before we do so however, two points should be made.

First, the above devices may be combined in a wide variety of ways, and any given individual will utilize one or more of them depending on his or her own situation. Thus a person may have created a dispersed village for himself, but utilize body management whenever he must move outside its boundaries. Or, a long-time city dweller who has lived in different areas of the city may have several neighborhoods which serve him as modified concentrated villages. And he may combine these with home territories outside the neighborhoods. Or, even the least skillful and most protected villager (for example, older women in ethnic ghettoes) may have several sites within the village that are more home territories than are other sections of the village. What I am suggesting then, is that we must not think of any given device as being used exclusively by any particular category or categories of persons.

Second, people who use one or more of these devices are not necessarily utilizing them all the time. The same person who sticks to his dispersed village one day may go adventuring the next. The same person who "avoids" the city one day with body management may feel quite adventurous three days later. I may be tired today and want nothing so much as to be left alone. Tomorrow, however, I may be delighted to get into a long conversation with some total stranger while eating my lunch. I may have just arrived in the city, a "respectable" young woman, frightened of the newness and strangeness of it all. Four months later I may feel like the most sophisticated city dweller around, confident of my powers to handle myself in all situations.

In sum, then, it should be borne in mind that any given city dweller may combine avoidance devices in a variety of ways, and that the same person may combine avoidance with adventuring. It is to that adventuring that we now turn.

CHAPTER EIGHT

USING THE CITY
The Adventures of Skilled Urbanites

I'll once in a while go to downtown San Francisco alone and the first feelings I usually get are tremendous feelings of my own smallness as a unit in
the universe and the second feelings I get are that I don't have to behave in
a manner that's consistent with my behavior among people whom I'm
known by. Because I'm not known; so I find the opportunity of being
alone in a really large public place as an opportunity to put on, and to act;
you're free to do something totally different, to try on a new identity.

I just swing my purse and walk and have a good time. I don't really feel
like a lot of people really feel, strange and encumbered, because it's such a
big place. I really like it. . . . It's so intriguing, there's always something
around the corner that you find and I like to experience it, a lot of times
by myself. You also have the possibility of encounters with different people
when you're alone. I was thinking when I'm in public places by myself, I'm
always apprehensive at the start of it and then once I become involved in it
and I can interact with people, immediately it's smoothed over; just to
meet someone, make a contact, establish some kind of play between you,
then I'm fine; but it's always the initial step of stepping into it that is always difficult when you go into a strange place.

Urbanites, as this interview extract suggests, are not always busily
engaged in "avoiding" the city. The city may also be, for those with
the knowledge and skills to make it so, a setting for adventure; a place
to confront new and diverse people and situations; a place to try out
new and diverse identities. The public space of urban settlements—
the world of strangers—may, for many persons some of the time
and probably for some persons all the time, be experienced as
"freeing," "exhilarating," "fun," "exciting." Human beings are not always and everywhere on the defensive. They are not always and
everywhere preoccupied with the protection of their fragile selves.

Armed with sufficient knowledge and skill, they, like the young woman whose words are reproduced above, sometimes find it enjoyable to seek out a little danger, to court a little fear, to engender a little anxiety. They sometimes find it enjoyable, that is, to go adventuring.[1]

We shall focus upon some of the ways that people use the city for "fun," and whenever possible, for "fun and profit," beginning with the "ideal" prototype of these adventurers: the urbane hero. Then we shall explore some unconventional and conventional forms of city fun and finally consider two highly improbable urban adventurers: hicks and eccentrics.

The Urbane Hero: Prototype of the Adventurer

There is in the Western world, an image, an idealized image, of a certain human "social type." This social type may be called the "urbane hero," but he (for the type is usually portrayed as masculine) may be known to the reader under a variety of names. He is the "city slicker." The "guy who knows his way around." The "cosmopolitan." The "real city person." He is the guy who might sell you the Brooklyn Bridge; he is never the guy who would buy it.

The dominating trait of the urbane hero is his coolness. No matter where he goes in the city (and he goes everywhere), no matter whom he encounters (and he encounters everyone), he is always unflustered, at ease, and in command. He is never thrown by diversity, whether it be diversity in the way people look or diversity in the way they behave.[2]

A secondary trait is tolerance. He not only is not thrown by diversity, he relishes it, finding in his city's wide array of life-styles, a source of genuine personal pleasure. While he is "justly angered" with cruelty, the exploitive use of power, and unfair physical violence, he looks with amusement and a certain fondness on the minor vices, his own or those of his fellow urbanites. He couples and tempers this tolerance, however, with toughness. He understands and is willing to accept that life, particularly urban life, is struggle, is conflict, is sometimes pain.

His secret weapon, the weapon that allows him to be cool, tolerant, and tough is knowledge; he is the star scholar of city know-how. He is likely to have established for himself a whole series of home territories, to have developed for himself a wide range of personal acquaintances. These are very useful to him, but they do not limit him. He can move as easily through public space that is "new" as through space that is "old hat"; he can move as easily among persons he has never met as among friends and acquaintances of many years. His grasp of urban meanings—appearential, locational, and behavioral—allows him to operate amidst strangers with minimal risk. His possession of urban skills—in how to dress, where to go, and how to act—allows him to take those minimal risks should he wish to.

Anyone who has not been locked in a bare room for the last thirty or forty years has met the urbane hero many times. He appears repeatedly on movie and television screens, sometimes disguised as a private detective, sometimes as a lawyer, sometimes as a plain-clothes policeman, sometimes as a big-city reporter, sometimes as a free-lance adventurer, sometimes as an "agent." He is Peter Gunn, Joe Mannix, "The Baron," James Bond, or one of the "Avengers" (Emma Peel being one of the few female versions of the type), or Humphrey Bogart as a reporter, Humphrey Bogart as a detective, or Humphrey Bogart as a not-quite-honest free-lancer. Those who have not met him on the screen have encountered him many times in the pages of books. He has the starring role in almost all mystery stories, where he may appear as Sherlock Holmes, Hercule Poirot, Perry Mason, or Philo Vance.[3]

The urbane hero is, of course, a fiction. But to say that he is a fiction is not quite the same as saying that he is unreal. If no actual human being is quite like him, there are, nevertheless, undoubtedly many human beings who approximate him or who emulate him or who admire him. He embodies the characteristics, the know-how, the command over his complex environment that many urbanites would like to possess; for he is the man who walks with ease through the world of strangers.

In the following pages, we shall be talking about flesh-and-blood human beings, not idealized heroes. But we shall be talking about flesh-and-blood human beings who, in varying degrees, are not so dissimilar from the urbane hero. They too are cool, tolerant, and tough. They too possess city know-how. They too "walk with ease." They are, in essence, the working adventurers of which the urbane hero is merely a plastic prototype.

Adventuring in the City

URBAN FUN: UNCONVENTIONAL "GAMES"

For a certain kind of urban adventure, the city's anonymity is a crucial prerequisite. I speak here of those adventures involving some element of deception. The city dweller, remember, makes judgments about—identifies—the strange others who surround him on the basis of the other's appearance, location, and, to a limited degree, behavior. He has nothing else to go on. He has no knowledge of the other's biography, no fund of gossip about the other, no personal experience of past interaction. He has, in short, no information with which he can "correct" the other's proffered identity or intent. For the most part, as we have seen, such immediate information is sufficient. For the most part, the strangers who surround the city dweller are what their appearances, locations, and behavior suggest that they are. If this were not the case, city living would be so unpredictable, chaotic, and confusing that it would cease to be a viable human option. For the most part, I have said—but not always. The world of strangers is a world ripe for deception. And the city contains its share of those who are willing to pluck.

Let us consider two sorts of deceptive or "unconventional" games that urban adventurers play: *identity games* and *interactional games*. Identity games involve deception vis-à-vis who one is. Interactional games involve deception vis-à-vis what one is up to. The distinction is somewhat artificial, however, in that each sort of game also involves the other. Deception regarding identity necessarily involves deception as to intent, and vice versa. The difference between the two sorts of games, then, is primarily a matter of emphasis and they are separated only for analytic convenience.

Identity Games. There are probably as many ways to play fast and loose with "who one is" as there are human beings; three ways, however, seem especially popular: passing, performing, and pretending.[4]

Passing is the most encompassing of the identity games. Not only the strangers one encounters in public are deceived but one's friends and acquaintances, as well. It is also the most risky. There is always the chance that friends and acquaintances will spot inconsistencies and guess the "truth" or that someone who "knew one when" will show up and "blow one's cover." It is also the game with which the reader is probably most familiar. Examples include the light-skinned American of African descent coming on as "white," the narcotics agent infiltrating a "commune," the reporter joining a distinct religious or political group, or the social scientist engaging in covert observation. The passing may be short-term or long-term, depending on such factors as the individual's original intent, whether or not unmasking occurs, satisfaction with the pretended identity, and so forth; but during the period of passing, the entire life-round of the individual is involved. Because this is such a familiar phenomenon, I shall not consider it further, except to point out that it is a game far more easily played in public space amidst strangers than in private space amidst friends. As with all sorts of deception, the less information available to others, the greater the chance for success.[5]

In contrast to passing, the game of *performing* is primarily played out in the public sectors of the city and it tends to encompass less of the individual's life-round. When the adventurer is finished with his game, he retires to private space and assumes again the identity which he claims as his own. In what is perhaps its most classic version, the game is played by those who utilize the public space of the city to beg. Its most skilled players were to be found among the various beggars of the preindustrial city. Masters of the appearential order, these ingenious individuals "practiced to deceive" in any way that seemed likely to increase their take. And the ways that seemed most likely primarily involved some manipulation of identity. Many of the beggars of the preindustrial city were, of course, exactly what they appeared. But the "others" were something else again. There were those, for example, who stood around crying a good deal, pretending to be "helpless orphans." There were those who "passed themselves off as merchants ruined by war, by fire or by having been robbed on the highway." There were the

malingreux . . . [who] were covered with sores, most of which were self-inflicted, or they pretended to have swellings of some kind, and stated that they were about to undertake a pilgrimage to St. Meèn, in Brittany, in order to be cured. . . . The *sabouleux* . . . were in the habit of frequenting fairs and markets, or the vicinity of churches; there, smeared with blood and appearing as if foaming at the mouth by means of a piece of soap they had placed in it, they struggled on the ground as if in a fit, and in this way realized a considerable amount of alms. . . . The *convertis* pretended to have been impressed by the exhortations of some excellent preacher, and made a public profession of faith; they afterwards stationed themselves at church doors, as recently converted Catholics, and in this way received liberal contributions. (Lacroix, 1963:469–70)

An early seventeenth century writer describes a not uncommon scene in French cities of the time:

"Rogues . . . and others, who have all day been cripples, maimed, dropsical, and beset with every sort of bodily ailment, come home at night, carrying under their arms a sirloin of beef, a joint of veal, or a leg of mutton, not forgetting to hang a bottle of wine to their belt, and, on entering the court, they throw aside their crutches, resume their healthy and lusty appearance, and, in imitation of the ancient Bacchanalian revelries, dance all kinds of dances with their trophies in their hands, whilst the host is preparing their suppers. Can there be a greater miracle than is to be seen in this court, where the maimed walk upright?" (Quoted in Lacroix, 1963:471)

Let me hasten to assure the reader that the French had no corner on alms-taking con-men. Medieval Italy certainly had its share:

Thus the *affrati*, in order to obtain more alms and offerings, went about in the garb of monks and priests, even saying mass, and pretending that it was the first time they had exercised their sacred office. . . . The *accatosi* deserve mention on account of the cleverness with which they contrived to assume the appearance of captives recently escaped from slavery. Shaking the chains with which they said they had been bound, jabbering unintelligible words, telling heart-rending tales of their sufferings and privations, and showing the marks of blows which they had received, they went on their knees, begging for money that they might buy off their brethren or their friends, whom they said they had left in the hands of the Saracens or the Turks. . . . (Lacroix, 1963:477)

And Sjoberg tells us that:

An American doctor who practiced in Chungking, China, a few decades ago records that when he attempted to rid a beggar of his sores, the latter resisted on the grounds that his deformities were essential to his occupation. (Sjoberg, 1960:204) [6]

In the modern city, begging has largely passed from the scene. And with it have gone also those who had truly perfected this version of the game of performing. Nevertheless, there is some indication that they may not be gone forever. An increasingly frequent sight in the modern city is the young, rather shabbily dressed white "floater" standing on street corners asking all who pass by for their "spare change." The extent to which these young beggars are as destitute as they sometimes appear is not known. Many, having cut their ties with home, having gotten "strung out" on drugs or having simply rejected Western materialism, may, in fact, be as poor as their pitiable appearances would suggest. But one cannot help but suspect that here and there, in this individual or that, the spirit of the preindustrial con-man has surely been resurrected. One cannot help but suspect that some of these young people, like their Parisian counterparts of old, shed their pitiable conditions at the end of the day to "dance all kinds of dances with their trophies in their hands, whilst the host is preparing their suppers." [7]

Passing and performing are both rather serious identity games. They encompass major portions of the individual's life round and the stakes involved are frequently rather high. The consequences of losing these games, (that is, being "unmasked") include such unpleasant experiences as imprisonment, job loss, physical and mental abuse, status reduction, and so forth. Fortunately for those urbanites with a bent for adventure but a distaste for catastrophe, there is another option. *Pretending* is a game that may be played only sporadically and then only for short periods of time. The most serious consequence of failure is mild embarrassment, and that is unlikely to be of long duration.

To play the game, one may or may not plan to do so ahead of time (in contrast to both passing and performing which involve rather careful planning). Often, the opportunity to play "just happens" but even when it does, the individual is under no particular obligation to take advantage of it. And since the game is always played with strangers and always in public space, one can often, if things go poorly, simply leave the scene.

The essence of the game is a kind of "Walter Mitty" wish-fulfillment.[8] The individual expresses in public for the ratification of surrounding strangers an identity or an aspect of identity that he or she feels cannot be expressed among personally-known others. Thus, for example, the individual may "pretend" to belong to some admired occupational group as with a young woman informant who told me that she had always rather wanted to be a stewardess and that she had once gotten into a conversation with a man in a restaurant in the course of which she told him she was a stewardess. She said that she then proceeded to describe her life to him in some detail, talking about all the places she had seen, the advantages and disadvantages of being always on the go, and so forth. She commented that at the end of the conversation she had almost convinced herself that it was true.

Or the individual may "take on" some occupation, not because the occupation is desired for itself but because of the status which it carries. In the following passage, a group of young men of peasant origin, being for the moment "in the money," visit an exclusive and expensive restaurant in the city of Lodz where they proceed to spend lavishly:

We sat down at a table and Alesky ordered a bottle of cognac and *zakaski*. As soon as the waiter went away, girls began to turn around us and to flirt, each prettier than the other, and with large decolletes, so that almost the whole breast was to be seen. Soon we selected one each and sat at a larger table. Alesky pretended to be an employee of the treasury office from Petersburg, although he had never seen Petersburg; Pawel, a merchant of the first guild, although he was only of the third; I a travelling Polish-American agent, although I had no idea about it; Lucas, the son of a rich manor-owner, although he was only the son of a tavern keeper. (Thomas and Znaniecki, 1919:381)

In the friendly darkness of the anonymous bar, how easily does the teaching assistant become a professor; the clerk, an executive; the lowly private out of uniform, a man of substance. One informant told me that during his stint as an enlisted man in the Air Force, he would occasionally make dinner reservations under the name of Dr. ———. Arriving at the restaurant early, he would wait in the bar until the speaker system announced that the "doctor's" table was ready and then walk into the dining room, the oppression of his "actual" status momentarily lifted.

Sometimes the game is played in a more subtle, a more inward manner. I refer here to the expression of identity that accompanies being present in the appropriate location and/or dressing for the part. Here the individual makes no verbal claim to the identity in question. Nor does he receive any verbal ratification for it. Instead, his knowledge of urban meanings allows him to assume that if he appears in a certain place and/or in a certain way, those about him will make the appropriate "identification" and this "assumed" ratification is sufficient. The shy young man, ill at ease and unsuccessful with women, can, at least for a moment, "be" the swinger of his secret dreams by the simple expedient of standing about in a body bar "looking cool." The adolescent female could, in the 1960s, don her "hippie" outfit on a Saturday afternoon and parade the streets of the Haight-Ashbury, with the certain knowledge that the gawking tourists would take her to be one of the area's exotic inhabitants. And the out-of-town matron may, for a few brief minutes, become a New York City sophisticate:

Again, especially in New York City because that is the epitome of an urban area, there's something about, to me, walking down the street and buying theater tickets or you know doing anything that makes me feel very sophisticated or very worldly. Simply because it's New York City and it can give you that feeling. . . . But that's a very exhilarating feeling for me . . . to feel very sophisticated.

One suspects that much of the appropriation of dress styles and identity badges that goes on in the modern city involves this mild version of the game of pretending.

Interactional Games. As I suggested earlier, identity games and interactional games are very much intertwined. To be deceptive regarding what one is up to is always to be deceptive to some degree regarding "who" one is. That is, one aspect of identity involves the motivations and goals assumed to be appropriate to it. This interrelationship will be apparent in the examples of interactional games discussed below.

I want here to consider only two kinds of interactional games, although presumably there are many more. We shall look first at haggling, then at hustling.

In the preindustrial city of times past and in many preindustrial and early industrial cities in the contemporary world, the game of *haggling* is played with relish. Its focus, as the reader is undoubtedly aware, is the buying or selling of some given piece of merchandise, each participant working as hard as possible to conceal what he is willing to sell for, or what he is willing to buy for. The game, of course, may be played between persons who know one another and in a private setting (as in its modern but diluted version: labor-management bargaining), but in its purest form, the participants are strangers, and the setting is public. Under these latter circumstances, each must use his urban know-how to deceive the other while simultaneously penetrating the other's deceptive front. Sjoberg describes the general process:

In the haggling process the seller sizes up the customer by his dress and mannerisms to determine whether the latter has any notion of the "real value" of the article in question and what he is probably able to pay. The seller then states a price considerably higher than what he expects to receive. The buyer in turn offers an amount considerably less than he expects to pay. Gradually each party raises or lowers the figure, as the case may be, until a meeting point is reached.

In the process the verbal duel may wax violent. Usually the customer belittles the item in question and tries to evince little interest in purchasing it, while the seller uses counterarguments to persuade the customer to buy it at the asking price. Occasionally friends, even strangers, will join in, interposing remarks as to the probable worth of the article. . . . (Sjoberg, 1960:205)

With the general rationalization of business in the modern city, haggling, in its pure form, has largely disappeared. Many contemporary urbanites, even those with great knowledge of, and skills in, city ways, cannot play this game—as any number of tourists have discovered to their sorrow.

Hustling on the other hand, is alive and well. The goals of hustling are many and varied; its essence, however, is to get the other to do what one wants him to do without his being aware of just what that is. Past master at the hustle is the "cat":

Despite the location of his social world in the "asphalt jungle" of the "Black-belt" he strictly eschewed the use of force and violence as a technique for achieving his ends or for the settling of problematic situations. He achieved his goals by indirection, relying, rather, on persuasion and on a repertoire of manipulative techniques. . . . His idea was to get what he wanted through persuasion and ingratiation; to use the other fellow by deliberately outwitting him. . . .

The cat gets by without working. Instead he keeps himself in "bread" by a set of ingenious variations on "begging, borrowing, or stealing." Each cat has his "hustle" and a "hustle" is any nonviolent means of "making some bread" which does not require work. One of the legendary heroes of the cat is the man who is such a skillful con-man that he can sell "State Street" to his victim. Concretely, the cat is a petty thief, pickpocket, or pool shark, or is engaged in a variety of other illegal activities of the "conning" variety.[9]

Despite the implications of the above passage, the game of hustling does not always involve illegality. It is a game indulged in for a whole array of probable and improbable purposes:

One of Bertha's favorite strategies [to gain access to potential converts for the millenarian sect of which she was a member] was to patronize coffee shops and snack bars and to feign the appearance of the single girl lingering long over her coffee. By unabashedly making eye contact and acknowledging smiles, she invited men to initiate access to her. She recognized the sexual assumptions of these contacts and consciously sought to exploit them [for her religious group]. She would explain the male's conduct to him in veiled religious terms, noting that many people were seeking for *something* today. The play between her and her erstwhile partner typically culminated in an invitation to dinner. The ambiguity of these overtures can perhaps best be judged by the occasion on which a young sailor appeared for dinner with a bottle of wine for two, only to find a rice-based meal set for seven, chaperoned by a Korean lady. (J. Lofland, 1966:115)

URBAN FUN: CONVENTIONAL ENCOUNTERS

The city dweller seeking adventure in public space is not limited to involving himself or herself in deception; he or she is not limited to unconventional gaming. Public spaces may also be the settings for the mild but quite pleasant adventures of simply encountering and conversing with people one has never met before; that is, with strangers. I refer here not to those stylized task-oriented exchanges between waiter and customer, bus driver and rider, and so forth. Even persons utilizing body management to keep themselves aloof and apart must occasionally speak in these situations. I refer, rather, to the verbal encounters between strangers that are not simply "built in" to the role that either is playing; to such experiences as exchanging pleasantries with the person sitting next to one on the bus, as joining one's cafeteria tablemate in conversation, as passing a few words with the people with whom one is waiting in line, as picking up a date in a bar, as meeting someone in a grocery store and inviting him home to dinner.

Experiences such as these are a constant aspect of city living. They are frequently observed and are reported with frequency by informants and by historians of urban life (for example, Carcopino, 1940:250). They vary, as the reader may have noted, in terms of extent of involvement: the exchange which begins and ends in a single setting is probably more frequent than that which continues in a series of settings or which eventuates in the movement of the involved participants into private space, since the latter, of course, is more risky. The stranger one meets in a bus depot and takes home may turn out to be wanted for murder; [10] the woman one meets in a coffee shop may have religious not sexual experience in mind; or the friendly guy one met at the coffee house and invited home for a "smoke" may turn out to be a narcotics agent.

When these conventional encounters occur repeatedly in a single public locale, they become part of the process by which the individual establishes a patron or, even, a colonizer relationship to the locale. But even when they are not part of this process, they are one of the mechanisms by which total strangers are transformed into personally-known others.

A major question regarding these conventional encounters is this:

how does the individual decide with whom to initiate an encounter? How does he or she judge whether any given strange other is safe and/or accessible, or at least sufficiently safe and sufficiently accessible to risk making an interactional opening? The risk of making such an opening is not really great. At most the other may simply ignore one, or tell one to "buzz off." But these are unpleasant and embarrassing experiences and presumably ones the individual would wish to avoid. (Note that those individuals who wish to engage in unconventional gaming must make the same initial decision. After the opening, however, these persons are involved in more complex interaction calling for much greater skill than is he who only wants to engage in some conventional talk.)

Interview and observational materials suggest that in making the decision, the individual engages in an extremely complex calculus, weighing this fact against that, under these circumstances given those factors. There appear to be at least three highly interrelated issues involved in the decision calculus: desirability, legitimacy and appropriateness. Let us briefly consider each in turn.

Desirability. In determining desirability, the individual is "identifying" the other and calculating whether this person, as identified, is someone he or she really wants to talk with. The calculation, like the identification, is based on the information received from the intersection of cues relative to the other's location, appearance,[11] and behavior, but is then coupled with the individual's own mood and purposes. Thus, for example, young unattached male informants invariably report that the people they are most likely to talk to in public are young attractive females. Skid row bums, persons obviously drunk, and persons acting "oddly" are frequently listed as persons one prefers not to talk to, although this latter is not an invariable rule. One young man who was enrolled in a social psychology class, reported that he enjoyed talking to people everyone else was avoiding so as to "experiment with what would happen." (Desirability also plays a part in the decision of the person being encountered to respond, as when a young woman informant reported that she agreed to go out with a man she had just met in a camera store because he "looked like Sonny Tufts." In fact, all of the following discussion is as applicable to the responder as to the initiator.)

Legitimacy. Calculations of legitimacy involve consideration of the chances that the other will define the encounter as expected and all right under the circumstances. In contemporary America, for example, there do appear to be a number of situations in which interaction between total strangers is "expected" to occur. (Interactions between public-space service personnel and their stranger clients are, of course, always of this character, but they will not be discussed here.) Thus, persons engaged in legal and "respectable" solicitation, such as collecting signatures on a petition, selling Veterans' Day poppies, or seeking funds for a worthy cause are usually thought to have legitimate access to all. So, too, persons seeking minor assistance are seen to have good reason for initiating an encounter. And it has frequently been noted that in America, persons accompanied by dogs or children appear to be legitimately "open" to other persons similarly encumbered. In addition, whenever the everyday routine is disrupted, whenever conditions are collectively defined as extraordinary, almost all stranger interaction is expected and legitimized. An electrical blackout may be one such "disruption":

It seemed to me that the blackout quite literally transformed the people of New York. Ordinarily smug and comfortable in the high hives of the city where they live and work, they are largely strangers to one another when the lights are on. In the darkness they emerged not as shadows, but far warmer and more substantial than usual. Stripped of the anonymity that goes with full illumination, they became humans conscious of and concerned about the other humans around them. (L. Wainwright, "A Dark Night to Remember," *Life*, November 23, 1965:35)

The most pressing problem was to rescue all the people trapped in subways and elevators. A few women fainted and there were some hysteria cases, but most of the imprisoned strap-hangers rose to the occasion. Aboard one train, a man who called himself Lord Echo got everybody to join him in calypso songs; two hours later astonished rescuers found 50 passengers dancing in the aisles. ("The Disaster that Wasn't," *Time*, November 19, 1965:41A)

However, the suspension of ordinary routine is not limited to crisis situations. San Franciscans report, for example, that being crowded aboard a cable car provides a great opportunity to talk to people. Being part of a crowd watching a parade or demonstration or other less-than-routine occurrence also legitimizes encounters. And so does being present in some highly specialized locales, such as body bars where "prowling" is the expected and approved activity.

A determination that any given encounter would not be legitimate does not necessarily lead to a negative decision. If it did, strangers would rarely talk to one another.[12] Such a determination is simply thrown into the hopper and weighed against desirability and appropriateness. Under situations where encounters are defined as legitimate, however, such a definition may be the determining factor. I suspect that a good many people who spend most of their time avoiding the city, may actually have an adventure when the conditions are right.

Appropriateness. Simultaneously with questions of desirability and legitimacy, the issue of appropriateness must be considered. That is, an encounter may be seen as appropriate even though "illegitimate," or as legitimate but inappropriate. Thus, for example, the resident colonizers we met in the foregoing chapter seem frequently to feel that it is appropriate for them to talk to anyone and everyone in their respective home territories. And if they make their relationship to the locale very clear, the encountered other is likely to grant the appropriateness, if not legitimacy, of their actions, as in the following:

A young woman is seated in the very last seat of a bus; the seat extends the entire width of the bus. She has been on the bus since it started out from the depot and took the seat she now occupies at the time she boarded. After the bus has been traveling for some five minutes, it stops at an intersection and a working class middle-aged male comes aboard. After paying the driver, he moves toward the rear, and as he is about to reach the back seat, he looks at the woman seated there and says, "This is my favorite place. Will I be in the way?" The woman smiles and replies that of course he will not. He seats himself on the same seat but somewhat to the left of her, next to the window. During the next twenty or thirty minutes they engage in on again, off again conversation. Finally, they begin to talk and do not interrupt their conversation until the male leaves the bus.

The important thing to note here is that despite the not infrequent concern of females with keeping themselves aloof from surrounding males, this young woman was quite willing to engage the older man in conversation. With the words, "This is my favorite place," he made it very clear that he was the host and she the visitor.

In assessing the appropriateness of initiating an encounter, the individual must consider not only his own relationship to the locale in question but such other matters as the openness to interaction being signaled by the other. Thus, for example, one woman reported that she hated to eat alone and enjoyed talking to strangers in restaurants. However, if the person whose table she joined (in a cafeteria, where lone persons must often sit with strangers) never looked at her when she sat down, remaining engrossed in his or her food or book or whatever, her response was to say nothing, granting him his "right" to be left alone.

Even in situations of fully legitimized encounters, body language may suggest that interaction is inappropriate, as with a store clerk who reported that she could tell just by the way persons handled themselves whether or not they wanted to be waited on.

Calculations of appropriateness, like those of desirability and legitimacy, also involve consideration of the character of the particular public space itself. Encounters between males or between males and females, for example, may be more "appropriate" in some settings than in others. In his study of a millenarian cult, John Lofland found that the male members of the sect who attempted to initiate contact with persons in libraries and museums (as a first step in proselytizing for converts) met with very little success:

In the winter of 1962–3, Elmer and Alfred attempted access in libraries and museums. Elmer liked to station himself near the psychology section of a library, observe in what books people were browsing, and wander about the reading rooms noting what books were being read. Upon finding a person involved in a book imagined to be "cosmic" in concern (books on psychology, religion or world affairs), he would stay close by the person, waiting for an occurrence that could bring about a conversation. Elmer did much looking but he rarely found an opportunity to talk and often complained about the difficulties of striking up a conversation with strangers. Access was equally difficult in museums. While walking around looking at the exhibits, Alfred's ploy was to station himself next to a co-patronizer and hope for a likely opening. He complained that it was difficult to. make such an opening. If you looked at a work while standing beside a stranger and said, "That is certainly an interesting bear" (or whatever), they tended to "look at you as if you are some kind of nut" and walk away. (J. Lofland, 1966:115–16)

Temporal considerations also play a part in calculations regarding appropriateness. As we have seen, patrons of a given locale, by reason of their repeated presence, come to recognize and eventually to talk with other patrons. The amount of time that will be required for any given pair of patrons to start talking will probably vary, however, depending on sex, age, locale, and so forth. In the following rather sad story, a young man waited three months for the appropriate moment to approach a young woman:

I had been working in Chicago for three months and during all that time it had been my practice to stop at the same coffee shop near my office each morning for about a half hour before going to work. On the very last day of my job, I was in the coffee shop as usual and was preparing to leave when a young man approached me. I had noticed him before but we had never spoken. He said that he had seen me every morning for the past three months and had not wanted to approach me earlier but felt that it was alright to do so now. He said he would very much like to get to know me and perhaps to go out on a date. He introduced himself and I replied by giving him my name in return. I told him that it was very nice of him to have approached me but that this was the very last day I would be on the job; that, in fact, I would be leaving Chicago tomorrow. The interesting part of all this is that I felt it was quite proper for him to have talked to me in this way, and had I been remaining in Chicago, I might even have agreed to go out with him.

Improbable Adventurers: Hicks and Eccentrics

In the foregoing pages, we have been watching highly skilled urbanites involving themselves in a series of city adventures. Before concluding this chapter, however, we must devote a few moments of attention to two types of adventurers who manage to have a great time in the city despite their lack of, or disattention to, urban know-how. I refer to hicks and eccentrics.

Hicks are persons who don't know how to get along in the city but don't know or don't care that they don't know. The consequences of their ignorance are often rather astounding. They talk to all kinds of people and find that all kinds of people will talk back; they make fast-friends in the most unlikely locales and under the most unlikely circumstances; they ask for and receive assistance in situations in which even skilled urbanites would hesitate. They move through the city with confidence, protected from its dangers and pitfalls by the simple shield of ignorance. Just how long this blissful ignorance can be sustained is questionable. While it lasts, however, the person least well equipped for city living may find that "city folks are just like the people back home."

Eccentrics, like hicks, appear to have no conception of how one is "supposed" to act in the city, but, unlike hicks, this ignorance may be more apparent than real. It may be, in fact, that they have discovered a great urban secret: in the city, he who behaves most oddly, is often treated most kindly.

We have seen in Chapter Seven and in this chapter that persons who behave oddly in the city are likely to be avoided. However, as we also have seen, in situations where avoidance is impossible, normalization is the rule. In the following example, note how hard the more conventional urbanites must work to keep the eccentric from suspecting that her behavior is seen as even slightly odd:

A working class woman, late forties or early fifties, is seated at one of the horseshoe counters in a large coffee shop in a bus depot. She is cleanly dressed, wearing a sweater and print dress. As she is drinking her coffee, a woman in her mid-seventies comes out of an adjoining cafeteria and greets her. The newcomer is dressed in a rather motley collection of unmatched, apparently second-hand and terribly wrinkled and dirty items of apparel. Her dress is of shiny satinlike material and is badly tattered. It hangs loosely around her as though it were several sizes too large. Over this, she wears a shiny, equally shapeless satin coat, apparently designed for wear on formal occasions. It contains a very large hole in one elbow. A badly bedraggled hat, with a tiaralike frame sits on her head. She is carrying a large paper shopping bag which appears to be almost full although nothing within it is identifiable. The old woman stops beside her acquaintance. "Enjoying hot coffee, huh?" They exchange a few words. The old woman looks about her and notices that on the counter are several dirty small paper plates, used by the coffee shop for serving sandwiches and pie. She picks up one nearest to her and asks her acquaintance, "Do you think I can have it? They usually give them to me. I have a collection of them you know?" The acquaintance says nothing for at this point the waitress approaches them. The old woman asks the waitress if she may have the plate. The waitress nods, her face showing neither surprise nor puzzlement. Another plate setting further down the counter comes to the old lady's attention but before she can reach it, the waitress has picked it up and placed it in the waste can. Noticing this, the lady asks the waitress if she may have the second plate. Again the waitress remains expressionless, pulls it out from the trash and hands it to her. Noticing other plates in the waste can, she asks if she might have those too, and in a short time she has all the dirty plates available in that section of the coffee shop in her possession. As she receives each one, she wipes it off slightly with a napkin and places it in her shopping bag. After she completes wiping off and packing the last plate, she bids good-bye to her acquaintance and disappears. A few moments later the waitress approaches the other woman and asks her what the old lady does with all those paper plates. Her face is not expressionless now, and she quite clearly means to indicate that she thinks the now departed lady is a little crazy. The woman answers that she thinks the old lady has children to visit her and uses the plates, after cleaning them up, to serve refreshments to her visitors. Having verbalized this explanation, she apparently finds it unsatisfactory even to herself, shrugs her shoulders and laughs, and says to the waitress: "I don't really know what she does with them." The two women exchange knowing smiles and the interaction between them ends.

There is a marvelous paradox in all this. As we have seen in this and the preceding three chapters, city dwellers work very hard at acquiring urban know-how so that they may either avoid the city altogether or adventure in it with a minimum of risk. And yet, here are these two improbable adventurers, hicks and eccentrics, illiterate in, or inattentive to, city ways. And what is their reward? Sometimes, at least, friendliness, protection, normalization. The most inept participants in the world of strangers are, on occasion, its most pampered citizens.

CHAPTER NINE

THE ROUTINE WORLD
OF STRANGERS

As noted in the preface, I conceive of a book as a journey, with the author as guide. Continuing that analogy, we have now reached our destination. The journey has been long, with many side trips, but, I hope, not uninteresting. At this juncture, it seems appropriate, befitting the role of a guide, to offer some general thoughts regarding what we have encountered along the way.

Two major themes have permeated the foregoing pages. The first, and perhaps more obvious one, is that the social psychological conditions for urban life cannot be taken for granted; that the situation of living as a stranger in the midst of strangers has within it the logical potential for a chaotic unpredictability that no human would find tolerable. We can live in the world of strangers only because we have found a way to eliminate some of the "strangeness." We can live in the world of strangers only because we have ordered our cities such that it is possible to identify these personally-unknown others with some degree of accuracy.

If I am correct in this assertion, it follows that the situation of contemporary life—an urban situation—necessitates some continuing arrangement for making identities visible. It necessitates, that is, some continued denial of the great humanistic urge to obliterate "categorization." Humans, if they are to live in the world of strangers (and given the present population of the earth, there would appear to be no other choice) need to know a great deal more than the simple fact of common humanity about the people who surround them.

The appearential order, which dominated the preindustrial city, was, as we have seen, one way in which the possibility for relatively accurate identifications could be assured. But the viability of this type of order depended upon a relatively rigid class or caste system, buttressed by tradition and/or an extremely powerful elite group. The congruence between appearance and identity required more than mere voluntaristic "self-expression"; it required enforcement. Thus, the contemporary blossoming of such appearential identity indicators as bumper stickers, lapel buttons, and expressive dress styles does not herald the reemergence of the appearential order. A situation where I have only to change my dress style and paste an American flag on my car window in order to pass as a member of the "silent majority" does not guarantee a very stable order, especially when three days later I may switch again by replacing the flag with a peace sign. I repeat: the appearential order was possible only because the linkage of identity to appearance was not a matter of individualistic whim but a matter of coercive and traditional power.

So, too, the spatial order which dominates the modern city derives its stability and, therefore, its usability, from the fact that it is not merely voluntary but enforced—enforced by shared beliefs, by shared preferences, by shared customs, *and* by law. The paradox of the situation is that having created the spatial order, we now throw up our hands in horror at its continuing unfolding, and speak in hysterical tones of the "urban crisis." What is the urban crisis but the inexorable expression of the spatial segregation of persons and activities—the essence of spatial ordering. That this order has created poverty-stricken central cities ringed by sprawling suburbs hooked together by pollution-creating transportation devices does not gainsay its serviceability in keeping the urban world social psychologically, if not physically, livable.

I am not suggesting that some alternative, some more humane alternative, to either the appearential or spatial order cannot be found. I am suggesting, however, that utopian plans for the heavenly city must, if they are to be viable, contain within them a heavy dose of social psychological realism about the very unheavenly creatures who will be its inhabitants.

The second, and perhaps less obvious, theme is that the city created a new kind of human being—the cosmopolitan—who was able, as his tribal ancestors were not, to relate to others in the new ways that city living made not only possible but necessary. *The cosmopolitan did not lose the capacity for knowing others personally. But he gained the capacity for knowing others only categorically.* The cosmopolitan did not lose the capacity for the deep, long-lasting, multifaceted relationship. But he gained the capacity for the surface, fleeting, restricted relationship.

It is true, of course, that the transformation from the world of personally-known others to the world of strangers has been, and continues to be, an emotionally painful one. It is one thing to make abstract statements about the great changes that have taken and continue to take place in the world: about the massive growth of population and urbanization, about increasing spatial mobility, about the growing numbers who put down their roots not in a place, but in a profession. It is quite another thing to talk about these changes in terms of their emotional meaning for, and effect on, the day-to-day lives of human beings. The tribalist does not easily become a cosmopolitan, and the cosmopolitan, having been transformed, looks back wistfully to a life that will not come again. A brief personal reminiscence will perhaps make clearer what I mean.

Some years ago, I made one of my infrequent return visits to the relatively small and isolated town in which I was raised. It had grown in the years since I first left, but it had not grown very much. When I lived there, the population was somewhat less than 8,000. It is now somewhat more. But it is still a small town, or at least it seems so to me.

During this visit, I spent some time with a woman who has been my friend since we were toddlers. She is married now and has two young sons, and she and her husband intend to remain in the town the rest of their lives. Because of the husband's military commitments, they had lived elsewhere for a while—in a more populous area—but they had returned as soon as they were free to do so. Happy as she is in this town in which she has spent almost all of her life, she senses that somehow things are not as they were. She feels the winds of change, and she finds them disquieting. "Do you remember when we were children," she asked me, "and we used to walk downtown? Do you remember how we always knew everyone we passed on the street? Why, it took forever to make the walk because we had to stop and talk to so many people. It's not like that at all anymore," she said; "there are so many new faces. People seem always to be coming and going. I can walk down the street now without hardly ever seeing anyone I know. It's really changing." And there was a certain sadness in her voice. "It's not the same at all."

For my friend, being a participant in great historical transformations has had a very personal meaning. It has meant an unsettling alteration in her formerly solid world. The change in that world is hardly a massive one, but it is perceptible to her. She can see, and recognizes that she must cope with the fact, that what was once an environment of personally-known others, is becoming, however limited the degree, a world of unknown others. "People are always coming and going," she says. They arrive, but they never seem to stay long enough to be recognizable. They come, not as settlers, but as transients; they come because one of the great governmental or private bureaucracies of which they are a part asked them to come, and they will go when the great bureaucracies want them to be someplace else. Even this still small and still isolated town is beginning to feel the shockwaves of history. Its citizens are discovering that there are strangers in their midst. Even there the world of strangers has penetrated, and even there it must be coped with.

What is true for this one small town is, of course, many times more so for the more urbanized and less isolated areas of the globe. American humans, for example, retreat to the suburbs, ostensibly to escape the crowding and anonymity of the city. But once outside their immediate suburban neighborhoods, in the great shopping centers which dot their landscapes, they find themselves surrounded by as many strange faces as they ever confronted in the city. A few contemporary American villages may still be classic *gemeinschaft* societies in the winter, but with the coming of summer and its influx of tourists, part-time residents, and occasional visitors, many of these villages are transformed into almost urban settlements. In short, while the world of strangers may be particularly characteristic of great cities and their surrounding metropolitan hinterlands, it is not limited to them. The necessity to cope with large numbers of personally-unknown others, the emotionally painful, wrenching shift from tribalist to cosmopolitan, is part of the texture of modern life.

I have said that this wrenching shift is emotionally painful. It is also intellectually difficult. Whatever the stresses and strains inherent in the small personal world—and if we can believe its many critics, these are not insignificant—it is nonetheless a world rather easily and naturally grasped by its inhabitants. The world of strangers, in contrast, is almost overwhelming in its complexity. To master the intricacies and subtleties of urban meanings, to excel in the development of urban skills, these are no mean accomplishments; to become not merely urban but urbane, this is an exacting task.

In the face of this pain and difficulty, it is perhaps not surprising that so many of us should attempt retreat. Retreat into the pseudotribalism of the concentrated or dispersed urban village. Retreat into the regenerated tribalism of the rural commune or the "out of the way" small town. Retreat into dreams of somehow "re-creating" in the "community" the binding brotherhood and sisterhood of "communion." [1] For some, such attempts may prove successful. For most, however, given the three billions of us now inhabiting this globe, there simply is no retreat. For most of us, the world of strangers is a permanent home. For most of us, the world of strangers must become routine. I hope we shall be equal to the task.

NOTES

CHAPTER ONE

1. Childe, 1942; Lenski, 1970:164–65, 196–97; Redfield, 1953; Wood, 1934:chap. III; R. Wright, 1971:2–3.

2. Whether a human being will appear very "different" from oneself is clearly a matter of perspective. From the point of view of modern science fiction, all humanity appears remarkably similar. But from the point of view of totally isolated humans, who have knowledge of only their own existence, anyone new would likely appear very "different" indeed—even if that new arrival seemed, to the cosmopolitan eye, similar to his host in color, facial and body structure, and clothing. For centuries, Western men believed that "monstrous races" inhabited many areas of the globe, and actual sightings of the residents of these areas did not always disconfirm the belief. Some early European explorers of the New World reported seeing Indians who were fully as terrible in appearance and habits as they had expected. For a fascinating review of this long-lasting belief in "Homo Monstrosus" see Malefijt, 1968.

3. A scanning of Old Testament references to strangers suggests the existence of a similar ambivalence among the ancient Hebrews. On the one hand, Jehovah is constantly enjoining them to treat strangers with friendliness and hospitality. On the other hand, strangers are a dreaded instrument of punishment, as in the Book of Prophets, which contains repeated dire threats of what God will allow strangers to do to his chosen people if they don't behave.

4. Where not otherwise indicated, quoted materials are from the author's interviews or observational field notes.

5. In here reviewing a part of the literature on the responses of small settlements of isolated peoples to strangers, I have been guided by my own conceptual purposes and have consequently ignored and obscured many of the distinctions and concerns which are centrally important to scholars of these matters. I have not been interested, for example, in systematically accounting for the variation in responses. Nor have I attended to others' extant conceptualizations which seek unity in variety (Van Gennep, 1960, for example). The reader who may be interested in such matters is referred to all the works mentioned above and the bibliographies contained therein, especially Wood, 1934. An additional source of descriptive material, if not of concepts or explanations, is Darwin's fascinating account of the *Beagle* crew's encounter with the inhabitants of Tierra del Fuego (1906:chap. X).

6. In his interesting and insightful paper, Rolland Wright (1971) has suggested that people living in personal worlds are either "totally unable to handle strangers" or able to handle them only with difficulty. I think this is

not quite accurate. To say that a people are not equipped to deal with strangers routinely is not to say that they are not equipped to deal with them at all or are equipped to do so only with great difficulty. As long as strangers appear infrequently, there is no need for routine handling and thus, the lack of a capacity for it poses no difficulty. One might even argue that killing the stranger, for example, not an uncommon response in times past, was a rather efficient method of "dealing with" unwanted visitors. It is only when strangers appear routinely among a people unarmed with routine handling procedures that we can begin to talk meaningfully about "difficulties." This is just the situation that is of interest to Wright, and his focus upon it has led him, I think, to a slightly inaccurate generalization. For a discussion of "tribal people in an urban world," see Chapter Six.

7. There are admitted exceptions to this. As Lenski (1970) has pointed out, as a consequence of some rather special circumstances, cities did arise (in Central America and China, for example) in societies with a horticultural (pre-plow) economic base. The exceptions, however, are not usually seen as invalidating the general rule.

8. Adams, 1960; Ceram, 1968; Childe, 1942; K. Davis, 1955; Lenski, 1970; Mumford, 1961; Redfield, 1953.

9. Until very recently, this new social situation was one which only a minuscule proportion of the earth's population ever had to face. Massive urbanization is a very new phenomenon. Even in the great city-building civilizations of the Mediterranean area, most people went about·their business encased in the kinds of little personal worlds described above.

10. In part, this variation in capacity may be due to basic differences in memory abilities. In part, it is probably also due to differences in motivation. For many reasons, an individual can come to consider it extremely important to know large numbers of people. To the degree that this is important to him, his "capacity" is thereby increased. In a personal communication, Gerald Suttles has suggested that the "average individual" might well be able to recognize as many as several thousand persons. However, social groupings must be engineered such that "the least clever at recognition can also negotiate in a known social world." Consequently, the actual size of extant personal worlds may be poor indicators of the human capacity for personal knowing.

11. Cities, contemporary and historical, vary in the "fluidity" of their populations. In general, fluidity probably increases with size, but this is not invariable. Two cities of the same size might differ considerably in this regard because of such factors as economic specialty or geographical location. However, the emphasis here is on the contrast between cities and smaller, isolated settlements. From this viewpoint, all sorts of variations among cities shrink to irrelevance.

12. Let me emphasize that this apparent definitional reliance on sheer numbers does not gainsay my appreciation of the fact that a "city" is not merely a large settlement. As Louis Wirth (1964) early pointed out and as many others have since emphasized, size is merely one among numerous elements, the constellation of which creates that unique phenomenon we designate as a city. Concerned as I am here, however, with the transformation of a world of personally-known others into a world of strangers, the numerical increase of a settlement's population becomes particularly crucial.

Its importance, of course, as should be clear from the text, resides not in itself, but in its social-psychological consequences.

13. Sociologists have not, I think, paid sufficient detailed attention to the effects of numerical increase on either human consciousness or the organization of social life (although popular social science literature [for example, Hall, 1966; Morris, 1969] abounds with terrible warnings of impending doom if high population densities are allowed to continue or increase). Recognition of numerical increase as a basic explanatory variable is, of course, implicit in the classic sociological dichotomies, *gemeinschaft–gesellschaft*, status–contract, mechanical solidarity–organic solidarity, folk society–urban society, and so on, which represent attempts to capture globally enormous historical changes. It is also implicit in much of the modern writing on urbanization and city life. But *detailed* consideration of just what happens and why, when groups or settlements of societies grow larger, is rarely dealt with. The exceptions to this general disattention only highlight its widespread character. Simmel's work is perhaps the best known. Aside from the essays dealing directly with numerical effects (Wolff, 1950:87–177), two further pieces are of note: "Sociology of the Senses: Visual Interaction" and "The Metropolis and Mental Life" (Simmel, 1924, 1950a). More modern exceptions include Barker and Gump's sensitive and insightful *Big School, Small School* (1964) and Mott, 1965.

14. On the situation of "strangers amid strangers," the classic stranger literature in sociology is oddly silent. In thinking about strangers, writers from Simmel (1950b) to Schutz (1944) have limited themselves in the main to two situations: (1) the newcomer approaching an established group and becoming assimilated and (2) the newcomer approaching an established group and remaining marginal. While these are certainly fruitful analytic foci since they recur in all places and times, they are hardly the only "stranger situations" worthy of consideration. Wood (1934) made an early attempt to specify other possibilities, but she has been largely ignored. For a recent review and critique of the sociological stranger literature, see McLemore (1970).

15. When the rules and the repertoires prove to be erroneous, despite a sufficient supply of information, the individual experiences what is commonly called "culture shock." See Oberg, 1954, and Hall, 1959. On cultural variation in coding, see Lee, 1950.

16. This view of humans sketchily presented here draws heavily upon the interactionist tradition in sociology. For a more detailed and thus more accurate understanding of this view and the tradition from which it springs, the reader is referred to the following works: Strauss (ed.), 1964; Blumer, 1969; Rose (ed.), 1962; Manis and Meltzer (eds.), 1972; Strauss, 1959; Berger and Luckmann, 1966; J. Lofland, 1969; Lindesmith and Strauss, 1968; Goffman, 1959, 1967. On the biological basis of human fear and anxiety, see Hebb and Thompson, 1968. On the relations between threats to self, self-esteem and anxiety, see E. Becker, 1962.

17. For a discussion of the human capacity and propensity to categorize, see J. Lofland, 1969:122–28, 303–7.

18. It seems possible that much of the personal knowing in small settlements is of this character. That is, not all residents who claim to "know everyone in town" may actually have such inclusive acquaintanceships.

What they have, rather, is extensive knowledge of or about many of their fellow citizens—recognizing some by face and/or name, others only by placement in some sort of relational network (Bill's friend who sold him that car, Emily's sister, and so forth). This type of knowing probably greatly increases the size of a settlement that can be experienced as non-anonymous. I am grateful to Virginia Olesen and Gerald Suttles for sharing with me their thoughts on this matter.

19. It is interesting to speculate whether face-to-faceness is a prerequisite for the fullest development of personal knowing. Common sense would suggest that it is. How can I possibly "know" someone I have only read about or heard about more intimately than I know persons I see daily? And yet, some biographers might claim to "know" their subjects better than even the most intimate of the latter's contemporaries. The biographer, after all, is likely to have access to a wider range of biographical information, covering a longer period of time than did the subject's contemporaries. However interesting, such speculation thrusts one into the philosophical quagmire of questions about what it means to "truly know" another. For my purposes, such questions may safely be put aside.

20. These two sets of distinctions (personal knowing/categoric knowing; personally-known others/strangers) are similar but not identical to the traditional sociological scheme for classifying forms of human association: primary group or relationship/secondary group or relationship. Primary groups are certainly groups made up of persons who have personal knowledge of one another. But these persons also have categoric knowledge of one another. Primary groups are clearly groups of personally-known others, but so, in the main, are secondary groups. The fact that secondary relationships may be characterized as "formal, impersonal and institutional" (E. Faris, 1932:46) does not at all imply that these are relationships between "strangers," at least not in the sense in which I am using the term. In addition, as Faris has made very clear, in distinguishing between primary and secondary groups, the essential element is the former's "emotional character which binds its members into a relation" (1932:50). My two sets of distinctions, in contrast, are concerned exclusively with cognitive experience, with "knowing," to which affective states of one sort or another may or may not be attached. If love-at-first-sight is possible, then personal knowing is hardly a prerequisite for positive affect. On the other hand, personal knowing is also no guarantee of the existence of affect, positive or negative. In sum, then, the traditional sociological distinction between primary and secondary groups and relationships cross cut and are cross cut by my two sets of distinctions too extensively for any arguments regarding their essential isomorphism to be maintained. The same can be said relative to Schutz's famous sets of distinctions: predecessors, contemporaries, and successors; consociates and other than consociates; course-of-action types and personal types (1962:15–22).

21. I here use the term "space," rather than the more traditional "place" simply to convey a less precise, less "bounded" or enclosed locus. Despite its widespread usage, the phrase "public place" does seem to connote a specific and easily definable setting, a connotation I wish to avoid. In using "public space," however, I refer to the same sorts of locations as does one municipality which defines a "public place" as "any street, alley, park, pub-

lic building, any place of business or assembly open to or frequented by the public, and any other place which is open to public view or to which the public has access" (*Ann Arbor, Michigan Ordinance Code,* Ann Arbor, Michigan: Municipal Codification Service, Inc., 1957, Chapter 108, Paragraph 9:61). Goffman admits to a similar definition: "Traditionally, 'public places' refer to any regions in a community freely accessible to members of that community; 'private places' refer to soundproof regions where only members or invitees gather . . ." (1963a:9). Oddly enough, he then goes on to consider not behavior in public places, as the title of his work would suggest, but the analytic unit, gatherings: "all occasions when two or more persons are present to one another" (1963a:9), which may occur in areas traditionally designated as either public or private.

22. The way in which I am using "public" and "private" crudely to differentiate areas of a city in no way suggests that the terms cannot be used meaningfully in other contexts. Thus, one may distinguish between public and private space *within* an area common-sensically and legally defined as private. A family home can be seen as having public and private areas within it. Or differing house arrangements and designs may be compared in terms of the degree of privacy or public openness afforded. See, for example, D. Smith, 1971; Rapoport, 1969:66–69. Conversely, one may consider the degree of privacy available in common-sensically designated public areas. B. Schwartz (1968:743) suggests that privacy is an object of exchange which may be purchased in public settings such as transportation facilities and theaters.

23. The Australians did have one slot for unrelated persons—the sacred messenger—who carried some agreed-upon visible artifact to signal his identity (Wood, 1934:66–68). In this, the Aborigines anticipated one urban solution to the problem of strangers. Early anthropologists utilized a variety of strategies to gain access to groups likely to be hostile to unrelated persons or all newcomers. In the main, their success was probably due to their support by European colonial powers, under whose force of arms and numbers group restrictiveness either broke down or was rendered impotent.

24. Simmel's comments on the rapidly expanding cities of the nineteenth century are equally apropos of large settlements of earlier eras, excepting, of course, his references to transportation.

> Social life in the large city as compared to the towns shows a great preponderance of occasions to see rather than hear people. Before the appearance of omnibuses, railroads, and street cars in the nineteenth century, men were not in a situation where for periods of minutes or hours they could or must look at each other without talking to one another. Modern social life increases in ever growing degree the role of mere visual impression which always characterizes the preponderant part of all sense relationships between man and man and must place social attitudes and feelings upon an entirely changed basis. (Simmel, 1924:360)

25. One highly select urban group was, however, thus enabled; that is, female members of the elites in some of the more excessively male-dominated cultures. Kept in lifelong protective custody behind high walls, these

women rarely, if ever, had to confront the problem of dealing with strangers. In some respects they were not unlike some rather peculiarly located suburban matrons today. See Sjoberg, 1960: chap. VI, as well as, Putnam, 1970, on "The Greek Lady."

26. The question of causation here raises its ugly head. Did the human's "need" to know who the strangers were who surrounded him *cause* the ordering which permitted him to do so? This sort of question will appear again in Chapter Three when the historical transition from one sort of ordering to another is discussed. There it will be easier to hazard a possible answer. But with regard to the cities of the premodern era, one can only say that the issue is clouded by historical ignorance. It is quite probable that the historical urban order developed independently of any "need" for it. That probability, however, does not gainsay its crucial role in making city life livable.

CHAPTER TWO

1. As should be clear from the text, I use the term "public order" in a relatively restrictive sense. I am concerned with public order only in the limited sense of relatively stable arrangements of persons and places in urban public space. I do not intend to imply anything about the overall organization of a society or subunit of that society. Nor do I intend to imply anything about the basic normative or legal structure on which a society is built. There are, of course, relationships between public order in the sense in which I use the term and public order in these broader, more inclusive senses. But the tracing of these relationships is beyond the scope of this study. For an example of the term's usage in one of its broader senses, see McDougal and Lasswell, "The Identification and Appraisal of Diverse Systems of Public Order" (1959).

2. The reader should bear in mind, however, that when I speak of the preindustrial city exhibiting certain characteristics, I refer to *tendencies* toward exhibiting such characteristics. There is no question but that some actual cities exhibit one or the other characteristic more strongly than do others. As I suggested in Chapter One, abstractions from reality should never be confused with the concrete reality itself.

3. For the historical works from which this composite picture is drawn, see the references throughout the remainder of this chapter.

4. Unless otherwise indicated, references to Rome refer to Imperial Rome, especially late in the first and early in the second century A.D.

5. Not only were executions likely to be public in the preindustrial city but they occurred with considerable frequency. Most social orders throughout much of history have found enormous numbers of reasons for putting humans to death. See Laurence (1960) on the history of capital punishment.

6. See, for example, Chastenet, 1952:226; Holmes, 1966:40–41.

7. Holmes, 1966:80; Sjoberg, 1960:209; Tanzer, 1939:55.

8. Byrne, 1961:258; Comhaire and Cahnman, 1962:102; Sjoberg, 1960:287.

9. See, for example, Comhaire and Cahnman, 1962:80; Cunard, 1952:182; Sjoberg, 1960:96, 274.

10. As we shall see in the next chapter, these persons play an important role in early industrial cities where their numbers swell to enormous proportions. They were also a crucial source of the membership of the recurrent revolutionary religious movements which shook Medieval and Reformation Europe. See Cohn, 1961.

11. Carcopino, 1940:226; see also Chastenet, 1952:221, on Paris.

12. In many parts of the non-Western, nonindustrial world, such publicly displayed suffering is still frequently encountered. It seems likely, however, that the spread of Western medicine, the change in forms of punishment, and the widespread development of various sorts of health institutions have reduced its proportion in the general population as compared with that in the historic preindustrial city.

13. There is some scholarly disagreement regarding the residential mixing of classes in the preindustrial city. Comhaire and Cahnman, for example, suggest that in Ancient Rome, the poor tended to concentrate in the central city, the rich moving outward to private homes built on the slopes of the surrounding hills (1962:52). That is, they suggest, at least for Rome, a pattern similar to that found in the modern city. On the other hand, Sjoberg argues that in the preindustrial city, generally, the reverse was true: the rich concentrated in the center of the city, while the poor were forced to the outskirts (1960:98–99). It is probably the case that some *tendency* toward segregation was always to be found. Yet the necessary compactness and density of the pretrolley, preautomobile city must surely have kept this tendency in check.

14. Mel Scott, 1959; see also Byrne, 1961:94–96, on London; and Schnore, 1967:123, on the general historical trend toward work–home segregation.

15. See also, Lenski, 1970:272, 278.

16. See Bowra, 1952; G. & C. Charles-Picard, 1961; Haarhoff, 1948.

17. In addition to the references given below, see Rörig, 1967:128–30; Berreman, 1969. I do not mean to suggest that all the costuming, body marking, and linguistic practices about to be described were limited to urban areas. The reader should bear in mind that city people always share many beliefs, activities, and practices with their rural neighbors, and city influences always extend outward. As should already be clear, my concern is not with uniquely urban activities and practices but with unique meanings and functions which these activities and practices have in urban settings.

18. Lacroix, 1963:516; see also Barber and Lobel, 1953:324.

19. In addition to permanent and temporary body markings (a kind of "labeling"), Colonial Americans also utilized "costuming" in their punishments:

> Besides using letters to designate the nature of the crime, a convicted person was sometimes compelled to wear a rope or halter around his neck, or in the case of rape, an iron collar. For cursing or swearing, the offender's tongue was put in a cleft stick. (Miller, 1966:258)

20. M. Depping, quoted in Lacroix, 1963:436; see also, Sjoberg, 1960:100–101. In a personal communication, Gerald Suttles has suggested that the fact that "people were confined to their ghettoes primarily during

the hours after curfew suggests that the main object was to segregate them during those periods when (1) the appearential order was least visible; (2) supervision and surveillance were weakest; and (3) casual relations and love making were at their height."

CHAPTER THREE

1. This fact does not, of course, gainsay its value to all preindustrial city dwellers in making their world knowable and thus livable. As we shall have occasion to note again, the interests and forces which create or maintain a given public space order seem quite independent from the social psychological use to which that order, once created, is put.

2. This appears to be the case despite the supposed asceticism (M. Weber, 1958) of early capitalism. Even such exemplary carriers of the "protestant ethic" and the "spirit of capitalism," as the Colonial American Puritans were not immune to the sin of vanity:

> The Puritans were torn between their conviction that plain unadorned apparel was prescribed for God's people and their equally strong conviction that differences in dress must be maintained between classes. (Miller, 1966:114)

3. There were exceptions to this. Some cities in Medieval Europe, for example, were relatively independent of the surrounding agricultural order and were controlled by commercial interests (Mumford, 1938; Rörig, 1967). So too were the cities of "maritime societies," such as Venice (Lenski, 1970:300–4).

4. See Lenski, 1970:Part III; Smelser, 1959, and the bibliographies contained therein.

5. See, for example, Briggs, 1965; Fried and Elman (eds.), 1968; George, 1965; Mayhew, 1950; Smelser, 1959.

6. Goffman's "Symbols of Class Status" (1951) is one of the more penetrating analyses of the frantic activities of the elites in their struggle to differentiate themselves from their persistent imitators by means of continually changing external display. From the point of view of the elites, the most distasteful aspect of this appropriation has probably always been that he who takes on the dress may also, in the anonymous city, decide to take on the "rights." Note the tone of righteous indignation in the following account from the London *St. James Chronicle* of June, 1763:

> A very impudent young fellow, a journeyman cabinet maker, upon the presumption of a ruffled shirt, and a gold button and loop to his hat, took the liberty of accosting two ladies of fashion in the Park last Tuesday evening, and was not a little vehement in his declaration of a prodigous passion to one of them, who he earnestly begged to favour him with an assignation. The lady, after in vain requesting him to go about his business, seemed at last overcome by his importunities, and after desiring leave to speak for a moment to her companion aside, he was permitted to see them home. Overjoyed at this concession our subaltern Don Juan attended them to a private door in the Park, which led to a house near Queen Square. This one of the ladies opened, and desiring the spark to follow her, conducted him to a very elegant drawing-

room, whilst the other stayed below giving some orders to the servants. The whole Elysium of the lover's happiness was now opening in our hero's imagination when o dire mischance, four lusty servant-men appeared with a blanket, in which the gay lothario was instantly put, and carried downstairs into the yard. Here, after his passion had been pretty hard tumbled about . . . he was permitted to depart very quietly, and desired to reflect on the consequence of his impudence and presumption. (Quoted in Larwood, 1881:431–32)

7. Among scholars of the origin of cities as types of human settlements, the term refers to a much earlier period of explosive transformation. See Childe, 1950; Adams, 1966.

8. See, for example, Briggs, 1965; Chancellor, 1907; Fried and Elman (eds.), 1968; Lane, 1969:366; Larwood, 1881; Mayhew, 1950. It is quite possible that the floating populations of some rapidly growing contemporary non-Western cities (in nonindustrial or "developing" nation states) do now or will soon greatly exceed in numbers, and perhaps in proportion, the organizationally unaffiliated of the early industrial city. Some economists predict, for example, that by 1986 Calcutta will have, out of its projected 12.5 million population, 1 million people out of work and 3 million people with not enough work (*Newsweek*, April 6, 1970:60–61). Present day Nairobi, Kenya, struggles with the problem of 65,000 to 100,000 squatters who come to the city seeking work that is not to be found (*San Francisco Chronicle*, April 30, 1970). Bombay may have as many as 30,000 beggars (*San Francisco Chronicle*, April 11, 1970), and in Caracas, Venezuela, abandoned children (numbering more than a million nationally) make their home in the street. "They keep alive scavenging, stealing and begging by day and sleeping at night anywhere they can—in doorways, under bridges, in public parks" (*San Francisco Chronicle*, June 6, 1970). Nathan Keyfitz (1967) has suggested that populations of many non-Western cities are being artificially swelled far beyond the capacity of economic structures to absorb them—largely because of Western imports of food.

9. On technological developments, see Fitch, 1966; Meikelham, 1845; Sigerist, 1956; Simon, 1854; Usher, 1929; L. Wright, 1960.

10. Engels, 1950; Flexner, 1970:chap. IX; Smelser, 1959:chaps. IX–XI.

11. Chancellor, 1907:8–9, 18, 26, 105–6, 195–97; Roberts, 1969; Silver, 1967:3–5.

12. During a somewhat later period, the situation in the growing cities of America was quite similar. See, for example, Asbury, 1928, 1968, on nineteenth century New York and New Orleans; and Ferdinand, 1967, and Lane, 1967, 1969, on nineteenth century Boston.

13. On casual labor in nineteenth century London, see Fulford, 1952:273.

14. As van den Berghe (1970) has noted, some form of distance is a "functional prerequisite in any social situation involving authority, hierarchy or stratification." Where distance is not maintained socially, through etiquette or sumptory laws, for example, it can be maintained spatially, through segregation.

15. I do not mean to suggest that the industrial elites were uninvolved in the creation of a "policed society"—to use Allan Silver's phrase. Indeed, both in the United States and England, it was very much in their interest to be involved. The "floating population" that was harassing the middle

class was also challenging the industrial elites—not interactionally, but politically. The police force was created not merely to handle crime and disorder, but to control *rebellion*. See Roberts, 1969; Silver, 1967; Gorer, 1969; Tilly, 1969; Lane, 1967, 1969; and Brown, 1969. Chancellor (1907) contains some graphic descriptions of eighteenth and nineteenth century London political riots.

16. In addition to the works cited throughout this chapter, see Ashton, 1954; Toynbee, 1908; Tobias, 1967; Allen, 1929; G. Young, 1934; Hays, 1957; and the novels and essays of Dickens for a taste of this enormous literature.

CHAPTER FOUR

1. The preindustrial city could, more easily than can the modern, be located within its political boundaries. The twentieth century phenomenon of "massive metropolitanization" pushes the meaningful limits of a city far beyond those which are legally designated. The concept of the "modern city," then, as it is used herein, includes not only the actual "political" entity, but its surrounding satellites and semisatellites as well. The exact end points of the modern city, of course, remain indeterminant.

2. See, for example, Schwab, 1965, on African cities.

3. It should come as no surprise that sociologists "discovered" the spatially segregated city at the same time and in the same place that the spatially segregated city was coming into its own: early twentieth century America. For some peculiar reason, however, sociologists came to believe that spatial segregation was an inevitable "given" in urban development. They even produced a special subarea to handle one of nature's social "constants"; they called it ecology. For a brief history of this development, see R. E. L. Faris, 1967, especially Chapter 4, "Research on the Ecological Structure of the City."

4. Along Rio de Janeiro's Copacabana beach, the problem has been solved in a typically modern way by setting aside specialized space for specialized activity. The first "pipi-dog" or dog toilet is under construction ("A Place for the Dogs to Go," *San Francisco Chronicle*, June 30, 1972).

5. I am here, and throughout this chapter, perhaps overly cynical regarding the humanitarian and reform movements of the nineteenth and twentieth centuries. Many sincere and honestly dedicated individuals were unquestionably involved in them. Nevertheless, a purview of continued injustices and inhumanities in modern industrial nation states suggests to me that such movements succeeded more in hiding cruelty than they did in alleviating it. Relevant works on these movements include Lane, 1967; Schlesinger, 1968; Gusfield, 1963; Flexner, 1970; Gursslin, Hunt, and Roach, 1959–1960; and Adrian, 1961:chap. 3.

6. On the development of this practice in nineteenth century Boston, see Lane, 1967:54. See also Anderson, 1961:42 and throughout.

7. It is hardly a coincidence that contemporary riots erupt among the remaining unaffiliated floaters. In the United States, these are the young and the poor. The elderly might also be considered in this category. Their reduced physical vigor, however, makes them unlikely candidates for the kind of energy-exertion required in rioting.

8. The peculiarly middle class character of urban spatial segregation is attested to by the ironic fact that those with greater access to private recreational space also are likely to have greater access to public recreational space. (The elites, of course, have little need for such facilities as public parks. Their resources enable them to build their own private "parks," and to use the entire world as a playground.) Thus, it is in the most densely packed and economically deprived sections of a modern city that we can still see the kind of public-space activity pile-up so characteristic of the preindustrial urban settlement.

9. I do not mean to suggest here that segregation is an innate and therefore inevitable human tendency. It is surely true that among lower-status persons segregation is more likely to be imposed than preferred. Nevertheless, as recent attempts at school and neighborhood racial integration in the United States have demonstrated, the higher-status group can make life so uncomfortable for the "integrator" that being with one's own—however despised one's own may be—becomes psychologically preferable.

10. Briggs, 1965; Dickens, 1961, described nineteenth century London's lower class areas in detail.

11. Wilson, 1967. As a basis for the spatial segregation of neighborhoods in the United States, ethnicity (as distinct from "color") has never been very stable and continues to decline in importance (see Cressey, 1971). And it seems possible that racial differentiation may follow the same course. In their stead, age and life-style, especially as they combine with class, appear to be emerging as major bases of segregation. For an insightful commentary on this trend, see Suttles, 1972:especially 262.

12. Toll, 1969. It remains to be seen how successful recent attempts in the United States to "scatter" public housing among affluent neighborhoods will be. But at least in one European city where access to housing is governmentally controlled, the segregation of social groups by neighborhood appears to be waning (Musil, 1968).

13. Greer, 1965. For a description of one of the processes by which, under conditions of modern land development practices in the United States, large-scale specialized neighborhoods emerge, see Suttles, 1972:86–90.

14. Containment, of course, is not intended to keep respectables out; only to keep outcastes in.

15. In their analysis of San Francisco's world-famous tolerance for deviance—its "culture of civility"—Howard S. Becker and Irving Louis Horowitz (1970) suggest that this tolerance is largely due to a willingness among various groups to "accommodate" to the desires of each other. In essence, although they do not say so explicitly, this means spatial segregation.

16. It seems highly unlikely that the average preindustrial urbanite was as interactionally ill-at-ease with the omnipresent "visibly handicapped" as are many of his modern counterparts. For sensitive analyses of these contemporary interactional problems, see F. Davis, 1961, and Goffman, 1963b.

17. Thus Goffman is able to devote one entire section of a book on *Stigma* (1963b:chap. 2) to those "stigmas" which cannot be seen.

18. See, for example, Form and Stone, 1964; J. Lofland and Lejeune, 1960.

19. John Irwin (1973), in his analysis of the Southern California surfing

"scene," describes an earlier instance of costume appropriation. Male high school students, who never went near the water, nevertheless decked themselves out to look like surfers—even to the extent of peroxiding their hair.

20. See, for example, "The Taxicab Hair Dispute," *San Francisco Chronicle*, April 14, 1970; "The Hippie Hackies," *Newsweek*, May 4, 1970.

21. On the identity-bestowing power of space, see J. Lofland, 1969:162–73, 234–43.

22. In San Francisco at least, mass arrests of prostitutes appear to proceed on the basis of location rather than appearance. A local resident reports being called for jury duty on the case of a young "very straight-looking" college girl who was picked up in the "Tenderloin" during a daytime "cleanup." J. Lofland, personal communication.

23. On the controversial decision to uniform policemen in the first place, see Lane, 1967. For a general discussion of the functions of uniforms in modern society, see Joseph and Alex, 1972. While the elimination of uniforms seems a general tendency in the modern world, there is also some evidence of movement in the opposite direction. Numerous retail stores, banks, and savings and loan associations in the United States have introduced standardized "career apparel," especially for their female employees (see Beverly Stephen, "Will Uniforms Work," *San Francisco Chronicle*, January 24, 1972). Whether this trend will continue, and if it does, the extent to which these uniforms will be useful in signaling occupation, remain to be seen.

24. Parsons, 1914:55. Such relegation to nonperson status which the uniform makes possible would seem to be most likely to occur when the wearer is lower in the social hierarchy than the observer. As Walter Klink has noted in a personal communication, uniforms may also function to open up the possibilities for interaction between strangers, as when similarly garbed but unacquainted soldiers feel free to converse with one another.

25. Goffman, 1963b; F. Davis, 1961:120–32.

26. Foote, 1969:301. On control of skid row generally, see Bittner, 1969. On the history of vagrancy laws and the various uses to which they have been put, see Chambliss, 1969.

27. See further on the origin of modern police systems in England and the United States, Brown, 1969; Gorer, 1969; Lane, 1967, 1969; Roberts, 1969; and Tilly, 1969. On the police as surrogate norm enforcers in "aggregate" situations, see Greer, 1962:59–60.

Chapter Five

1. The relevant literature is enormous. See, for example, Lindesmith and Strauss, 1968; J. Lofland, 1969; Brim and Wheeler, 1966; McCall and Simmons, 1966; Shibutani, 1961, and the bibliographies therein.

2. This suggests that those humans reared in the city may have a "head start" on their country-cousins-turned-urbanites. It would be interesting to learn if the former—as a group—are generally more knowledgeable about, and more skillful in, their urban environment than the latter.

3. From another point of view, however, one might argue that it matters

a great deal; that, in fact, the urbanite loses much by avoiding areas incorrectly defined as dangerous. Freedom of movement is lost. The area in which one may pursue urban adventures (see Chapter Eight) is constricted. The sense of being "at home" in all parts of the city is forgone. And, as in the modern world, when the dangerous label is applied to total cities, not just areas within them, who can count the cost?

4. A similar calculus obtains in the relations between "normals" and deviants. Humans find it advantageous to believe that a normal may easily become deviant but that it is extremely difficult for a deviant to be "normalized." See J. Lofland, 1969:210–12.

5. The same may be said of social scientific guide books. In fact these latter are probably superior, for they tend to concentrate on specifying the indicators of locational types, rather than merely describing actual locations. On "tearooms," see Humphreys, 1970; on bars, Cavan, 1966; on racetracks, Marvin B. Scott, 1968.

6. In the contemporary United States, franchising greatly lessens the risk of generalizing from one experienced location to others "of its type." Having ever been to a Howard Johnson's, Holiday Inn, or McDonald's, for example, the individual can know with great certainty just what to expect in another one.

The fact that the spatial order makes the learning of locational meanings possible, does not, of course, guarantee how or if they will be learned. The size, shape, and number of the "locational maps" that city dwellers carry about in their heads obviously vary enormously from individual to individual. At one extreme is the individual for whom "the city" consists of a few well-understood streets—the surrounding area a large blank space on his single map. At the other extreme is the individual who carries in his head extremely detailed maps of locational meanings for many cities. Lynch (1960) makes one of the few attempts to understand this little-explored aspect of urban phenomenology.

7. Which perhaps accounts for the widespread popularity of a recent book on this topic (see Fast, 1970). Humans are delighted suddenly to discover how terribly clever they had been all along. On the other hand, bringing the subject of "body language" into conscious awareness may also make people uncomfortable, as with those who report that psychiatrists make them nervous because "they're always looking at you and reading all kinds of things into the way you sit." On the topic of coding behavior, generally, see Andrew, 1965; Labarre, 1947; Birdwhistell, 1952; Ruesch and Kees, 1956; Feldman, 1941; Critchley, 1939; Hall, 1959, 1966; Felipe and Sommer, 1966; Sommer, 1959, 1961, 1962, 1965, 1967, and 1969. For a sensitive analysis of the way in which cabdrivers use appearential, locational, and behavioral clues to "code" for trustworthiness among their passengers, see Henslin, 1968:138–58.

8. For a brilliant fictional account of the psychic terror engendered in a woman who understands what is involved in crossing a city street but lacks the skill to do it, see Jackson, 1960a:especially pp. 183–84.

9. It is probably easier in America to learn how to dress up than it is to learn how to dress down—perhaps because the whole system is geared to express its devout belief in upward mobility. On "self-presentation" generally, see Goffman, 1959.

10. On learning how to wait in line, for example, see Mann, 1969.

CHAPTER SIX

1. I speak here primarily of modern city dwellers. I do not have the materials to say very much about these or similar devices in the preindustrial city. In addition, as will become clear, a number of these depend on (and, in fact, contribute to) the modern city's penchant for spatially segregating activities and persons. Preindustrial urbanites did not have such segregation so widely available to them.

2. It is not my intent to suggest that this listing is exhaustive. City dwellers are an ingenious lot and they undoubtably have developed multitudinous methods for locationally privatizing urban public space.

3. I hesitate to say strategies, as the word implies, I think, somewhat more consciously calculated intent than is applicable here.

4. The most effective method for minimizing stranger contact would, of course, be to remain at home. But this option is not available to many persons, and by those to whom it is available (for example, young mothers), it is not usually seen as particularly desirable.

5. These "ways of knowing" are massively interrelated. Thus, having personally experienced a particular locale, the individual may then generalize to other places of that "type." So too he or she may use this experience to instruct others, either as to place "type" or as to the specific locale which the other has never visited.

6. The reader may recall that a similar distinction was made in Chapter One regarding ways of knowing people. Hearsay knowing may be likened to "knowing of" a person one has never met.

7. Fulford, 1952:285–86. See also Fried and Elman, 1968:224–26; Stone, 1954.

8. Miller, 1966:130–31. In the early decades of this century, many of Chicago's hobos developed such a patron relationship to a local bookstore and received the accompanying benefits. "Here many men who have no other address receive their mail. . . . The men meet their friends at the 'Proletariat' or they leave things there for safekeeping. They all know [the owner] Mr. Horsley, and he has the good will of all the 'bos.'" (Anderson, 1961:176.)

9. I here use the term resident rather than the more familiar habitué because the former term conveys, I think, more of the private and possessive character of the home-territory relationship.

10. McCandlish Phillips, "The Waiting Room for Death," *San Francisco Sunday Examiner and Chronicle*, June 21, 1970.

11. For a description of one sort of agreement which may be worked out between management and colonizers, see Cavan, 1963.

12. *Ann Arbor News*, Thursday, August 26, 1965. Interestingly enough, this situation was brought to the attention of officials *because* the colonizers were behaving as though the rest stops were home territory. Any lone males entering the rest stops were assumed to be fellow homosexuals and were approached as such. The complaint of one such misidentified male brought in the police. See further on this general topic, Humphreys, 1970.

13. For an excellent description of the utilization of the streets as private territory by street-gang members, see Wertham and Piliavin, 1967.

14. There may be more to the oft-noted propensity of truck, cab, and bus drivers to "act as if they owned the streets" than mere complaining. In fact, these "street residents" may feel quite proprietary toward their territories.

15. This is not to suggest that the two types of villages do not differ from one another in other significant regards as well. For my purposes, however, these can be safely disregarded.

16. Kotler (1969) makes an argument for the granting of autonomy to urban neighborhoods, for their being granted independence from the imperialistic center city.

17. See, for example, Gans, 1962; Suttles, 1968.

18. See, for example, Suttles, 1968:especially chaps. 4 and 5. On "villages" of Southern Mountaineer migrants, see Huelsman, 1969.

19. Young and Willmott, 1962:104–105; chap. 7 of this work contains much relevant material. See also Hoggart, 1970:especially chaps. 2 and 3. On the importation of tribal villages to African cities, see Plotnicov, 1967.

20. On variations in urban neighborhoods, see Bell and Boat, 1957; Dennis, 1968; Keller, 1968; Smith, Form, and Stone, 1954; Suttles, 1972.

21. See, for example, F. Davis, 1968a.

22. I am indebted to Anselm Strauss for initially suggesting this possibility to me.

CHAPTER SEVEN

1. See, for example, Goffman, 1963a; Suttles, 1970.

2. Sections of the following may also be found in L. Lofland, 1972. The discussion to follow is probably most applicable to the United States. Behavioral meanings, particularly body language, as we saw in Chapter Five, tend to be culture-specific.

3. During the brief period of time required for these preparations, the individual is usually not entirely out of the sight of others. There are, of course, exceptions. Sometimes entrances are designed in such a way as to afford the individual at least a modicum of real privacy. Thus, a woman leaving a darkened theater may yank at her girdle just before stepping out into the light. However, in most settings, readiness checks must be performed within the view of at least a few others. For this reason the check is necessarily superficial, and if major repairs should be required, they must either be postponed or made within the view of whatever persons happen to be about. In such cases, and certainly with most routine preparation, it is apparently preferable to be conspicuous in front of a few strangers at the entrance than to be even more conspicuous by being caught by the many strangers inside with one's presentation down.

4. In contrast, residents and persons traveling in packs demonstrate their feeling of being "at home" in the setting most clearly during this period of the approach. Both types are often observed standing just inside the entrance for a prolonged period of time, gazing about frankly and with apparent calm.

5. I was able to gather this data because of the remarkable ability of human beings to determine whether an eye—looking in their direction

—is focused or not. See, for example, Gibson and Peck, 1963; Argyle and Dean, 1965.

6. Goffman in all his work has made much of this tendency of urban humans to mask expressiveness. See, especially, *Behavior in Public Places* (1963a).

While the general goal of this first principle and later principles is to keep oneself as inconspicuous and as unapproachable as possible, just what is required to do this naturally varies from one sort of public space to another. If a setting is particularly crowded or noisy, for example, the individual may have more leeway in expressiveness than if the setting is quiet and contains only a few inhabitants. A fit of coughing is enough to attract attention in a library reading room; it is likely to go totally unnoticed at a football game when the crowd is screaming. So, too, the expected activities of a setting will alter the ambience of any particular act. Thus, accidentally catching another customer's eye in a drug store is less fraught with meaning than the same occurrence in a pick-up bar (see, for example, Cavan, 1966). Bumping into someone on an extremely crowded street is hardly conspicuous; doing so when there is plenty of room to avoid it is conspicuous indeed. Moving freely about an air terminal is not likely to attract anyone's attention; moving freely in an elevator is altogether another matter.

7. As Edward Hall has noted, Americans

> have a pattern which discourages touching, except in moments of intimacy. When we ride on a streetcar or crowded elevator, we will "hold ourselves in," having been taught from early childhood to avoid bodily contact with strangers. (Hall, 1959:149; see also, 1966:chap. X)

8. For a fascinating discussion of the meaning and use of seating and other spatial arrangements in bars, see Cavan, 1966:chap. 5.

9. Under certain conditions, a lack of props may be experienced as quite stressful. Robert Sommer has suggested that:

> Just as people moving about a house require resting places for solitude or individual concentration, people rooted to a given spot in a public area require places where their eyes can rest without stress. There is the apocryphal story of the stress produced by the newspaper strike in New York City where the seated men (in the subway) were unable to "retreat into" newspapers and had to look at the other occupants particularly women standing above them. (Sommer, 1965:347–48)

10. Georg Simmel, some fifty years ago, had recognized and written about the fact that eye contact between humans is fraught with meaning:

> The limits [of eye contact] are to be determined by the significant fact that the glance by which one seeks to perceive the other is itself expressive. By the glance which reveals the other, one discloses himself. By the same act, in which the observer seeks to know the observed, he surrenders himself to be understood by the observer. The eye cannot take unless at the same time it gives. The eye of the person discloses his own soul when he seeks to uncover that of another. What occurs in this direct mutual glance represents the most perfect reciprocity in the entire field of human relationships. (Simmel, 1924:356)

More recently Michael Argyle and Janet Dean (1965) have reported that eye contact serves a number of functions—one of the most important being a quest for feedback during social interaction, as well as a signaling that the communication channel is open. In addition, eye contact may be seen as a component of intimacy and is, in a significant way, the equivalent of physical proximity.

11. A display of sunglasses observed by the author carried this come-on: LOOK AT PEOPLE WITHOUT THEIR KNOWING IT!

CHAPTER EIGHT

1. For empirical evidence of anxiety-seeking in humans and other higher-order animals, see Hebb and Thompson, 1968. See also J. Lofland, 1969:chap. 5 on "The Adventurous Deviant Act," and Huizinga, 1955, on "man at play." For a description of anxiety-courting among adolescents, see Schwartz and Merton, 1967.

2. For an interesting analysis of coolness as a quality of self-presentation, see Lyman and Scott, 1968.

3. He is also, more recently, writing his own books. His genre is the sociological case study. His subjects are deviant people, groups, and behavior. His method is direct observation. He is cool, he is tolerant, and he is tough, and he is not for a minute going to let his readers forget it.

4. The emphasis here is on identity games involving conscious deception. The individual actually believes himself or herself to be something other than the identity he or she is proferring and the manipulation of identity symbols is highly calculated (see, for example, Goffman, 1963b). I recognize that there are similarities between this situation and the identity transformations which are so much a part of human life experience and which have been of so much interest to sociologists and social psychologists. The *sine qua non* of the identity transformation, however, is that the individual comes eventually not only to act "as if" and to appear "as if" but to believe in the new identity as well. The *sine qua non* of the identity game, quite to the contrary, is disbelief. It may be true, of course, that in the becoming process, the individual will experience some sense of "phoniness," some sense that he is "putting on an act," especially in the early stages (see, for example, F. Davis, 1968b:246–48; Olesen and Whittaker, 1968:263–67). It is also possible that persons indulging in identity games may, at some point, come to believe their own propaganda. To the degree that such things actually occur, identity games and identity transformations might fruitfully be analyzed as identical phenomena. For purposes of this discussion, however, I prefer to keep them separate.

5. The relevant literature includes Goffman, 1963b, on the general problem of information management; Greenburg, 1965:56–57, on tribal passing among migrants to African cities; Crichton, 1959, 1961, on the "great imposter"; and Griffin, 1962, on racial passing in reverse of the usual direction.

6. On similar begging tricks utilized by American hobos during the early decades of this century, see Anderson, 1961:44–46.

7. Sherlock Holmes was once called upon to locate a well-to-do English businessman who had mysteriously disappeared. In doing so, he also discovered the nature of the gentleman's business: begging. Having once tried it for a short period in order to collect material for a story, he had found it

so rewarding that he was evermore loath to set his hand to more demanding and less lucrative occupations. (See Doyle, 1930:229–44, "The Man
With The Twisted Lip.")

8. I am indebted to Leon Mayhew for suggesting this possibility to me.

9. Finestone, 1957:4–5. See also Suttles, 1970. Maurer, 1962, gives an excellent description of the techniques utilized by one of the city's most
skilled gamesmen: the con-man. See especially, Chapter 8 on "short-con
games." While interactional skill is paramount in the successful pursuance
of these swindles, there is also a strong element of identity-appropriation
involved. In them, the interrelationship between identity games and interactional games is clearly demonstrated.

10. Dick Hallgren, "The Man Who Turned Him In," *San Francisco
Chronicle*, January 15, 1970.

11. I suspect, although I have no supporting data, that despite the dominance of the spatial order in the modern city, many contemporary urbanites continue to rely rather heavily on appearance in making their identifications of surrounding strangers. In so doing, of course, they frequently
err, and thus find the city a more difficult, more inhospitable milieu than
might otherwise be the case.

12. Goffman (1963a:124) has suggested that:

> [While] acquainted persons in a social situation require a reason not to
> enter into a face engagement with each other . . . unacquainted persons
> require a reason to do so.

I am suggesting that they may require a reason to do so legitimately, but
hardly a legitimate reason to do so.

CHAPTER NINE

1. It is not my intent here to add my voice to the ongoing debate over
community—over its definitions; over its destruction, differentiation, or
alteration by urbanization; over its political or organizational complexities.
The relevant literature is already enormous, emerging from many disci-
plines and points of view. For a sampling of sociology's contributions, see
Sennett, 1970; Stein, 1960; Suttles, 1972; and Zablocki, 1971.

BIBLIOGRAPHY

Adams, Robert M., 1960, "The Origin of Cities." *Scientific American*, September.
———, 1966, *The Evolution of Urban Society*. Chicago: Aldine Publishing Co.
Adrian, Charles R., 1961, *Governing Urban America*. 2nd ed. New York: McGraw-Hill Book Co.
Allen, George C., 1929, *The Industrial Development of Birmingham and the Black Country: 1860–1927*. London: G. Allen and Unwin, Ltd.
Amory, Cleveland, 1950, *The Proper Bostonians*. New York: E. P. Dutton & Co., Inc.
Anderson, Nels, 1961, *The Hobo*. Chicago: The University of Chicago Press, Phoenix Edition. First published 1923.
Andrew, Richard J., 1965, "The Origins of Facial Expressions." *Scientific American*, October, pp. 88–94.
Argyle, Michael, and Janet Dean, 1965, "Eye Contact, Distance and Affiliation." *Sociometry*, September, pp. 289–304.
Asbury, Herbert, 1928, *The Gangs of New York*. New York: Knopf.
———, 1968, *The French Quarter*. New York: Capricorn Books. First published 1936.
Ashton, T. S., 1954, *The Industrial Revolution 1760–1830*. London: Oxford University Press.
Barber, Bernard, and Lyle S. Lobel, 1953, "Fashion in Women's Clothes and the American Social System." In Reinhard Bendix and S. M. Lipset (eds.), *Class, Status and Power*. Glencoe, Illinois: The Free Press, pp. 323–332.
Barker, Roger G., and P. V. Gump, 1964, *Big School, Small School: High School Size and Student Behavior*. Stanford: Stanford University Press.
Becker, Ernest, 1962, *The Birth and Death of Meaning*. New York: The Free Press of Glencoe, Inc.
Becker, Howard S., and Irving L. Horowitz, 1970, "The Culture of Civility." *Trans-action*, April, pp. 12–19.
Bell, Wendell, and Marion D. Boat, 1957, "Urban Neighborhoods and Informal Social Relations." *American Journal of Sociology*, January, pp. 391–398.
Berger, Bennett M., 1960, *Working Class Suburb: A Study of Auto Workers in Suburbia*. Berkeley: University of California Press.
Berger, Peter L., and T. Luckmann, 1966, *The Social Construction of Reality: A Treatise in the Sociology of Knowledge*. New York: Doubleday & Company, Inc.
Berreman, Gerald D., 1969, "Social Categories and Social Interaction in a North Indian City." Unpublished paper.

Birdwhistell, Ray, 1952, *Introduction to Kinesics*. Washington, D.C.: Department of State, Foreign Service Institute.

Bittner, Egon, 1969, "The Police on Skid-Row: A Study of Peace Keeping." In W. J. Chambliss (ed.), *Crime and the Legal Process*. New York: McGraw-Hill Book Co., pp. 135–155.

Blumer, Herbert, 1969, *Symbolic Interactionism: Perspective and Method*. Englewood Cliffs, New Jersey: Prentice-Hall, Inc.

Bowra, Maurice, 1952, "Athens: The Periclean Age." In M. Bowra et. al., *Golden Ages of the Great Cities*. London and New York: Thames & Hudson.

Boykin, Eleanor, 1940, *This Way Please*. New York: The Macmillan Co.

Brant, Ethel Cushing, 1925, *Standard Etiquette*. New York: J. H. Sears & Company, Inc.

Briggs, Asa, 1965, *Victorian Cities*. New York: Harper & Row. British publication, 1963.

Brim, O. G., Jr., and S. Wheeler, 1966, *Socialization After Childhood*. New York: John Wiley & Sons, Inc.

Brown, Richard M., 1969, "Historical Patterns of Violence in America." In Hugh Davis Graham and Ted Robert Gurr, *Violence in America: Historical and Comparative Perspectives, Vol. 1*, A Staff Report to the National Commission on the Causes and Prevention of Violence. Washington, D.C.: U.S. Government Printing Office, pp. 35–64.

Byrne, M. St. Clare, 1961, *Elizabethan Life in Town and Country*. New York: Barnes & Noble, University Paperbacks. First published 1925.

Carcopino, Jerome, 1940, *Daily Life in Ancient Rome: The People and the City at the Height of the Empire*. Edited with bibliography and notes by Henry T. Rowell; translated from the French by E. O. Lorimer. New Haven: Yale University Press.

———, 1952, "Rome Under the Antonines." In M. Bowra et. al., *Golden Ages of the Great Cities*. London and New York: Thames and Hudson.

Cavan, Sherri, 1963, "Interaction in Home Territories." *Berkeley Journal of Sociology*, pp. 17–32.

———, 1966, *Liquor License*. Chicago: Aldine Publishing Co.

Ceram, C. W., 1968, *Gods, Graves and Scholars: The Story of Archaeology*. 2nd rev. ed. Translated by E. G. Barside and Sophie Wilkins. New York: Alfred A. Knopf. First published in English 1951; first German ed. 1949.

Chambliss, William J., 1969, "The Law of Vagrancy." In W. J. Chambliss (ed.), *Crime and the Legal Process*. New York: McGraw-Hill Book Co., pp. 51–63.

Chancellor, E. G., 1907. *The History of the Squares of London: Topographical and Historical*. London: Kegan Paul, Trench, Trübner & Co., Ltd.

Charles-Picard, Gilbert, and Colette Charles-Picard, 1961, *Daily Life in Carthage at the Time of Hannibal*. London: George Allen & Unwin Ltd.

Chastenet, Jacques, 1952, "Paris, Versailles and the 'Grand Siecle.'" In M. Bowra et. al., *Golden Ages of the Great Cities*. London and New York: Thames and Hudson.

Childe, V. Gordon, 1942, *What Happened in History*. Harmondsworth, Middlesex: Penguin Books.

————, 1950, "The Urban Revolution." *Town Planning Review*, Vol. 21, pp. 3–17.

Cohn, Norman, 1961, *The Pursuit of the Millennium*. 2nd ed. New York: Harper Torchbooks.

Comhaire, Jean, and W. J. Cahnman, 1962, *How Cities Grew*. Madison, New Jersey: Florham Park Press.

Cox, O. C., 1969, "The Preindustrial City Reconsidered." In Paul Meadows and E. H. Mizruchi (eds.), *Urbanism, Urbanization and Change: Comparative Perspectives*. Reading, Mass.: Addison-Wesley Publishing Company, pp. 19–29.

Cressey, Paul F., 1971, "Population Succession in Chicago: 1898–1930." In James Short (ed.), *The Social Fabric of the Metropolis*. Chicago: The University of Chicago Press, pp. 109–119.

Crichton, Robert, 1959, *The Great Imposter*. New York: Random House, Inc.

————, 1961, *The Rascal and the Road*. New York: Random House, Inc.

Critchley, M., 1939, *The Language of Gesture*. London: Edward Arnold.

Cunard, Victor, 1952, "The Venetian Republic." In M. Bowra et. al., *Golden Ages of the Great Cities*. London and New York: Thames and Hudson.

Darwin, Charles, 1906, *Voyage of the Beagle*. London and New York: J. M. Dent & Sons Ltd., and E. P. Dutton and Co., Inc.

Davies, Trevor, 1952, "Madrid Under the House of Austria." In M. Bowra et. al., *Golden Ages of the Great Cities*. London and New York: Thames and Hudson.

Davis, Fred, 1961, "Deviance Disavowal." *Social Problems*, Fall, pp. 120–132.

————, 1967, "The Cabdriver and His Fare: Facets of a Fleeting Relationship." In Gerald D. Bell (ed.), *Organization and Human Behavior*. Englewood Cliffs, New Jersey: Prentice-Hall, Inc., pp. 264–272. Originally published in *The American Journal of Sociology*, September, 1959, pp. 158–165.

————, 1968a, "Heads and Freaks: Patterns and Meanings of Drug Use Among Hippies," with Laura Munoz. *Journal of Health and Social Behavior*, June, pp. 156–164.

————, 1968b, "Professional Socialization as Subjective Experience: The Process of Doctrinal Conversion Among Student Nurses." In H. S. Becker, B. Geer, D. Riesman, and R. S. Weiss (eds.), *Institutions and the Person: Papers Presented to Everett C. Hughes*. Chicago: Aldine Publishing Co., pp. 235–251.

Davis, Kingsley, 1955, "The Origin and Growth of Urbanization in the World." *The American Journal of Sociology*, March, pp. 429–437.

Dennis, N., 1968, "The Popularity of the Neighborhood Community Idea." In R. E. Pahl (ed.), *Readings in Urban Sociology*. Oxford: Pergamon Press.

Dickens, Charles, 1961, *Oliver Twist*. New York: New American Library. First published, 1838.

————, 1964, *Great Expectations*. Indianapolis: Bobbs-Merrill Co., Inc. First published 1860–61.

Douglas, Davis, 1952, "Medieval Paris." In M. Bowra et. al., *Golden Ages of the Great Cities*. London and New York: Thames and Hudson.

Doyle, A. Conan, 1930, *The Complete Sherlock Holmes*. Garden City, New York: Doubleday & Co., Inc.

Drake, St. Clair, and H. R. Cayton, 1962, *Black Metropolis*, Vols. 1 and 2. New York: Harper & Row. First published 1945.

Ellis, Dean S., 1967, "Speech and Social Status in America." *Social Forces*, pp. 431–437.

Ellison, Robert, 1968, *This Book Can Save Your Life*. New York: Signet.

Engels, Frederick, 1950, *Condition of the Working Class in England in 1844*. London: Allen and Unwin. First published 1892.

Faris, Ellsworth, 1932, "The Primary Group: Essence and Accident." *American Journal of Sociology*, July, pp. 41–50.

Faris, Robert E. L., 1967, *Chicago Sociology, 1920–1932*. San Francisco: Chandler Publishing Company.

Fast, Julius, 1970, *Body Language*. New York: Evans Publishing.

Feldman, S., 1941, *Mannerisms of Speech and Gestures in Everyday Life*. New York: King's Crown Press.

Felipe, Nancy Jo, and Robert Sommer, 1966, "Invasions of Personal Space." *Social Problems*, Fall, pp. 206–14.

Ferdinand, Theodore N., 1967, "The Criminal Patterns of Boston Since 1849." *American Journal of Sociology*, July, pp. 84–99.

Finestone, Harold, 1957, "Cats, Kicks and Color." *Social Problems*, July, pp. 3–13.

Fitch, James M., 1966, *American Building: The Historical Forces That Shaped It*. Boston: Houghton Mifflin Co.

Flexner, Eleanor, 1970, *Century of Struggle: The Woman's Rights Movement in the United States*. New York: Atheneum. First published 1959.

Foote, Caleb, 1969, "Vagrancy-type Law and Its Administration." In W. J. Chambliss (ed.), *Crime and the Legal Process*. New York: McGraw-Hill Book Co., pp. 295–330.

Form, William H., and Gregory P. Stone, 1964, "Urbanism, Anonymity and Status Symbolism." In Richard L. Simpson and Ida H. Simpson (eds.). *Social Organization and Behavior*. New York: John Wiley & Sons, Inc., pp. 335–345.

Frazer, Sir James George, 1922, *The Golden Bough*. One-vol. abridged ed. New York: The Macmillan Co.

Freedman, Ronald (ed.), 1964, *Population: The Vital Revolution*. Garden City, New York: Doubleday & Co., Inc.

Fried, Albert, and Richard Elman (eds.), 1968, *Charles Booth's London: A Portrait of the Poor at the Turn of the Century, Drawn From His Life and Labour of the People in London*. New York: Pantheon Books.

Fulford, Roger, 1952, "Jubilee London." In M. Bowra et. al., *Golden Ages of the Great Cities*. London and New York: Thames and Hudson.

Gans, Herbert, 1962, *The Urban Villagers*. New York: The Free Press.

George, M. Dorothy, 1965, *London Life in the Eighteenth Century*. New York: Capricorn Books. First published 1925.

Gibson, James J., and Ann D. Peck, 1963, "Perception of Another Person's Looking Behavior." *American Journal of Psychology*, September, pp. 386–394.

Goffman, Erving, 1951, "Symbols of Class Status." *British Journal of Sociology*, December, pp. 294–304.
——, 1959, *The Presentation of Self in Everyday Life*. Garden City, New York: Doubleday & Company, Inc.
——, 1963a, *Behavior in Public Places*. New York: The Free Press of Glencoe.
——, 1963b, *Stigma*. Englewood Cliffs, New Jersey: Prentice-Hall, Inc.
——, 1967, *Interaction Ritual*. New York: Doubleday and Company, Inc.
Gorer, Geoffrey, 1969, "Modification of National Character: The Role of the Police in England." In W. J. Chambliss (ed.), *Crime and the Legal Process*. New York: McGraw-Hill Book Co., pp. 412–420.
Greenberg, Joseph H., 1965, "Urbanism, Migration and Language." In Hilda Kuper (ed.), *Urbanization and Migration in West Africa*. Berkeley and Los Angeles: University of California Press.
Greer, Scott, 1962, *The Emerging City*. New York: The Free Press.
——, 1965, *Urban Renewal and American Cities*. Indianapolis: The Bobbs-Merrill Company, Inc.
Griffin, John Howard, 1962, *Black Like Me*. New York: New American Library, Signet Books.
Gursslin, O. R., R. G. Hunt, and J. O. Roach, 1959–60, "Social Class and the Mental Health Movement." *Social Problems*, Winter, pp. 210–218.
Gusfield, J. R., 1963, *Symbolic Crusade: Status Politics and the American Temperance Movement*. Urbana, Illinois: University of Illinois Press.
Haarhoff, T. J., 1948, *The Stranger at the Gate: Aspects of Exclusiveness and Co-operation in Ancient Greece and Rome, with Some Reference to Modern Times*. Oxford: Basil Blackwell. First published 1938.
Hall, Edward T., 1959, *The Silent Language*. Greenwich, Connecticut: Fawcett Publications, Inc.
——, 1966, *The Hidden Dimension*. Garden City, New York: Doubleday and Company, Inc.
Harris, Mark, 1968, "The Self-Made Brain Surgeon." In Penney C. Hills and L. Rust Hills (eds.), *How We Live: Contemporary Life in Contemporary Fiction*. New York: The Macmillan Company, pp. 441–453.
Hart, C. W. M., and Arnold R. Pilling, 1966, *The Tiwi of North Australia*. New York: Holt, Rinehart and Winston.
Hays, Samuel P., 1957, *The Response to Industrialism, 1885–1914*. Chicago: University of Chicago Press.
Hebb, D. O., and W. R. Thompson, 1968, "The Social Significance of Animal Studies." In G. Lindzey and E. Aronson (eds.), *Handbook of Social Psychology*, Vol. 2. 2nd ed. Reading, Mass.: Addison-Wesley Publishing Co., Inc.
Henslin, James M., 1968, "Trust and the Cab Driver." In M. Truzzi (ed.), *Sociology and Everyday Life*. Englewood Cliffs, New Jersey: Prentice-Hall, Inc., pp. 138–158.
Hoggart, Richard, 1970, *The Uses of Literacy*. New York: Oxford University Press. First published 1957.
Holmes, Urban Tigner, Jr., 1966, *Daily Living in the Twelfth Century:*

Based on the Observations of Alexander Neckam in London and Paris. Madison: University of Wisconsin Press.

The Housekeeper's Helper, 1892. New York: Union Publishing House.

Huelsman, Ben R., 1969, "Southern Mountaineers in City Juvenile Court." *Federal Probation,* December, pp. 49–54.

Hughes, Everett C., 1964, "Good People and Dirty Work." In Howard S. Becker (ed.), *The Other Side: Perspectives on Deviance.* New York: The Free Press of Glencoe, pp. 23–36.

Huizinga, Johan, 1955, *Homo Ludens: A Study of the Play Element in Culture.* Boston: The Beacon Press. First published 1950.

Humphreys, Laud, 1970, *Tearoom Trade: Impersonal Sex in Public Places.* Chicago: Aldine Publishing Co.

Irwin, John, 1973, "Surfing: The Natural History of an Urban Scene." *Urban Life and Culture,* July, 1973.

Jackson, Shirley, 1960a, "Pillar of Salt." In *The Lottery.* New York: Avon Books, pp. 172–184. Originally published by Farrar, Straus & Giroux, Inc., copyright 1949 by Shirley Jackson.

———, 1960b, "The Villager." In *The Lottery.* New York: Avon Books, pp. 40–55. Originally published by Farrar, Straus & Giroux, Inc., copyright 1949 by Shirley Jackson.

Jacobs, Jane, 1963, *The Death and Life of Great American Cities.* New York: Vintage Books.

———, 1969, *The Economy of Cities.* New York: Random House.

Joseph, Nathan, and Nicholas Alex, 1972, "The Uniform: A Sociological Perspective." *American Journal of Sociology,* January, pp. 719–730.

Keller, Suzanne, 1968, *The Urban Neighborhood: A Sociological Perspective.* New York: Random House.

Kephart, Horace, 1913, *Our Southern Highlanders.* New York: Outing Publishing Company.

Keyfitz, Nathan, 1967, "Population Density and the Style of Social Life." *Proceedings of the XVII International Horticultural Congress,* Vol. 2, pp. 29–41.

Kotler, Milton, 1969, *Neighborhood Government: The Local Foundations of Political Life.* Indianapolis and New York: The Bobbs-Merrill Company.

Kroeber, Theodora, 1967, *Ishi in Two Worlds: A Biography of the Last Wild Indian in North America.* Berkeley and Los Angeles: University of California Press.

Labarre, Weston, 1947, "The Cultural Basis of Emotions and Gestures." *Journal of Personality,* September, pp. 49–68.

Lacroix, Paul, 1963, *France in the Middle Ages.* New York: Frederick Ungar Publishing Co. First published as *Manners, Customs and Dress During the Middle Ages and During The Renaissance Period,* 1876.

Lane, Roger, 1967, *Policing the City: Boston, 1822–1885.* Cambridge: Harvard University Press.

———, 1969, "Urbanization and Criminal Violence in the 19th Century: Massachusetts as a Test Case." In Hugh Davis Graham and Ted Robert Gurr, *Violence in America: Historical and Comparative Perspectives, Vol. 2,* A Staff Report to the National Commission on the Causes and Prevention of Violence. Washington, D.C.: U.S. Government Printing Office, pp. 359–370.

Larwood, Jacob [L. R. Sadler], 1881, *The Story of the London Parks*. London: Chatto & Windus, Piccadilly.

Laurence, John, 1960, *A History of Capital Punishment*. New York: The Citadel Press.

Lee, Dorothy, 1950, "Lineal and Nonlineal Codifications of Reality." *Psychosomatic Medicine*, March–April, pp. 89–97.

Lenski, Gerhard, 1970, *Human Societies: A Macrolevel Introduction to Sociology*. New York: McGraw-Hill Book Co.

Levy-Bruhl, Lucien, 1923, *Primitive Mentality*. Translated by Lilian A. Clare. New York and London: The Macmillan Company and George Allen & Unwin, Ltd.

Lewis, Oscar, 1962, *This Was San Francisco*. New York: D. McKay Co.

Lewis, Sinclair, 1961, *Lewis at Zenith (A Three Novel Omnibus: Main Street, Babbitt, Arrowsmith)*. New York: Harcourt Brace Jovanovich, Inc.

Lindesmith, A. R., and A. L. Strauss, 1968, *Social Psychology*. 3rd ed. New York: Holt, Rinehart & Winston, Inc.

Lofland, John, 1966, *Doomsday Cult: A Study of Conversion, Proselytization and Maintenance of Faith*. Englewood Cliffs, New Jersey: Prentice-Hall, Inc.

———, 1968, "The Youth Ghetto: A Perspective on the 'Cities of Youth' Around Our Large Universities." *Journal of Higher Education*, March, pp. 121–143.

———, 1969, *Deviance and Identity*, with the assistance of L. H. Lofland. Englewood Cliffs, New Jersey: Prentice-Hall, Inc.

Lofland, John, and Robert LeJeune, 1960, "Initial Interaction of Newcomers in Alcoholics Anonymous: A Field Experiment in Class Symbols and Socialization." *Social Problems*, Fall, pp. 102–111.

Lofland, Lyn H., 1971, "A World of Strangers: Order and Action in Urban Public Space." Ph.D. dissertation, University of California, San Francisco.

———, 1972, "Self-Management in Public Settings: Parts I and II." *Urban Life and Culture*, April and July, pp. 93–108 and pp. 217–231.

Love, Edmund G., 1957, *Subways Are For Sleeping*. New York: The New American Library.

Lyman, Stanford M., and Marvin B. Scott, 1968, "Coolness in Everyday Life." In M. Truzzi (ed.), *Sociology and Everyday Life*. Englewood Cliffs, New Jersey: Prentice-Hall, Inc., pp. 92–101.

Lynch, Kevin, 1960, *The Image of the City*. Cambridge: The M.I.T. Press.

McCall, G. J., and J. L. Simmons, 1966, *Identities and Interactions*. New York: The Free Press of Glencoe.

McDougal, Myres S., and H. D. Lasswell, 1959, "The Identification and Appraisal of Diverse Systems of Public Order." *The American Journal of International Law*, pp. 1–29.

McLemore, S. Dale, 1970, "Simmel's 'Stranger': A Critique of the Concept." *Pacific Sociological Review*, Spring, pp. 86–94.

Malefijt, Annemarie de Wall, 1968, "Homo Monstrosus." *Scientific American*, October, pp. 112–118.

Manis, Jerome G., and Bernard N. Meltzer (eds.), 1972, *Symbolic Interaction: A Reader in Social Psychology*. 2nd ed. Boston: Allyn and Bacon.

Mann, Leon, 1969, "Queue Culture: The Waiting Line as a Social System." *American Journal of Sociology*, November, pp. 340–354.

Maurer, David W., 1962, *The Big Con*. New York: The New American Library.

Mayhew, Henry, 1950, *London's Underworld*. Edited by Peter Quennell. Selections from "Those That Will Not Work," Vol. 4 of *London Labour and the London Poor*, first published, 1862. London: Spring Books.

Meikelham, Robert, 1845, *On the History and Art of Warming and Ventilating Rooms and Buildings*. 2 vol. London: G. Allen & Unwin, Ltd.

Mellaart, James, 1964, "A Neolithic City in Turkey." *Scientific American*, April.

Miller, John C., 1966, *The First Frontier: Life in Colonial America*. New York: Dell Publishing Company.

Moholy-Nagy, Sibyl, 1968, *Matrix of Man*. New York: Frederick A. Praeger.

Morris, Desmond, 1969, *The Human Zoo*. New York: McGraw-Hill Book Co.

Mott, Paul E. 1965, *The Organization of Society*. Englewood Cliffs, New Jersey: Prentice-Hall, Inc.

Mumford, Lewis, 1938, *The Culture of Cities*. New York: Harcourt Brace Jovanovich, Inc.

———, 1961, *The City in History*. New York: Harcourt Brace and World.

Musil, J., 1968, "The Development of Prague's Ecological Structure." In R. E. Pahl (ed.), *Readings in Urban Sociology*. Oxford: Pergamon Press, pp. 232–259.

Oberg, Kalervo, 1954, "Culture Shock." Bobbs-Merrill Reprints in Anthropology, A-329, copyright K. Oberg. Indianapolis: Bobbs-Merrill.

Olesen, Virginia L., and Elvi W. Whittaker, 1968, *The Silent Dialogue*. San Francisco: Jossey-Bass, Inc.

Origo, Iris, 1957, *The Merchant of Prato*. London: Jonathan Cape.

Pahl, R. E., 1970, *Patterns of Urban Life*. New York: Humanities Press.

Parsons, Elsie Clews, 1914, *Fear and Conventionality*. New York: G. P. Putnam's Sons.

Peterson, William, 1961, *Population*. New York: The Macmillan Company.

Pirenne, Henri, 1925, *Medieval Cities*. Translated by F. H. Halsey. Princeton: Princeton University Press.

Plotnicov, Leonard, 1967, *Strangers to the City: Urban Man in Jos, Nigeria*. Pittsburgh: University of Pittsburgh Press.

Power, Eileen, 1955, *Medieval People*. Garden City, New York: Doubleday Anchor Books. First published 1924.

Pruitt, Ida, 1967, *A Daughter of Han: The Autobiography of a Chinese Working Woman*, as told to the author by Ning Lao T'ai-t'ai. Stanford: Stanford University Press. First published 1945.

Putnam, Emily James, 1970, *The Lady: Studies of Certain Significant Phases of Her History*. Chicago: University of Chicago Press. First published 1910.

Queen, Stuart A., and Robert W. Habenstein, 1967, *The Family in Various Cultures*. 3rd ed. Philadelphia: J. B. Lippincott Co.

Radcliffe-Brown, A. R., 1931, "The Social Organization of Australian Tribes." *The "Oceania" Monographs*, No. 1, Melbourne.

Rapoport, Amos, 1969, *House Form and Culture*. Englewood Cliffs, New Jersey: Prentice-Hall, Inc.

Redfield, Robert, 1953, *The Primitive World and Its Transformation*. Ithaca: Cornell University Press.

Roberts, Ben C., 1969, "On the Origins and Resolution of English Working-Class Protest." In Hugh Davis Graham and Ted Robert Gurr, *Violence in America: Historical and Comparative Perspectives, Vol. 1*, A Staff Report to the National Commission on the Causes and Prevention of Violence. Washington, D.C.: U.S. Government Printing Office, pp. 197–220.

Rörig, Fritz, 1967, *The Medieval Town*. Berkeley and Los Angeles: University of California Press.

Rose, Arnold (ed.), 1962, *Human Behavior and Social Processes*. Boston: Houghton Mifflin Company.

Rowling, Marjorie, 1968, *Everyday Life in Medieval Times*. London and New York: B. T. Batsford, Ltd., and G. P. Putnam's Sons.

Ruesch, Jurgen, and Gregory Bateson, 1951, *Communication: The Social Matrix of Psychiatry*. New York: W. W. Norton and Company, Inc.

Ruesch, Jurgen, and W. Kees, 1956, *Nonverbal Communication: Notes on the Visual Perception of Human Relations*. Berkeley: University of California Press.

Runciman, Steven, 1952, "Christian Constantinople." In M. Bowra et al., *Golden Ages of the Great Cities*. London and New York: Thames and Hudson.

Russell, J. C., 1958, "Late Ancient and Medieval Population." *Transactions of the American Philosophical Society*. Philadelphia: American Philosophical Society.

Schlesinger, Arthur M., 1968, *The American As Reformer*. New York: Atheneum Paperback.

Schnore, Leo F., 1967, "Community." In Neil J. Smelser (ed.), *Sociology: An Introduction*. New York: John Wiley and Sons, Inc., pp. 82–150.

Schutz, Alfred, 1944, "The Stranger: An Essay in Social Psychology." *American Journal of Sociology*, May, pp. 499–507.

———, 1962, *Collected Papers I: The Problem of Social Reality* (edited by Maurice Natanson). The Hague: Martinus Nijhoff.

Schwab, William B., 1965, "Oshogbo—An Urban Community?" In Hilda Kuper (ed.), *Urbanization and Migration in West Africa*. Berkeley and Los Angeles: University of California Press.

Schwartz, Barry, 1968, "The Social Psychology of Privacy." *American Journal of Sociology*, May, pp. 741–752.

Schwartz, Gary, and Don Merton, 1967, "The Language of Adolescence: An Anthropological Approach to the Youth Culture." *American Journal of Sociology*, March, pp. 453–468.

Scott, Marvin, 1968, *The Racing Game*. Chicago: Aldine Publishing Company.

Scott, Mel, 1959, *The San Francisco Bay Area: A Metropolis in Perspective*. Berkeley: University of California Press.

Sennett, Richard, 1970, *The Uses of Disorder: Personal Identity and City Life*. New York: Alfred Knopf.

Shibutani, T., 1961, *Society and Personality*. Englewood Cliffs, New Jersey: Prentice-Hall, Inc.

Sigerist, Henry E., 1956, *Landmarks in the History of Hygiene*. London and New York: Oxford University Press.

Silver, Allan, 1967, "On the Demand for Order in Civil Society: A Review of Some Themes in the History of Urban Crime, Police and Riot." In David J. Bordua (ed.), *The Police*. New York: John Wiley and Sons, Inc., pp. 1–24.

Simmel, Georg, 1924, "Sociology of the Senses: Visual Interaction." In Robert E. Park and Ernest W. Burgess (eds.), *Introduction to the Science of Sociology*. Chicago: University of Chicago Press, pp. 356–361.

———, 1950a, "The Metropolis and Mental Life." In Kurt H. Wolff (ed.), *The Sociology of Georg Simmel*. Glencoe, Illinois: The Free Press, pp. 409–424.

———, 1950b, "The Stranger." In Kurt H. Wolff (ed.), *The Sociology of Georg Simmel*. Glencoe, Illinois: The Free Press, pp. 402–408.

Simon, John, 1854, *Reports Relating to the Sanitary Condition of the City of London*. London: G. Allen and Unwin, Ltd.

Sjoberg, Gideon, 1960, *The Preindustrial City*. New York: The Free Press.

Smelser, Neil J., 1959, *Social Change in the Industrial Revolution*. Chicago: University of Chicago Press.

Smith, Dorothy E., 1971, "Household Space and Family Organization." *Pacific Sociological Review*, January, pp. 53–78.

Smith, Joel, W. H. Form, and G. P. Stone, 1954, "Local Intimacy in a Middle-Sized City." *American Journal of Sociology*, November, pp. 276–284.

Sommer, Robert, 1959, "Studies in Personal Space." *Sociometry*, September, pp. 247–260.

———, 1961, "Leadership and Group Geography." *Sociometry*, March, pp. 99–110.

———, 1962, "The Distance for Comfortable Conversation: A Further Study." *Sociometry*, March, pp. 111–116.

———, 1965, "Further Studies of Small Group Ecology." *Sociometry*, December, pp. 337–348.

———, 1967, "Sociofugal Space." *American Journal of Sociology*, May, pp. 654–660.

———, 1969, *Personal Space: The Behavioral Basis of Design*. Englewood Cliffs, New Jersey: Prentice-Hall, Inc.

Sprackling, Helen, 1944, *Courtesy, A Book of Modern Manners*. New York: M. Barrows & Co.

Stein, Maurice R., 1960, *The Eclipse of Community*. Princeton: Princeton University Press.

Stinchcombe, Arthur, 1963, "Institutions of Privacy in the Determination of Police Administrative Practice." *American Journal of Sociology*, September, pp. 150–158.

Stone, Gregory P., 1954, "City Shoppers and Urban Identification: Observations on the Social Psychology of City Life." *American Journal of Sociology*, July, pp. 36–45.

Strauss, Anselm, 1959, *Mirrors and Masks: The Search for Identity*. Glencoe, Illinois: The Free Press.

——— (ed.), 1964, *George Herbert Mead on Social Psychology*. Chicago: University of Chicago Press.

Suttles, Gerald D., 1968, *The Social Order of the Slum*. Chicago: University of Chicago Press.

———, 1970, "Deviant Behavior As an Unanticipated Consequence of Public Housing." In Daniel Glaser (ed.), *Crime in the City*. New York: Harper and Row, pp. 162–176.

———, 1972, *The Social Construction of Communities*. Chicago: University of Chicago Press.

Tanzer, Helen H., 1939, *The Common People of Pompeii: A Study of the Graffiti*. Baltimore: The Johns Hopkins Press.

Thomas, W. I., and F. Znaniecki, 1918, *The Polish Peasant in Europe and America, Vol. 2*. "Primary Group Organization." Chicago: University of Chicago Press.

———, ———, 1919, *The Polish Peasant in Europe and America, Vol. 3*. "Life Record of an Immigrant." Boston: Richard G. Badger, The Gorham Press.

Tilly, Charles, 1969, "Collective Violence in European Perspective." In Hugh Davis Graham and Ted Robert Gurr, *Violence in America: Historical and Comparative Perspectives, Vol. 1*, A Staff Reporter to the National Commission on the Causes and Prevention of Violence. Washington, D.C.: U.S. Government Printing Office, pp. 5–34.

Tobias, J. J., 1967, *Crime and Industrial Society in the 19th Century*. London: B. T. Batsford, Ltd.

Toll, Seymour I., 1969, *Zoned American*. New York: Grossman Publishers.

Toynbee, A., 1908, *Lectures on the Industrial Revolution of the Eighteenth Century in England*. London: Longmans, Green & Co.

Trollope, Frances, 1960, *Domestic Manners of the Americans* (edited by Donald Smalley). New York: Vintage Books. Originally published, 1832.

Usher, A. P., 1929, *A History of Mechanical Inventions*. New York: McGraw-Hill Book Co.

van den Berghe, P., 1970, "Distance Mechanisms of Stratification." In *Race and Ethnicity: Essays in Comparative Sociology*. New York: Basic Books, Inc., pp. 42–53.

Vanderbilt, Amy, 1962, *New Complete Book of Etiquette*. Garden City, New York: Doubleday & Co., Inc.

Van Gennep, Arnold, 1960, *The Rites of Passage*. Chicago: University of Chicago Press.

Weber, Adna F., 1899, *The Growth of Cities in the Nineteenth Century: A Study in Statistics*. New York: Published for Columbia University by Macmillan Co.

Weber, Max, 1958, *The Protestant Ethic and the Spirit of Capitalism*. Translated by Talcott Parsons. New York: Charles Scribner's Sons. First published 1904–1905.

Werthman, Carl, and Irving Piliavin, 1967, "Gang Members and the Police." In David J. Bordua (ed.), *The Police*. New York: John Wiley and Sons, Inc., pp. 57–65.

Williams, Robin, Jr., John P. Dean, and E. A. Suchman, 1964, *Strangers Next Door*. Englewood Cliffs, New Jersey: Prentice-Hall, Inc.

Wilson, James Q., 1967, "A Guide to Reagan Country: The Political Culture of Southern California." *Commentary*, May, pp. 37–45.

Wirth, Louis, 1964, "Urbanism as a Way of Life." In A. J. Reiss, Jr. (ed.), *Louis Wirth on Cities and Social Life*. Chicago: University of Chicago Press, pp. 60–83.

Wolff, Kurt H. (ed.), 1950, *The Sociology of Georg Simmel*. Glencoe, Illinois: The Free Press.

Wood, Margaret M., 1934, *The Stranger: A Study of Social Relationships*. New York: Columbia University Press.

Wooley, Leonard, 1954, *Excavations at Ur*. London: Ernest Benn.

Wright, Lawrence, 1960, *Clean and Decent: The Fascinating History of the Bathroom and the Water Closet*. New York: Viking Press.

Wright, Rolland H., 1971, "The Stranger Mentality and the Culture of Poverty." In Eleanor Leacock (ed.), *The Culture of Poverty: A Critique*. New York: Simon and Schuster, pp. 315–344.

Young, George M. (ed.), 1934, *Early Victorian England: 1830–1865*. 2 vol. London: Oxford University Press.

Young, John H., 1881, *Our Deportment*. Detroit: F. B. Dickerson & Co.

Young, Michael, and Peter Willmott, 1962, *Family and Kinship in East London*. Baltimore: Penguin Books. First published 1957.

Zablocki, Benjamin, 1971, *The Joyful Community*. Baltimore: Penguin Books.

ACKNOWLEDGMENTS

I should like to acknowledge the assistance of numerous persons in the conception and construction of the manuscript. Howard S. Becker, Phillip Hammond, Walter Klink, Peter Manning, Albert J. Reiss, Jr., Anselm Strauss, and Gerald D. Suttles all read versions of this work and provided both encouragement and helpful criticism. The faculty of the Graduate Program in Sociology at the University of California, San Francisco, gave me the freedom to pursue my interest in the "world of strangers" and the inspiration to do so. Barney Glaser's analysis seminar, in particular, was a continual source of new ideas and a constant spur to intellectual discipline. Fred Davis, Virginia Olesen, and Leon Mayhew, my dissertation committee, were consistently helpful, supportive, and constructively critical, even in the face of my stubborn resistance to suggested changes. To my "cohort" at UCSF, Pat Biernacki, Kathy Calkins, Laura Reif, Richard Rizzo, Betsy Robinson, and Tay Vaughan, I am grateful for two years of intellectual excitement, constructive commentary on this and other projects, and general support. Bill Gum, formerly of Basic Books, provided enthusiasm, editorial assistance, and an occasional much needed prod. I thank him.

A portion of the research upon which this study is based was conducted while I was a National Institute of Mental Health Training Fellow in the Department of Sociology, University of Michigan and a National Defense Education Act Fellow in the Graduate Program in Sociology, University of California, San Francisco.

Finally, this work is dedicated to two people who have been enormously important to both my intellectual and emotional life. Everett K. Wilson first introduced me to sociology at Antioch College during the years 1956–1959. He is a master teacher, an inspiring intellect, and a fine sociologist. I owe him an unpayable debt. Since our meeting in 1964, John Lofland has been my friend, my intimate, my colleague, and, most relevantly in this instance, my teacher. He knows, I trust, the love, respect, and thanks that are contained in this dedication.

As is always the case, what is of value in the foregoing owes much to the persons mentioned above, but since I often did not follow their advice, what is worthless must be attributed entirely to me. One rather wishes the opposite were true.

Grateful acknowledgment is also made for permission to quote from the following copyrighted material:

Caen, H. 1964. From his column in *The San Francisco Chronicle*, June 14. Reprinted by permission of the publisher.
Carcopino, J. 1952. "Rome Under the Antonines" in M. Bowra et al.,

Golden Ages of the Great Cities. London: Thames & Hudson. Pp. 33–34, 35. Reprinted by permission.

Cavan, S. 1963. "Interaction in Home Territories," *Berkeley Journal of Sociology*. Berkeley: University of California. Pp. 21, 24–25. Reprinted by permission.

Fred Davis, "The Cabdriver and His Fare: Facets of a Fleeting Relationship." © copyright 1959 by The University of Chicago Press. Reprinted by permission.

Finestone, H. 1957. "Cats, Kicks, and Color," *Social Problems 5:* #1 (Summer). Notre Dame: Society for the Study of Social Problems. Reprinted by permission of the author and the publisher.

Foote, C. 1969. "Vagrancy-type Law and its Administration," in W. J. Chambliss (ed.) *Crime and the Legal Process*. New York: McGraw-Hill. Pp. 297, 301. Reprinted by permission of the publisher. Originally published in the *University of Pennsylvania Law Review 117*. Reprinted by permission of Fred B. Rothman & Co., South Hackensack, New Jersey.

Fulford, R. 1952. "Jubilee London" in M. Bowra et al., *Golden Ages of the Great Cities*. London: Thames & Hudson. Pp. 285–286. Reprinted by permission.

The Silent Language by Edward T. Hall. Copyright ©1959 by Edward T. Hall. Reprinted by permission of Doubleday & Company, Inc.

Harris, Mark, "The Self-Made Brain Surgeon," in P. C. Hills and L. R. Hills (eds.), *How We Live: Contemporary Life in Contemporary Fiction*. New York: The Macmillan Company, 1968, pp. 441–453. Reprinted by permission of the author.

Ferris Hartman, "French Way to Keep the Girls Honest," *The San Francisco Chronicle*, April 10, 1970. ©Chronicle Publishing Co. 1970. Reprinted by permission.

Jackson, Shirley, "The Villager" in *The Lottery*. Originally published by Farrar, Straus & Giroux, Inc. ©1960. Reprinted by permission of the publisher.

Ishi in Two Worlds: A Biography of the Last Wild Indian in North America by Theodora Kroeber, University of California Press, 1961. Originally published by The University of California Press; reprinted by permission of The Regents of the University of California.

Lewis, Sinclair, *Lewis At Zenith (A Three Novel Omnibus: Main Street, Babbitt, Arrowsmith)*, New York, Harcourt Brace Jovanovich, Inc., 1961, p. 358. Reprinted by permission.

John Lofland, *Doomsday Cult: A Study of Conversion, Proselytization, and Maintenance of Faith* ©1966. Reprinted by permission of Prentice-Hall, Inc., Englewood Cliffs, New Jersey.

Lofland, J. 1968. "The Youth Ghetto: A Perspective on 'Cities of Youth' Around Our Larger Universities," *Journal of Higher Education*. Pp. 127, 129. Columbus: Ohio State University Press. Reprinted by permission.

Lofland, J. and Lejeune, R. 1960. "Initial Interaction of Newcomers in Alcoholics Anonymous: A Field Experiment in Class Symbols and Socialization," *Social Problems: 8:* #2 (Fall). Notre Dame: Society for the Study of Social Problems. Pp. 105–106. Reprinted by permission of the authors and the publisher.

The First Frontier: Life in Colonial America by John C. Miller. Copyright © 1966 by John C. Miller. Reprinted by permission of the publisher, Dell Publishing Co., Inc.

Patterson, R., "Violence Strikes a Street Called Terror Terrace," *The San Francisco Examiner*, December 15, 1969. Reprinted by permission.

"The Waiting Room for Death" by McCandlish Phillips. © 1970 by The New York Times Company. Reprinted by permission.

Runciman, S. 1952. "Christian Constantinople" in M. Bowra et al., *Golden Ages of the Great Cities*. London: Thames & Hudson. Pp. 62, 67, 70, 77, 78. Reprinted by permission.

Simmel G., "Sociology of the Senses: Visual Interaction" in Robert E. Park and E. W. Burgess, *Introduction to the Science of Sociology*. Copyright © 1924 by The University of Chicago Press. Reprinted by permission of the publisher.

The Preindustrial City by Gideon Sjoberg. Reprinted by permission of The Macmillan Company. © The Free Press, a Corporation 1960.

Zoned American by Seymour I. Toll. Copyright © 1969 by Seymour I. Toll. New York: Viking Press, Publishers. Reprinted by permission of Grossman Publishers.

"Gang Members and the Police," by Carl Werthman and Irving Piliavin in *The Police*, edited by David J. Bordua. Copyright © 1967 by John Wiley & Sons, Inc. By permission of John Wiley and Sons, Inc.

"Action Line," *Detroit Free Press*, July 2, 1966. Reprinted by permission.

"The Carmel Anti-Hippie Law Upheld," *The San Francisco Chronicle*, March 28, 1970. © Chronicle Publishing Co. 1970. Reprinted by permission.

INDEX

accatosi (preindustrial beggars), 163

acquaintance, and personal knowing, 16–17

action: and information, 14–15; learning, 111–117; *see also* behavior; behavioral repertoires

activities: limited segregation of, 51–52; pile-up, 70; spatial segregation of, 67–73

adolescent gangs, proprietary attitudes of, 129–130, 139

adventurer (urban): games played by, 161–168; traits of, 159–160

advertising: in preindustrial city, 38–39; and public space, 69

affect, and personal knowing, 184n

affluence, and clothing, 80

affrati (preindustrial beggars), 163

Afghanistan, status clothing in, 45–46

age, and spatial segregation, 76–77, 191n

age-sex units, 77

America (Colonial), 121; bourgeois in, 57; branding in, 47–48; clothing in, 45, 54, 187n; Southern hospitality in, 7; whipping in, 35

American Frontier, attitude toward strangers on, 7–8

American Southern Mountaineers, attitude toward strangers, 6–7

Amory, Cleveland, 136

Amsterdam (Holland), hippies in, 87

Andaman Isles, treatment of strangers in, 5

Anderson, Nels, 194n

animals, scavenger duties of, 37

anonymity (of city), related to population size, 10, 161

appearance: coding, 98–101, 106; and ordering of urban populace, 22

appearential meanings, in modern city, 99

appearential ordering, 176–177; decline of, 57–60; defined, 27; limited use in modern city, 84–87; in preindustrial city, 28, 29, 48–49, 52–55

appropriateness, of conventional encounter, 171–173

areal factors, and spatial ordering, 60–61

Argyle, Michael, 196n–197n

Athens, 45; political meetings in preindustrial, 39

Australia, strangers of, 4–5

Australian aborigines, 185n; attitude toward strangers, 6; coding schemes of, 21

automobile: and dispersed urban village, 136–137; privacy of, 73

"Avengers" (as urbane heroes), 160

Babbitt (Lewis), 132

Babylon, population under Chaldean rule, 12

backstage behavior, and on-stage situation, 141

backstage language: and camouflaged colonization, 126, 128; of group members, 139; of residents, 124, 127–128

"Baron, The" (as urbane hero), 160

Barron, Jack, 79

Bateson, Gregory, 6

bathroom activities, in preindustrial city, 34–35

Becker, Ernest, 13

Becker, Howard S., 191n

"beeline tactic," in reaching position, 145–146

Beelzebub, 63

begging: in modern city, 72; in preindustrial city, 40, 162–164

behavior: coding, 105–107; and etiquette books, 116–117; odd, 174–175; range of, and group size, 139; *see also* action

behavioral meanings: culture-specific, 107; identity-specific, 106–107

behavioral repertoires, 14, 27, 96, 111; and coding rules, 97; and placement of other, 21

Berger, Bennett, 74

Berkeley (California), 137

Beroena (Javanese God of the Sea), 6

biophysical limitation, to knowing, 10

birth rates, in cities, 59

floating population, 59; as colonizers, 123; in early industrial city, 99; vs. middle class, 62–65; in modern city, 71, 189*n*–190*n;* in preindustrial city, 42; and spatial ordering, 60
Foote, Caleb, 89
Form, William, 28
France: beggars in preindustrial, 162–163; clothing in preindustrial, 46, 54; executions in preindustrial, 35–36
Franks, hair length and status of, 46
Frazer, Sir James George, 7
Freedman, Ronald, 59
freedom, complications of, 13
Fulford, Roger, 59

games, *see* identity games; interactional games
gangs, *see* adolescent gangs
Gans, Herbert, 74
garbage and waste disposal: in modern city, 38; in preindustrial city, 37–38; and private space, 68
George, M. Dorothy, 61, 74
Gleason, Ralph J., 81
Goffman, Erving, 28, 86, 124, 185*n*, 188*n*, 191*n*, 196*n*, 198*n*
goliards, in Medieval Europe, 99–100
Grant, Lee, 69
group, members: backstage language of, 139; and newcomer, 183*n; see also* primary groups; secondary groups
group size: and mobile home territory, 138–139; and range of behavior, 139
Guatemala City, unemployment in, 64
guide books, and coding location, 104–105
Gunn, Peter (as urbane hero), 160

Haarhoff, T. J., 6, 45
Habenstein, R. W., 28
Hackett, Joan, 69
haggling, as interactional game, 166–167
hair length: as appearential clue in modern city, 100; and status, 46
Hall, Edward T., 68, 106, 107, 196*n*
"hanging about," in preindustrial city, 40
Harris, Mark, 133
Hart, C. W. M., 5
Hartman, Ferris, 78
Hebrews (ancient), and strangers, 181*n*
heterogeneity of populace: masked, 79–82; overt, 44–48
hicks, as urban adventurers, 173
hippies, 83–84, 87–88, 135, 165; costum-

ing of, 81–82, 99; ordinances in modern city against, 71–72
Holmes, Sherlock (fictional character), 197*n*–198*n;* as urbane hero, 160
Holmes, Urban Tigner, Jr., 11, 34, 40, 42, 43, 46
Homer (Greek poet), 6
home territories, 137; creation of, 119–132; defined, 119; mobile, 137–139; and proprietary rights, 129–131; and spatial ordering, 131–132, 171; and urban villages, 132
Horowitz, Irving Louis, 191*n*
hospitality and personal knowing, 21; Southern, 7
host attitude, and proprietary rights, 128–129
Housekeeper's Helper, The, 116
Hughes, Everett C., 91
human beings, nature of, 13–15, 52
"humanitarian movements," and industrialization, 68
"humanitarian organizations," as instrument of middle class, 65
hustling, as interactional game, 167–168

identification, and ordering, 29; *see also* appearential ordering; spatial ordering
identity and behavior, 111; and ordering, 27–28; transformations, 197*n*
identity games: defined, 161; forms of, 161–166; and identity transformations, 197*n;* and interactional games, 166, 198*n*
industrial city, defined, 57; *see* early industrial city; modern city
industrialization, related to distribution, 58
Industrial Revolution, 57–58
information: and coding rules, 14–15, 96–97; and human action, 14–15
interaction, and "body language," 172; *see also* encounters, conventional; interactional games
interaction (avoidance of): distance and, 153; entrance sequence and, 141–146; waiting styles and, 146–151
interactional games: defined, 161; forms of, 166–168; and identity games, 166, 198*n*
interaction distance, in Latin America, 107
interrogation (direct), and personal knowing, 21
intimate knowledge, and residents, 122–131